Also by Craig J. Heimbuch

*Chasing Oliver Hazard Perry*

# AND NOW
# WE SHALL DO
# MANLY
# THINGS

### Discovering My Manhood Through the
### Great (and Not-So-Great) American Hunt

## CRAIG J. HEIMBUCH

*wm*

WILLIAM MORROW
*An Imprint of* HarperCollins*Publishers*

AND NOW WE SHALL DO MANLY THINGS. Copyright © 2012 by Craig Heimbuch. All rights reserved. Printed in the United States of America. No part of this book may be used or reproduced in any manner whatsoever without written permission except in the case of brief quotations embodied in critical articles and reviews. For information address HarperCollins Publishers, 10 East 53rd Street, New York, NY 10022.

HarperCollins books may be purchased for educational, business, or sales promotional use. For information please write: Special Markets Department, Harper-Collins Publishers, 10 East 53rd Street, New York, NY 10022.

FIRST EDITION

*Designed by Diahann Sturge*

Library of Congress Cataloging-in-Publication Data has been applied for.

ISBN 978-0-06-219786-3

12 13 14 15 16  OV/RRD  10 9 8 7 6 5 4 3 2 1

*For Rebecca, the love of my life*

Well, you sure do have an interesting
way of looking at the world.

−Jim Heimbuch

# CONTENTS

**PART I: WINTER**

1. An Unexpected Beginning     3
2. Three Months Earlier     10
3. I Want to Hunt     24
4. My Sporting Life     30
5. Coming Out of the Hunting Closet     45

**PART II: SPRING**

6. Long Road to Iowa     61
7. Into the Lion's Den     77
8. Consider the McRib     98

**PART III: SUMMER**

9. Comfort Breeds Carelessness     113
10. Education     122
11. The Interstitial Time     151
12. Instruction     161

## PART IV: FALL

| | | |
|---|---|---|
| 13. | Preparation | 187 |
| 14. | The Drive to Iowa and My Missing License | 196 |
| 15. | Hemingway's Shot | 214 |
| 16. | The Asterisk* | 240 |
| 17. | Hunting Alone | 253 |
| 18. | Lust | 273 |
| 19. | Karma | 287 |
| 20. | Vindication | 311 |
| | EPILOGUE | 321 |
| | ACKNOWLEDGMENTS | 325 |

# PART I

# WINTER

# 1

## AN UNEXPECTED BEGINNING

We were just finishing packing up the car to head back to our place in Cincinnati when Dad asked me to go downstairs with him.

When I was young and my dad would call me down into his workshop, it usually meant trouble. Maybe my grades had been less stellar than I had led him to believe. Or maybe I had stretched the truth a bit about completing my chores. Either way, a trip into the workshop with Dad seldom resulted in warm, fuzzy father-son bonding—more likely it was a disappointed glare and a good long talking-to.

But that was then. Now that I'm married and have three children, visits to the workshop usually involve a woodworking project with the kids or the never-ending retrieval of my college belongings that have been stored there for more than a decade— you never know when that freshman term paper on Chaucer might come in handy during a job interview.

I followed Dad down the stairs past the stuffed northern pike and the bearskin mounted on the wall. I've never been comfortable with the bear. The fish is one thing. I grew up fishing, and while I may have chosen a different pose than the curled-and-about-to-strike one opted for by the taxidermist, I recognize Dad's pride in that particular fish. There's also a tasteful piece of driftwood. I like that very much.

The bear, on the other hand, gives me the creeps. It's all soft fur, claws, and teeth. And the eyes—I swear it's looking at me, pleading with me to be taken down from the wall of the dim basement. "Put me in a ski lodge," it's saying to me. "I want bikini models lying on me. I want to be the set of a late-night Cinemax movie. Please!"

"Dad," I said, "we have to get going. I don't want to get home too late. What do you need?"

"I want to give you something," he said.

"What?"

"Just something."

Fine, I thought, let Dad be mysterious. Since my dad doesn't often veer toward the sentimental, I figured it was something practical. A coupon for Home Depot, perhaps, or an extra set of hex wrenches.

Instead, Dad reached into the rafters and pulled down the keys to the gun safe, which was mounted on a wall in the back corner of the workshop. He unlocked it without a word and pulled out a twelve-gauge Winchester over-under shotgun and handed it to me without much fanfare or flourish.

"What's this?" I asked rather dimly.

"It's a twelve-gauge Winchester over-under shotgun," Dad said.

"Yes, but what is it for?" I asked.

"For shooting."

Dad has always had a way with words.

"No," I said as I tried to clarify, "why are you giving it to me?"

"I just thought you might appreciate it," he said.

I must admit, it was a beautiful gun. The deep-brown wood, the dark-gray barrels and brushed silver-colored parts. I liked the way it felt in my hands—its heft and size, the particular angularity of the grip and stock.

I have a certain familiarity with guns. I understand their basic workings, having grown up in a gun-loving extended family, and can appreciate a beautiful gun when I see one. But don't confuse familiarity with comfort. Although I have fired more guns than most of my suburban peers, I have never fully immersed myself in the shooting and hunting culture of my family. My dad is a hunter. He's killed deer and bear and all sorts of birds. But even his bounty pales in comparison to that of his brothers. My uncles are the kinds of guys who spend rainy Saturday mornings watching worn VHS tapes of Alaskan hunting adventures (one in particular involving the downing of a wolverine seems to be the favorite). They spend their vacations hunting, plan for their trips all year long, and have passed their enthusiasm on to their own sons, my cousins.

This moment, however, marks the first time in my life Dad has made an overt gesture to welcome me into the fold. That I didn't ask for a gun, and am entirely too old to be receiving my first one, doesn't seem to have factored into his thinking. It's as if my dad just woke up that morning and decided it was time for me to be armed. I imagined him standing over the sink, a fresh cup of black coffee—he only ever drinks it black and told me that I'd better learn to do the same as you never know when someone might be out of cream—in hand, and with a manly stretch groaning, "I'm going to give Craig a gun today. Yup, that's what I'm going to do."

My dad is not a man who prides himself on his possessions.

He always taught us that doing was better than having, that a man is measured by the sum total of his experiences not his net worth. He does not have a large collection—eight guns total—but this is the only one I remember him buying. He showed it to me right after he bought it, holding it up in front of him, examining it under the bare bulb hanging from the workshop ceiling like a museum curator holding an ancient relic.

I always assumed it was his favorite. He's used it maybe twice, so giving it to me was beyond generous; it was confounding.

"Dad," I said, "don't take this the wrong way, but you aren't dying, are you?"

"No," he said with a chuckle.

"You sure? No cancer? Heart disease? Diabetes?"

"Nope," he said. "I'm fine."

"Because if you've had a myocardial infarction, you can tell me," I said. "Or if you're going blind . . ."

This went on for ten whole minutes—me running through every debilitating disease and condition I could think of only to be reassured time and again that he was in perfect health and that everything was in order. No, he and Mom did not have a suicide pact and, to the best of his knowledge, there was no mob contract out on either him or me.

I remained incredulous.

"You're just coming to an age," he finally said, "when you might get interested in these kinds of things, and I wanted you to have this."

I'd never owned a gun—never even had the thought of owning one. Sure, I've enjoyed shooting at soda cans and paper targets in my uncle's yard, both as a kid and as an adult. But shooting was a vacation thing for me, something I did while visiting my relatives in Iowa. Sort of like people from Kansas who spend their holidays skiing in Colorado—it's an activity so tied to a specific place in my mind as to not be considered anywhere else.

So the idea of having a gun was completely foreign. I didn't have the slightest idea of what to do with it. I was excited (who isn't when receiving an unexpected gift?), but I also had some trepidation. Where would I keep it? It's not as if I had bought a gun safe in anticipation of the day when I might randomly be given a shotgun. It was as if he had just handed me the keys to a bulldozer. It was great and exciting, but using it would require an adjustment to my day-to-day life.

Not dwelling on the why of the situation any longer, Dad launched into a lengthy list of hows—how to take the gun apart and put it back together, how to clean it and maintain it, how to store the ammunition and how to use the trigger guards. He covered so much ground so quickly, I should have been taking notes.

"This is how it comes apart," he said, flipping a recessed switch forward and breaking the gun into three pieces. "And this is how it goes together." With a couple quick snaps it was whole again.

"Got it?"

"Um," I said, "can you show me one more time? You know, I just want to be sure I really got it."

Again, a flick of the switch and the gun was in three pieces. This time he handed the pieces to me and I fumbled with them for a while before he grabbed the pieces and snapped them together as if by rote. Twice more he demonstrated, and with each successive flick and snap my confidence waned.

It was a master's class in firearms taught over the span of five minutes. I couldn't recall my father giving me so much detailed instruction and insight in such a dense burst before. I mean, Dad was always there if you needed help with homework or your taxes, but he wasn't the kind to give instruction or un-prompted life lessons. As a teenager, the only advice I got about sex was an admonishment to not die of a venereal disease.

So Dad's effusive instruction on how to care for and handle this gun, while wildly out of character, was also oddly touching. I felt like he really cared. This was the father-son moment I had always been suspicious of in those movies of the week, and yet, here it was, happening right before me. Okay, so, at thirty-two, it wasn't exactly a scene from *The Wonder Years,* but I'll take what I can get.

I asked him to cover one more time the necessary implements to clean the weapon and demonstrated that, finally, I could indeed take it apart and put it back together. He gave me a case, geometric and sturdy with shiny metal sides and two hefty locks—I was tempted to handcuff it to my arm—and a hundred rounds of ammunition.

He gave me one last bit of instruction, or perhaps it was more admonition before closing the safe and leading me back upstairs. "You better be careful," he said, "and not fuck this gun up."

A random gift, thorough instruction, and an unwarranted use of profanity? I began thinking of other medical conditions. Something was definitely out of the ordinary.

Mom must have known what Dad was doing, because when I came back upstairs, she gave me a big, excited hug, the same kind she gave me when my wife surprised me with a thirtieth birthday party. Mom and Dad said their good-byes to my wife and kids, and I went out to put my new gun in the car—along with the portable crib for our daughter and our sons' stuffed animals.

We pulled away, and I gave a second look back over my shoulder at my parents waving from the front porch. I believe Dad was smiling a little larger than usual.

"What was that all about?" my wife asked before we reached the end of the block.

"Um." I hesitated. "He gave me a shotgun."

"What?!"

"Yeah, he gave me his favorite shotgun."

"But you're not a gun guy. Why did he do that?"

"Because he wanted to."

"Well," she asked, "what's it for?"

I paused a second to consider the complicated answer. Should I tell her about family legacy? About fathers and sons? About his hopes that one day I would follow in his sporting footsteps? Should I tell her that I had no idea what prompted this generosity?

In the end, I gave the only answer I knew would not come across as dreamy or fanciful. I told her—

"For shooting."

# 2

## THREE MONTHS EARLIER

I thought the mustache looked pretty good.

It wasn't Clark Gable in *Gone with the Wind;* it wasn't even Tom Selleck in *Magnum P.I.* But it was my first attempt at real facial hair and I was surprised by how well it was coming in, even if it was a little more dirty sand in color than what I had hoped. Plus, it was for a good cause. Every November, men around the world sign up for the "Movember" program to help raise money and awareness for prostate cancer research and prevention, and as the editor of an online magazine catering to the lifestyles of an older male demographic—men right around the age when they schedule their first prostate exam—I felt it was my duty to kick in. The way it works is that men grow a mustache and ask people to sponsor them. It's sort of like one of those charity walk-a-thons they have on junior high tracks where walkers get pledges of money based on their performance. A dollar a mile or two bucks an hour. Except there was no real measurement of length or endurance with Movember. You just signed up and, by doing so, you committed to the full thirty days of growing, pruning, and cultivating a mustache. Some of the men I knew who were participating were lucky. They were natural-born facial hair growers. Two days in, they looked like Burt Lancaster, suave and sexy as if stolen right from the pages of a late 1970s *GQ*.

I thought mine looked all right, but my wife hated it. She didn't understand why I needed to grow facial hair in order to support prostate cancer.

"Can't you just give them some money?" she asked, and I told her that me having a mustache was like writing a check, except other people wrote them on my behalf and all I had to do was hold out until the end of the month. "Yeah, but what about the pictures? All the pictures we're going to have from when Molly was born and you're going to look like a porn star."

She had a point. I suppose that if I was able to look at myself the way she saw me, my proud crumb duster would look like little more than a dusty accident, a spot missed on consecutive face washings. Without a hat on or my glasses, I looked like a hobo. With them, I looked like a chimney sweep. Either way, it probably wasn't the best image. I could imagine my newborn daughter, years from then, looking back through pictures from childhood and wondering if dear old dad had gone on some sort of strike around the time of her birth.

I went into my mustache experiment with a little trepidation and an open mind and was pleased to see that after just a couple of weeks, it covered my entire lip in one long strip. No bald spots, no patches of cat hair. Not full, not thick. But good enough for the time being, even though I knew it had to go eventually. Marriage is like that. Stay with the same person long enough, love them deeply enough, and you find even your simplest fantasies and indulgences become less important than the other person's fancies.

I checked it out in the rearview mirror of our minivan one

last time as I pulled around from the long-term parking lot to the circular, covered drive. After a little more than two days in the hospital, Rebecca and our newborn angel, Molly, were coming home. I can't really explain my fascination with the mustache, particularly given its relative unimportance at this time in my life, but for some reason it felt novel and masculine in a way I have seldom ever felt. Just the night before as I was getting our sons, then six and three, ready for bed, our oldest, Jack, had asked me if I was going to be a cowboy. Not for Halloween, which had passed three weeks before, or for some exotic prank, but as a job. He wanted to know if I was going to leave my work as a writer and an editor to ride the open range. It was the first time I had ever felt like someone's hero and I had my mustache to thank for that. My plan was to keep it as long as possible, but shave before we had the first round of professional photos taken as a family.

Molly was a welcome addition to the family. My wife and I had held each other's hand tightly—uncomfortably—in the ob-gyn's office as the technician had sprayed her belly with warm, gelatinous goo and pushed the sonogram wand (a bit too forcefully if you ask me) into her stomach. The tech paused and asked if we wanted to know the sex of the baby and we shared a knowing and meaningful look for a split second before simultaneously saying yes. It wasn't that we would not have been happy with another boy. It wasn't that at all. We loved having boys.

Jack had been a surprise of sorts. We had been married just over a year. I was working as a newspaper reporter in a small once-great industrial city between Cincinnati and Dayton, covering local politics and writing the occasional humor column that was greeted with tepid reader response. My wife had been a first-grade teacher and after four years away for college and nearly two away following our wedding, we were trying to decide if the right thing to do was to move back to Cleveland where both our families lived and would, presumably, protect us from the strange anxiety of being a young couple facing the world all alone. We went out for dinner at a fancy restaurant we drove past in the three-block area our suburban community passed off as a downtown, talking over a bottle of wine and steaks. We came to the conclusion that five years was the key. We'd work a little while longer in southwest Ohio, then move home to Cleveland, where we would live near our parents—themselves separated by less than two miles as Rebecca and I were high school sweethearts. I would try to get a job working for the *Cleveland Plain Dealer* or apply to law school, and she would work in our old school district. At the end of five years, when we were in our late twenties and had, presumably, been to Europe and the Caribbean and purchased a house, we would start a family of our own.

That was on a Friday night. Tuesday, I got home late from work to find Rebecca pacing around the drive that circled our apartment complex, talking nervously on the phone to a friend from work and smiling timidly when I pulled up near her.

"Hi," I said.

"Hi, how was your city council meeting?" She was giggling like a girl who had just caught a glance of a teen idol buying milk at a convenience store.

"Fine," I said. "Are you okay?"

"Yeah, why?" She paused. "Just go home, we'll talk then."

"What is it?"

"Nothing."

"What is it?"

"Nuh-thing."

"It's something," I said, and suddenly a thought came to me as clear and unexpected as a bolt of lightning out of a cloudless sky. "Beck, are you pregnant?"

Nothing. She smiled, beamed really, and asked if I was okay. That night we talked for hours, about the future, about the news, about our now irrelevant five-year plan that had held for just over seventy-two hours. The next summer, Jack was born.

We settled into the life of young parents as best as we could. We never had any money—journalists are, in fact, the only people who marry teachers for the money—and were the first among our friends to have children by a long shot. My budding journalistic career took a sideways detour when we realized that we didn't have enough to make minimum payments on our burgeoning credit card debt and pay for a babysitter. And we couldn't afford for my wife, then making nearly twice my salary, to stay home. So I had to leave newspapers to take a job doing public relations for the city I had been covering. Not exactly my finest ethical hour, but I had presented my conundrum clearly to my editors and tried to find an alternate solution—including moving to the night shift to stay home with Jack during the day. We couldn't find one, so I took a job I had been offered several times by the city manager, who I got along with very well and who, by personality and profession, didn't like dealing directly with the press.

I wasn't in the job long when I began pining for journalism. A dull ache to write stories—about people, profiles, mostly—set in like an ulcer, and I tried to find magazine writing opportunities. Finding none, I borrowed some money from my dad and started my own. So in addition to my forty-five-minute commute each way and the hectic life of young parents trying to care for a child without the benefit of close friends or family, I found myself working as the editor, publisher, sales manager, photographer, and lead writer of a small bimonthly magazine. I produced three or four issues before a friend of a friend introduced me to a man who owned an advertising agency. He offered me more money and even expressed some interest in helping build the magazine. I took the job and, almost immediately, regretted having done so.

The magazine was never brought up and the slightly larger paycheck was often delayed in arriving. Once, I was told to hurry up and cash my check before others that had been sent out went through. Turns out the company, which was small, was writing checks it could not cover. I didn't get an opportunity to do a whole lot of writing at the agency, unless you count writing banal, mindless, screaming television and radio ads for a chain of discount carpet stores to be writing. I certainly didn't. I had made up my mind to quit, my magazine long gone and Dad's investment wasted, when my wife nudged me one morning from a sunny sleep with some news. She told Jack first and wanted him to tell me, but he was not yet three years old and, while gifted from a verbal intelligence standpoint, perhaps too young.

She was pregnant. Again.

I greeted the news with genuine excitement, even if I knew that it would kill any hopes I had of leaving my dungeonlike work in pursuit of something better. It would turn out that, four months before Dylan was born, the decision would be made for me when my boss, with whom I always had a good personal relationship even if there was no business chemistry, called me into his office and rather unceremoniously let me go. I called my wife to tell her I had been fired, and we both settled in to the tingling numbness of shock that often follows a car accident. You are happy to be alive, but beyond that not much makes sense.

Our lease was coming to an end and, without me gainfully employed, we could not afford nor did we want to renew. As luck would have it, a family of one of Rebecca's students was being sent overseas for six months and was looking for someone to house-sit their beautiful suburban home. So that's what we did. Most of our things went into a storage locker and we spent a long summer and fall sleeping in someone else's bed, using their kitchen, and mowing their lawn. I stayed home with Jack while Rebecca finished up the school year and looked for jobs online while he was napping. I gained twenty pounds from depressive eating and felt less prepared to be a patriarch than I ever had. Dylan was due two weeks before the family was set to arrive back in the States and, a few weeks out I still hadn't found a job.

I wanted to work in journalism, but that felt hopeless. Editors in the area were wary of my intentions given the circumstances of my departure from the newspaper. And, even if I did somehow manage to get a job, it would not pay enough to cover the bills and child care. I had a month left of unemployment benefits when I got an e-mail from the boss who had fired me saying that a man he knew was looking for a magazine editor. I will always have Sam Wilder to thank for giving me my big break by hiring me to be the managing editor of a chain of regional home-and-garden magazines he had founded.

Dylan was born the week I began working again, and in the mad rush of the next three weeks, we managed to find a three-bedroom condo, move our things, and arrange for child care. It was frantic and stressful, and I had an awful feeling of ill-preparedness and unworthiness hanging about me for months. Most of this had to do with Dad. Never once had he uttered a judgmental word in my time of unemployment. Never had he scolded or admonished me for not living up to my end of the familial bargain. Quite the opposite, actually. He had been very supportive. Still, I had a hard time looking him in the eye. He's one of those guys who always had a job, who always supported his family. He'd never, as far as I knew, been fired from anything and, after leaving the army, I'm pretty sure he had spent his entire adult life living in homes of his own.

By the time Molly came down the chute, I had left the magazine on my own good terms, done some stay-at-home freelance work and taken a position at the web magazine, which offered a generous enough salary for my dear enduring wife to stay home with the kids. We weren't well-off, but we were making it work. And the birth of my daughter signified the first time Rebecca and I had brought life into the world in something resembling stability.

The moment the sonogram tech confirmed that the baby growing inside my wife was indeed a girl, my eyes welled up— part pride, part relief, part the oh-shit feeling that I imagine washes over every man when he learns he will someday be responsible for instilling fear into would-be teenage suitors. And I began looking forward to meeting her, holding her in my arms, and lavishing her with affection and praise more with each passing day.

She was bundled tight against the chill November air, a square inch of skin exposed from beneath her blankets, and I carried her up the steps to our second-floor living space gently. The boys had been making faces and talking to their new little sister in the cloyingly cooey voice children use to talk to newborns and puppies on the entire ride home from the hospital—twenty-five minutes made much longer by lack of sleep and an overabundance of cuteness. Stepping into our home, a small second-story condo we'd been renting for three years with an eye on buying a place of our own for all but three days of that time, I felt, well, strange. My heart began pounding, my eyes dimmed. I had a hard time breathing. I was panicky, anxious as if I had just been told I was late for a college exam for which I had not studied.

"Molly's home!" the boys yelled.

"Mommy's home!" Dylan added.

I turned and looked at my wife. I learned from Jack and had it reinforced with Dylan and Molly how cruel childbirth is to a woman physically. Yet, she looked beautiful. I handed Molly to her, and they went to the back bedroom for a feeding and diaper change. The boys followed and I had a long moment alone in our living room/kitchen area. I felt somehow incomplete and jittery. I felt empty and lost and stood in the kitchen with my coat and shoes on, holding Rebecca's overnight bag, Molly's diaper bag, and two books the boys had been thumbing through in the car. It was like the opening scene of *American Beauty* where Kevin Spacey is going mindlessly through the minutiae of his day, pouring coffee, staring blankly out the window. And for a long moment, I found myself staring at a glass of water I had left on the counter absentmindedly before leaving to pick up my wife and daughter. I took three deep breaths to calm my nerves and was snapped from my stare by Dylan, who was pulling on my pant leg, wanting to take me into Molly's room and show me his little sister.

I didn't dwell on the moment in the coming days and weeks, but I found it happening again and again at the least expected times. During my evening commute, at the dinner table, sitting on the couch, watching the boys play on the floor and feeling Molly's warm breath on my neck while she slept on my chest. And each time, it was nearly the same. A sense of panic, a feeling of emptiness, anxiety, and incompleteness.

Anxiety is nothing new to me. When things were really tough, when money was tight and my career was going nowhere, I suffered a few times from panic attacks. At one point, a few years before Molly was born, fearing that I was dying of some undiagnosed condition, I went to a doctor, who told me that there was nothing physically wrong, apart from a few extra pounds and not enough rigorous activity—which I took to mean sex as, I'm sure, any man would. Try as I did to sell my wife on the idea that upping our romantic heat might have medicinal benefits, she remained unconvinced and recommended that I go see a therapist.

I should say right off that I have nothing against the mental health professions, but the idea of paying someone to talk about my feelings was about as appealing as paying someone to spit in my food. In my family, the only problems you talked about were those contained in your math homework. And even then it was an act of desperation. It's not that we don't have emotions. Quite the opposite, actually; it's just that our emotions tend to run the spectrum between pleasantly contented and pleasantly bored. If you were to map my family's emotional expressiveness through color, you'd only need eggshell and beige. When I was growing up, we always were a jovial bunch, if not a close one. My mom has a tremendous sense of humor—one of the best of all time—but I can probably count on a single finger the number of times I've seen her visibly angry. Dad's emotions are only slightly more contained. I remember the two times he got really angry with me when I was under his roof. The first was middling compared to most fathers. The second was when I was twenty and we were fishing in Canada, but we'll get more into that later.

Despite my misgivings, I had taken Rebecca up on her suggestion. I tried to explain all this to the therapist in our first session—my family's peculiar lack of emotional effusiveness—and was asked in return, "How does that make you feel?" Feel? How should I know? That's the point. And that's the biggest reason I knew I was not destined for a life of therapy. I steered the conversation toward the physical symptoms of my troubles, and it took her exactly three seconds to diagnose anxiety.

"Do you know what your problem is?" she asked over the brim of her overlarge, Annie-Potts-in-*Ghostbusters* glasses.

"No," I said. "I was hoping that's what you could tell me."

"Your problem is that you believe every little thing that crosses your mind. If your brain tells you that you're not good enough, you believe it. If your brain tells you you're not doing what you're supposed to, you believe it."

"Why wouldn't I?"

"Because it's bullshit."

She told me to imagine all my negative thoughts as news items on the ticker that crawls across the bottom of the television screen. See them, but dismiss them. And it worked. I hadn't had an anxiety problem for close to four years. Of course, I never went back to therapy, but that's because I figured I was done. I assumed the problem had been solved, that the thin woman's work was finished and guaranteed like an oil change from an ASC-certified mechanic. I was good to go, only to return on the occasion of a mechanical failure.

For four years, things worked well. Until Molly came home. Until I felt for the first time that dull ache of nothingness. It was in mid-December when I was standing in the upstairs bathroom of my parents' house in Cleveland, shaving off my wiry mustache in the mirror I used to pop zits in as a teenager, when I caught a glimpse of myself. All at once, the panic set in, the heavy breathing, the thumping chest, the aggressive ennui. I made a few careless final swipes at my face with the razor and cut my lip, then went downstairs, holding a blood-sodden piece of toilet paper to my wound. Dad was sitting where he normally sits, in his dark blue leather recliner next to the fireplace. The television was on—a Cavaliers basketball game. My sons were on the floor. Molly was sleeping on her grandfather's chest. Rebecca was talking to my mom in the kitchen. I stood in the doorway and looked at it all. My family, my father. My life laid before me in complete innocence. And then I realized what had been troubling me; I saw the words on the ticker in my mind.

*You are the same age your dad was when you were born and you feel nothing like him. You don't feel in control of your life. You don't feel like a man.*

It was as if I had been staring at a book in a foreign language and all of a sudden I understood what the words meant. And it wasn't bullshit. It was exactly the truth, fact, clarity.

It's hard to explain the profundity of that moment. All my life I had been my father's son, my mother's son, and despite marriage, a career, children, and bills, I never really felt like a grown-up. Whereas my dad, who was in fact a year younger than I was when his third child—me—came along, was always so grown-up; so put together; had such a clear grasp on the world.

And my uneasiness lingered with me for weeks, through the Christmas holiday and into the new year. The panic was gone, the physical symptoms abated, but there was this sense of not feeling up to the life I was leading, of not fulfilling my role.

Of course it's not fair to compare yourself to your parents. You come from different places, different times. My dad grew up in Iowa, working on farms and walking to a country school. He went to Iowa State where he studied chemical engineering, and he later joined the army and became an officer. He grew up with eight siblings in a three-bedroom house. He made his own sausage.

All this seems like so much mythology when I think of my own anticlimactic superhero creation story. I grew up in the suburbs, a child of the '80s and '90s. I was an English major, and the only thing I ever had to share with my siblings was a healthy regard for Guns N' Roses and John Cusack movies. The closest I ever came to raising my own food was when I planted and killed a small tomato plant as part of a Cub Scout project. It wasn't that I felt I had wasted my life or was unhappy with it. Far from it. I had a pretty good life. It was just that I felt somehow stuck in the hinterland between youth and adulthood, being a young man and simply being a man. I wasn't stuck in the middle. I was 85 percent of the way there. But I wanted to know what it felt like to be the man in my household, the way I had always viewed my dad. And the mustache hadn't done the trick.

I needed something. A change. A continued evolution. Having a family early meant drifting apart from my college friends, nearly all of whom were slower to get married and have kids. Living as we had under constant financial strain meant any hobbies I may have had, any aspirations to travel or try new things, bowed below the weight of an always-too-small budget. I had long been comfortable with the fact that I would never have any stories about sowing my wild oats, about crazy trips to Mexico, or about following the imprudent impulses of youth. And, to be honest, I was fine with that. I never wanted anyone other than Rebecca. I still don't. Having a family had been a surprise, but it was quickly a welcomed one and I knew, even in the midst of the heaviest ennui, that what I was feeling was nothing like regret. It was more like unfulfilled potential.

There isn't a mustache lush enough to make up for that.

# 3

## I WANT TO HUNT

It was late—maybe around midnight in February—and I was sitting up in bed, the TV on top of our dresser was tuned to the Travel Channel, and the host was buying a load of hunting gear from an upscale shop in Vienna, Austria. He seemed pleased, like a lot of men are when buying themselves new toys, particularly when those toys are being paid for by someone else. My wife was asleep on the couch in the living room, having passed out watching her favorite soap opera and surviving another day at home with our three kids.

I was tired, not feeling well, and I knew I should be asleep. But even the cold medicine that promises a good night's sleep wasn't helping. I was feeling listless. I felt like I had things to do, but I didn't know what. It was just a general sense of obligation. I watched the host tool through the Alps in a Land Cruiser with his hunting guide in search of deer. They spotted a few nice big bucks. They were well within range, but the host didn't take a shot. He can't, he explains to the camera, because the show blew their budget on hunting gear. They could afford to shoot a doe, but a buck was just too much money. He laments wryly, then heads home with the hunting guide to eat venison and sausages around a small family table.

He made the whole thing look so cool, so invitingly manly, and I was overcome by the need to buy hunting gear. A gun. Coat, pants, an orange hat. Boots with a gusseted tongue to keep out deer ticks and water. Specialty hunting gloves with slim-fitting trigger finger and tacky palm for gun control. A dog whistle—a dog for that matter.

That night, I dreamed about hunting for the first time in my entire life. I dreamed of a giant deer, like an animatronics dinosaur at one of those roadside walk-through theme parks, emerging from the woods gracefully and walking up to me with the sauntering grace of a ballet dancer. It looked down on me, its steaming breath covering me in warm fog. I looked up at it in awe, just before it raised an angry hoof and squashed me into the ground. The entire scene was painted in Surrealist Technicolor and it was, of course, absurd beyond belief. Yet it felt so real. I'm not one who puts a lot of stock in dreams and signs. I don't believe that seeing a black cat will bring me bad luck, and I'm not the kind who runs out to the local gas 'n' suds to buy a lottery ticket because a cricket made its way onto my dashboard.

But I couldn't help but feel like an answer to my lack-of-manliness malaise was revealing itself the next day when I checked my e-mail at work and found a message from a publicist at the Travel Channel asking if I might be interested in interviewing its newest star, Steven Rinella, the host of *The Wild Within*. I get requests like this often, but usually it's from the author of a terrible book on the intricacies of forensic stamp collecting or the inventor of a product designed to make the pesky task of storing Play-Doh a breeze who's looking for a little publicity. It comes with the territory. At this time, the online magazine I edited, *Man of the House,* had a fairly loyal following of half a million readers. We'd just been featured in the *New York Times*, the *Boston Globe,* and elsewhere, so the requests for stories and profiles had stepped up significantly and I had gotten in the habit of deleting most of them unread. But the Travel Channel? Here my favorite television network was offering me an opportunity to talk with one of their hosts. How could I pass it up?

I didn't know anything about Steven Rinella or his show when I accepted the invitation, so I went on a research bender. I discovered that he was the author of two books about food and hunting. I watched the demo videos the Travel people sent me of his show, which was about his adventurers as a hunter and outdoorsman, and found myself fascinated. Never before had I seen a man stalk, shoot, and eviscerate a moose. Especially not on television. The closest I had come to ever seeing something like that was in an old horror movie. And yet, I wasn't grossed out. I was interested. I read his second book, *American Buffalo,* which recounts his youth as a sportsman, his lifelong fascination with America's most unique and once-treasured species, the bison, and his once-in-a-lifetime hunt for the animal in Alaska.

One line in particular struck me. Near the climax of the book, Rinella finds himself all alone in the wild north, lying prone and setting his sights on a buffalo roaming below and in front of him. Just before he pulls the trigger, he says to himself, *This is how food is made.* Such simple profundity, such clarity of purpose. I thought, *Now there's a man who knows exactly who he is, what he likes, and what he wants to do.* In short, there is a man nothing like me.

We made arrangements via e-mail to chat on a Tuesday night. He'd call me. I'd ask some questions about the show and he'd answer. Half hour at the most. They always say that when you do these kinds of interviews, as if the celebrity has many more important things to do than talk to you.

I once did an interview with an actress who had a minor role on a popular cable show and had costarred in a movie with Sylvester Stallone. Prior to our interview—which was conducted over the phone late at night—I received no fewer than four e-mails from her publicist reiterating the importance of her getting off the phone within fifteen minutes. She was then more than twenty minutes late calling me, which made me wonder if I somehow owed her five minutes and how I would go about repaying it? Knock a cigarette out of her hand just before she flicked her lighter? Buy her a field greens salad? A round of Botox? When at last we did get on the phone, I found myself apologizing for taking up her time, which, I told her, I understood was so precious.

"What do you mean?" she said.

"Your publicist told me you have something very important to do tonight."

"No, I don't."

"Are you sure?"

"Positive. I'm in my pajamas and it's only seven thirty here."

"So publicists are liars?"

"Pretty much."

This early experience interviewing the famous—or sorta-kinda-if-you-squint-in-just-the-right-light famous—took the fear out of the process for me. In subsequent interviews, I was cool and calm, knowing that it wasn't about a brush with fame or coolness by association. It was a business transaction and would more than likely be about as interesting as depositing a paycheck in an ATM.

Yet I found myself nervous to talk to Rinella. My palms were sweating when I pulled into the parking lot of a Starbucks not far from home. I had decided to take the call there to avoid the inevitable interruptions that come when trying to do work around the kids (or my wife for that matter). When I'm at home, seldom do five minutes pass in the waking day when I am not being beckoned from another room. I wanted to concentrate, to focus. There was something about Rinella—in his books, on his show—that resonated in me. I didn't want to pay him short shrift.

The e-mail came ten minutes after the time we were supposed to talk. It was simple and to the point. He had gotten the date of our interview mixed up. He apologized and offered to talk again at a time of my convenience. He signed it "SR" as if we have known each other for years. Two, maybe three sentences. He didn't overelaborate or make up an excuse to make me feel better. I remember thinking, *This guy even apologizes like a man.* I sent a note back and suggested the same time two days later and so found myself sitting at a back table in the Starbucks, pen in hand, a spare nearby, a couple of notebooks and a copy of *American Buffalo* splayed about the makeshift workspace. I couldn't believe how nervous I was to talk to a guy who a few days earlier I had never heard of, and I tried to calm my nerves when I picked up the call on the third ring.

"Hello?"

"Hi, Craig, it's Steven."

And so began one of the most interesting conversations I've ever had with a complete stranger. We talked for an hour and a half and when we were done, I began writing furiously. I don't normally do this. I usually wait a couple of days for an interview to sink in, but there was something about the guy that inspired me. It was his perspective. His belief that people willing to eat meat should be willing to harvest it; that hunters are too insular, too cliquish, too defensive. They don't make room for the curious. They don't make it easy for people to try. They don't do a good job selling their passion as a viable pastime.

Interviewing Rinella, spending time with him on the phone and hearing about his complicated relationship with his father and how fatherhood has changed his perception of what it means to be a man, I felt like I was talking to a man further along in his evolution than me. And yet, I was inspired. I too had a complicated relationship with my dad. I too wondered if I could change enough to be the dad I wanted to be. I realized what I had to do that night. I had to learn how to hunt. I come from a long line of hunters—at least as far as I know. My dad is a hunter. His brothers are hunters. I don't know a lot about my grandfather—either of them—as they were both gone by the time I was in third grade and my mom's dad I never met. And yet I had resisted, but talking to Rinella, I became fascinated. It felt right, the exact thing my weary manhood needed. I would become a hunter. It was as simple as that. I would venture off into the woods, gun in hand, and kill something and then everything would be better.

Just wait and see.

# 4

## MY SPORTING LIFE

I know about fishing. I've been a fisherman for most of my life. Growing up in north-central Wisconsin, I remember cringing as my dad removed coarse black leeches from a Styrofoam container and put them on my hook. In the small aluminum boat with the Evinrude outboard, there was not enough room to slink away from the small beasts and I might not have ever been afraid of them had my dad not pulled one off his finger, exposing a small stream of blood.

"What happened?" I asked.

"They're bloodsuckers," he told me. He didn't need to say much more. A certain feeling of disdain for the smallmouth bass that live in tiny Wisconsin lakes grew in me, simply because the fish will eat the leeches. How could I want anything that would eat a bloodsucker? To this day, I have never used a leech, though I have caught a lot of fish. There were semiannual trips to western Ontario for pike and walleye and, after we had moved from Wisconsin to California back to Wisconsin and on to Ohio, there were countless summer and early fall days spent fighting off low-grade seasickness as we bobbed up and down on Lake

Erie in pursuit of walleye and perch. I had my own tackle box and rod and spent a good deal of time in the small hold of the ProLine boat my dad had always wanted, suffering from the sun and stagnant air.

I have always loved the outdoors and fancied myself an outdoorsman, though I don't have the experience to back it up. Behind our first house on the suburban west side of Cleveland was a dense woods of old oak and maples. The kids on the street would spend summer afternoons building forts and walking, running, biking, and simply wandering the twisted network of trails blazed by generations of kids who had come before us. I loved the woods. I loved the coolness, the shadows, and the dappled sun breaking through the leaves high overhead. I probably would have found a way to live in those woods had I not had an experience that soured me somewhat on being there.

We were playing a game of capture the flag. There were probably eight of us from the neighborhood, all spread out through the woods on one of those dreamy days that only exist in movie scenes when a character remembers something from their past fondly. I remember it being cool among the trees and running alone on a stretch of trail fifty yards behind our house. I heard something off in the distance and stopped to listen, to see if I could tell which direction it was moving. I didn't feel it immediately, so intently focused was I on eluding capture by the older boy from up the street. It was only after a couple long moments' pause that I had the sensation that the ground beneath my foot was moving, or struggling to move. I felt a tug and then a flap of something like heavy paper on my hairless shin. I looked down and there, pinned beneath my Nike, was a bat. It was brown and black, furry and lying on its back, its wing pinned to the ground and its other flapping as it tried to get free. I looked into its beady black eyes and saw its teeth as its jaw flapped up and down silently. I don't remember exactly what I said as I bolted out of the woods, through some low brush and into my backyard, but I imagine it was something like, "Shit! Shit! Holy shit! Fuck! Damn! Shit! Shit! Shit!" because I had only recently discovered the cathartic benefits of swearing and had been polishing my abilities at the bus stop and during games of pickup basketball with friends.

I vowed never again to return to those woods and managed to keep that promise until after I had graduated from high school, but the inclination toward nature, or at least the accoutrements of those who find themselves in the natural world, was ingrained in me. I knew early that my flat-footed awkwardness, pudgy midsection, and general aversion to exercise in any traditional, suburban form meant I would never play center field for the Cleveland Indians, shoot three-pointers for the Cavs, or strap on the orange and brown of the Browns—unless I was to be an offensive lineman and who, really, dreams of becoming an offensive lineman when they are a kid? But I had read Gary Paulsen's *Hatchet* and the issues of *Boys' Life* that continued to trickle in long after my Cub Scout den had disbanded from disinterest, and it was about this time that I discovered the L.L.Bean catalog and developed a fascination that lasts to this day.

I don't quite know what it was about L.L.Bean, but there was something about the catalog that left me transfixed. While all my friends were rushing home to get the new issue of a magazine called *Beckett,* which published values and prices of baseball cards—and some of the more developed ones were hijacking copies of the Victoria's Secret catalog and *Sports Illustrated*'s swimsuit issue from the mailbox before their parents got home—I found myself rushing to the box at the end of our driveway hoping to find a new catalog from Bean. I read the descriptions of tents and anoraks as if they were literature. The twenty-five words used to describe the functions of a particular pocketknife were my prepubescent poetry. Years later, when Rebecca and I had one of our first dates, I told her about the trip, about the store, and about my dreams of moving to Maine and working there. I would have a cabin in the woods and spend my days writing thoughtful descriptions of water purifiers and first aid kits. Did it matter that my outdoor experience was generally limited to catalogs, some Hemingway books, and a whole lot of daydreaming? Not to me. Before I left for college, she gave me a gift. She had told a mutual friend of ours, an art student and painter, about my dream life and commissioned a small painting to hang in my dorm room and remind me of her. It was a cabin near a mountain and well done, even if it was obvious that the artist had never seen the rolling hills of New England and instead interpreted the mountain as Everest's big brother. It's hard to imagine what life was like before Google, but topographical inaccuracies didn't matter. I was in love with the idea of Maine and L.L.Bean.

After my freshman year of college, I took my roommate and best friend from high school on a road trip to Maine, to the Bean store and to Mount Desert Island. We were underage but managed a few beers along the drive. We went to the store twice, and it would be the last time I was there until more than a year after graduation, when I finally managed to get Rebecca up to Maine for a visit. I proposed to her on our first night there. Right there. In the furniture section of the same store that I had begun dreaming about as a kid.

Okay, it was a little more romantic than that. We had been arguing. Tensions were high because the airports had just re-opened after the September 11 terrorist attacks. I had been planning the trip for the better part of a year, since long before I had bought the ring and asked her parents for their blessing. I wanted everything to go so smoothly. This place, this dream, had been central to our early relationship and a big part of my identity, so I was a little miffed when we arrived into Portland late and got into our rental car and she told me we needed to stop to see her cousin—a person I had never met and one she had not mentioned until that moment.

"Are you kidding me? No way are we going to drive around Portland at almost midnight to go find some cousin you haven't seen in five years," I said.

"Why not? I'd do it for you."

"I wouldn't ask you to. I wouldn't ask you to go meet a stranger in the middle of the night after seven hours in airports and on planes when you had been planning this trip for months and months."

She wasn't pouting, but her silence told me I had said the wrong thing. Family is first with Rebecca, pure and simple. There is nothing more important. Here I was being a jerk when all she wanted to do is stop by to see a family member. It was, unfortunately, a fight we would have more than once during the course of our marriage and in traveling together. It seems no matter where we are going, there's always a cousin on the way or an uncle or an aunt or a great-aunt she's never met before.

We went straight to Freeport, where I booked a room in a hotel. The plan was to go to Bar Harbor the next day and after six years together and finally making this trip, she would have had to have been three points beyond stupid not to suspect that I had planned to propose. And I had. The next day, on top of Cadillac Mountain, overlooking the Atlantic and my favorite vacation spot in the world. But first we needed to unwind. The L.L.Bean store is open 24/7 365 days a year. There aren't even locks on the doors. I was too excited not to take her there for a little middle-of-the-night shopping. I thought maybe some retail therapy would thaw her icy mood.

Traveling in those first heady days after 9/11 was rough. Security was beyond tight, and it had taken every little bit of ingenuity I could muster to hide the engagement ring I had stashed in my pocket through security checkpoints and at the car rental place. Sometime between landing and checking in at the motel, I had stashed it in my backpack and very nearly left it there in the car when we parked in the lot behind the Bean store shortly after one A.M. But I got nervous. She rushed ahead to the bathroom and I ran back to our rented Hyundai to retrieve it, putting it back in my pocket as we walked around the store.

She was tired. She was a little angry and I did what many men try to do—buy her affection. Though I was living in Section 8 subsidized housing and making a meager $20,000 as a junior reporter on a small daily newspaper, I bought her two coats and a few other items hoping to make her happy. I paid with a fresh credit card and we wandered through the store, upstairs, taking a seat at a farmhouse table with green legs and matching ladder-back chairs—a staple of the L.L.Bean "Home" catalog.

"I really like this table," I said. It was true. I liked the style and the fact that it seemed like it would fit well into my semi-rural life plan.

"Me too," she said, still a little coldly.

"We should register for it," I said. It came out on impulse, with no real forethought.

"We should," she said, and the tone got a little tenser. "Except we're not engaged."

"Well, what if we were?"

"But we're not," she said, firmly, but with a brightening smile.

"What if we were?"

"But we're not!" This time more emphatically.

"But what if we were?" I asked, bending onto one knee, pulling the ring from my pocket, and sliding it across the table. "What if we were? Will you marry me?"

Tears formed in the corners of her eyes and we embraced. She went to the restroom and used her cell phone to call her best friend. Operation "He Finally Asked" was set into motion. While she was off doing that, I asked a woman who was working in the section how much the table and chairs were and the price was slightly out of my budget.

"What about just the chairs?" She told me their price and offered to call the warehouse and have them dropped off for me to pick up. "Here's the thing," I said, and I recounted the story of what had just happened. The woman took heart and made a few phone calls. It was against store policy to sell the floor models, but she understood their sentimental value and made arrangements anyway. She had them boxed up and sent to my apartment in Virginia and you can find them today in our home.

We returned the next day to register for the table only to find out that Bean had discontinued its wedding registry just months before. After the greatest weekend of my life—eating, lounging, dreaming, and roaming with my new fiancée—I wrote a letter to the then chairman of the company, a grandson of the man who gave it its name. He responded with a handwritten note of thanks and congratulations. He apologized for the cancellation of the registry, but wished us well in our life together. If you visit our home, you'll find that letter there too.

\* \* \*

By that point, I was living in Virginia and had taught myself to fly-fish (I even worked, for a short time, in a fly-fishing shop after graduation and before my move south), something too snobby and New England to ever be considered by my deeply midwestern sportsmen relatives. Fly-fishing was for the fancy class, as was L.L.Bean. No, the Heimbuchs were Cabela's people. Cabela's is like a prairie version of Bean. Its catalog, I remember, was thick and utilitarian. There were no pictures of families camping along an inland lake, no campsite ice cream makers, just pages and pages of guns and camo and gun cases, locks, and cleaning kits. Cabela's was, and is in large part, for hunters and serious fishermen. I tried hard to get into it the same way I did Bean, but it wasn't the same. There was no nuance, no story. The Cabela brothers were real people, but you never got a sense of who they were. Bean prided itself on tradition. L.L. was a real person. Babe Ruth was a customer. Cabela's had, what? A myriad of options when it came to fish finders and floor mats for your truck, but no romance.

Fly-fishing and Bean represented a certain divergence from family sporting tradition for me. I liked the idea of backpacking the Blue Ridge more than of taking a buck from an Iowa cornfield, or of casting a weightless fly to a graceful trout instead of a heavy lure to a gnarly toothed muskie. And then there was the hunting thing.

My anxiety about hunting came from the fact that I had never, really, done it before. On three occasions, I had been privy to a hunt. The first was when I was around eleven or twelve. We were visiting my Iowa family, and my dad wanted to go pheasant hunting. He, my uncle Paul, a cousin, and I walked with a couple of dogs through a cornfield that had been partially harvested, hoping to scare some birds up. My uncle Mark stayed on the other end of the field with a black powder rifle waiting for any deer that might get scared up by us walking through the field. It must have been about three degrees outside, because I remember my breath condensing in the scarf my mom had wrapped around my head and freezing. My dad had told me that you almost have to step on a pheasant in order to get it to flush up out of the corn. He told me this so that I wouldn't be surprised when I stepped on a crushed stalk and it came alive with flapping wings, but what it actually did was make me terrified to put my feet down. I didn't have the same relationship to wildlife that my dad had growing up. He grew up hunting those Iowa fields, raising livestock, and engaging in other pursuits that allowed for hands-on interactions with beast and fowl. I grew up in the suburbs. We had a family dog and got our meat from the supermarket a mile or so from our house. The closest I had ever been to a pheasant was seeing Funk's G seed signs on the ends of cornrows when driving out to visit my grandmother near Mason City. We had a clock in our basement, a wooden clock with the Funk's G logo on it, and burned into the face was the image of three pheasant rising from a row of corn.

Understanding this, you can probably guess what an anxious afternoon that was, walking through a cornfield. Every step tightened my intestines, every footfall shrunk my sphincter. I wanted to leave and go back to the car, but I was afraid that, if I did, Uncle Mark might mistake me for a deer and blow me away. He wouldn't have, of course, but I was young and my youthful imagination often got the best of me, so I pictured my family standing around my lifeless carcass, staring curiously at my body and then silently and collectively coming to the conclusion that, "Well, it would be a shame to let this meat go to waste . . ."

My second experience hunting was around the same time, perhaps even on the same trip. Dad and Uncle Mark colluded and decided it was time for me to go deer hunting. I don't remember being excited, but I wasn't opposed to the idea. Not at first, anyway. Mark and I got bundled up into thirty-five layers of clothes and drove to a nearby wood abutting a cement plant, where we ensconced ourselves atop a ridge looking down through trees to a shallow ravine.

"Great," I said. "What's next?"

"Next," Mark said, after giving me instructions on where and when to shoot a deer, "we wait."

And so we did. For what felt like hours. We waited as the sun began to go down in the winter sky and the woods took on a cool, gray look. We waited, sitting on the hard ground in zero-degree temperatures. We waited and waited, then waited some more until it got dark, too dark to hunt, and time to go home. When we got back to my grandmother's house, my dad asked how I liked deer hunting and, though my opinion on the sport had been murky prior to going out with Mark, it had begun to crystallize after. "It sucks," I said. "I don't ever want to do that again."

And so it was. I was never again invited and never asked to be.

My third experience hunting was significantly more recent. I was in my late twenties and already a father. I was visiting my folks in Cleveland for a weekend. Dad told me he had been asked by a client to go pheasant hunting at a private club twenty minutes away. He took me and my little brother, Kosta, with him. I don't want to take away from the experience—especially because I did actually get three or four birds—but this club was the perfect combination of country club and petting zoo. There was a clubhouse, complete with requisite mounted animals and card tables, a bar, and photos of victorious men bearing arms.

The pheasant were kept in a pen, a low-ceiling chicken-wire circus tent. You tell the man at the front desk how many birds you'd like to shoot, a transaction is made, and you are given a field assignment. While you, the hunter, are sorting out your gear and, perhaps, enjoying a drink from the bar, workers from the club place your prepurchased birds in the field. I can't be sure, but I suspect this involves dosing the pheasant with adult-sized portions of NyQuil, then laying them among the scrub grass of the football-field-sized hunting lanes. Then, mighty hunter, you go out and wake the birds enough for them to jump in the air and, following a deft maneuver with your shotgun, die. It was not perhaps the most sporting of efforts, but I did manage to get a few birds, all of which were defeathered and prepared by the same club staff that placed them in the field while I toasted with a posthunt beer.

Those were my experiences with hunting to this point—a paranoid walk, a frigidly long sit in the woods, and a few birds that may as well have been tied to a tree.

It's possible that my hunting aversion has something to do with never needing to do it—for sport, entertainment, or provision. When I was looking for fun on a Saturday, I went to the movies, to a museum, to a coffee shop.

My conception of hunting has always been a bit, well, simplistic.

**Step 1:** Outfit yourself with a device designed to accelerate a projectile at an alarming rate.

**Step 2:** Position yourself in a place where animals like to hang out—either to eat, sleep, or breed.

**Step 3:** Identify creature with a beating heart and instinct to flee.

**Step 4:** Remove heartbeat.

**Step 5:** Serve with potatoes.

The subtleties, strategies, complexities, and, even, potential enjoyment of hunting have, for most of my life, been lost on me. I never got it. I never understood why my dad got so excited to go deer hunting with his brothers. I didn't get it in the same way I didn't get weight lifting. It all seemed so caveman to me, so midwestern and simple. Me make boom-boom. Me lift heavy rock. Me beat on me chest. I thought myself to be more sophisticated than that, more urbane.

A big part of that has to do with my youthful longing to be more sophisticated than that, to be more urbane, to be more Eastern. I thought being from the Midwest was akin to being an athlete born with legs of two different lengths. I thought being successful would be harder for me because I was from the Midwest. I wanted the ocean. I wanted New York and Maine. I wanted to feel like I was from somewhere instead of the nowhere that actually was home. And if not New England, what about the Pacific Northwest? Portland: land of hippies and homemade everything. The Cascades, a place so beautiful it takes your breath away. California even. Talk to someone from California and they will tell about their youthful proximity to really interesting places like Los Angeles or San Francisco.

Then, in college, it was the South. Walker Percy and Faulkner. I was fascinated by the strange dignity of the place, despite having never really been there. I managed a minor in college in the history of the American South, but I have never been to Alabama, Mississippi, Louisiana, or Arkansas (unless you count a brief layover at the Little Rock airport on my way home from my bachelor party in Las Vegas). I've managed brief visits to both Carolinas and Georgia. I've driven through Tennessee on a couple of occasions and, now that I live in Cincinnati, I often find myself having lunch in Kentucky. After college, I took a job writing for a newspaper in Winchester, Virginia, a tiny but historic hamlet in the northern thumb of the Old Dominion. I have to say I adored living there. I fell madly in love with the Shenandoah Valley, with biscuits and gravy, and the patois of the people, all friendly as an afternoon rain. I loved driving through the Blue Ridge and, after a couple of months living there, I vowed to never again live above the Mason-Dixon.

That lasted less than a year when marriage and a job (along with its relative proximity to family) brought me back to Ohio. Once again, I felt like a man stranded, a man who wanted no place else but someplace else. I had neither mountain nor city, neither ocean nor charm. I come from Wisconsin. I come from Ohio. I come from cornfields and the Rust Belt. How could I ever be interesting coming from places like that? How could I ever be happy?

Something happened in my late twenties, though. I began to appreciate where I come from, to love the Midwest. It used to be, when I was a child, boring and arduous to drive to Iowa to visit my grandmother, aunts, uncles, and cousins. There's nothing but cornfields, there's nothing but nothing. And when you get there, it's boring. There's no mall or distraction. There's only outside, and outside isn't that interesting. But when I had kids, I came to appreciate the nothing as being something. I found myself wanting to go there, wanting to drive among the cornfields for hours on end, to smell the earth and eat the food and be among the people who mattered most to me. I wanted that connection to the people and places that I come from, and I began to see the Midwest as something else entirely. I began to see it as home.

And yet, it is not home. Not really anyway. I come from the suburbs, the manicured outskirts of once-great cities. While I tend to tell people I am a Wisconsinite—having been born in the north-central region of the state and living there almost entirely through my first-grade year—I am really an Ohioan through and through. I claim cheese and birch forests, but I bleed the west side of Cleveland. I complain about the suburbs, with their matching minimalls, sidewalks, and above-average schools, yet the suburbs are the only place I feel at home. So even when I am among family in Iowa, I feel separated, from the place, from the legacy, from the two-dozen cousins. They all seem to fit in there, while I feel like a tourist.

I'm not fully midwestern. Instead, like the Starbucks/mattress store/Target/Claire's boutique combinations that seem to exist in the twenty-mile concentric circles that surround American cities, I am somewhere in between. I am the suburb personified. I am bland and predictable. I don't require a lot of work to understand, and I don't offer too much by way of insight or fascination.

So, if I am to reconcile with where I am from, if I am to become a real Midwestern Man, I have to up the ante. I have to learn the essential traits and inhabit the role; I must do something bold, brave, something I would never have considered when I was young and dreaming of elsewhere.

I have to hunt. It's the only way. There was, of course, more to it than that. I wanted to stand above a still-steaming carcass and think, *I did that.* It wasn't bloodlust or a need for wanton destruction; it was a desire to feel fully formed as a man, to go off into the woods and kill an animal, provide sustenance for my young family, accomplish something I had always been too afraid to try.

# 5

## COMING OUT OF
## THE HUNTING CLOSET

Try telling someone these days that you're going to learn how to hunt and see what kind of reaction you receive. You may as well tell someone that you're thinking about taking up self-mutilation or dabbling in the study of classic New England witchcraft. Up to this point, my mission had remained secret. I trolled websites late at night after Rebecca had fallen asleep on the couch watching recorded soap operas. I was giving myself private lessons in what it would take, what I would need, what it would mean to be a hunter.

In the world in which I lived, the comfortable world of suburbia, hunters were rare. At parties, Little League games, and family events, the men were much more likely to talk about the market and how the president's latest tax proposal/health care initiative/foreign policy initiative was playing havoc with their portfolio. Being a journalist, I could follow the headlines, but when it came to relating to their personal economic upheaval, I was blessedly unable to relate. My portfolio consisted mainly of savings bonds my grandmother had sent me every year on my birthday and the retirement account the HR director at work set up for me on my first day on the job. There were, of course, other topics of conversation—sports, other businessy stuff, and the dilemma of choosing between golfing at their country club or a friend's country club the following weekend. It's the curse of living in the toniest, newest suburb in town and spending time almost exclusively with people ten years your senior. It's not that I don't like these people. Quite the opposite in fact. I like them very much. It's just that I don't often have a lot in common with them. And in this world of twenty-four-hour grocery stores and health clubs, the idea of sharing my plans to take up arms and stalk animals didn't seem like the right thing to do.

Except for John.

John is the husband of the best friend Rebecca has ever had. We'd met five years earlier, after our wives had met and become instant friends. After a few months of getting together with the kids or going out for coffee, wine, or dinner, the girls decided it was time for John and me to get to know each other.

"I want you to meet Anne's husband, John," Rebecca told me one day.

"Why?"

"Because," she said, "he's nice and I think you two would get along."

"Really? What's he do?"

"He's some kind of engineer."

"Well, that's a lot like being a writer."

"But you guys have so much in common."

"Like what?"

"He likes sports and you like sports. You'll have a lot to talk about."

She didn't point out that John is a football fan and I'm a

tennis fan, but in the strictest sense of the word, I guess she was right. It was a man date and there was no getting around it. It was lucky John and I did get along. Sure, he's an engineer who grew up in a small town—or near it—in western Indiana. He's an athlete and he drinks beer where I prefer gin, but we had things in common beyond the usual hobbies and interests; namely, we were married to very similar women. I decided I would first tell John about my idea to learn to hunt, but I realized there would be some obvious questions I would need to answer. For what would I be hunting? Where? When?

I went to a used bookstore in a strip mall in our town and asked the woman behind the counter where they kept the books about hunting. She looked at me for a long moment. Was it disdain? Or was she searching her mental inventory? She pointed me in the direction of the sports books, a small shelf tucked away in a dusty corner. I got the sense that people who read about sports tend to buy their books new and keep them on their shelves because the selection was meager to say the least. There were books about football and rock climbing, a couple of rows dedicated to the martial arts, and a couple more about soccer. But in terms of the sports afield, there were very few titles; and a vast majority of those were about fishing.

I tried another bookstore, one that sold new books, and the local public libraries. It seemed there was not a great demand for hunting books in the suburbs north of Cincinnati, so I turned to the Internet. I began with a search for "Ohio Hunting Rules" and came across the Ohio Department of Natural Resources site and a page devoted to hunting regulations. I once read an article about hunters in Germany. Being at least half and probably more German, I have over the years come to respect that country's innate sense of rules and order. Getting a driver's license in Germany takes years, and those caught committing moving violations on the autobahn aren't just slapped with a ticket; they have their privileges removed. Mind you, not for something like causing a ten-car pileup or repeated offenses of driving under the influence of massive quantities of German beer, but moving violations like failing to yield in the left lane for cars attempting to pass. Knowing this, it's no surprise to learn that hunting is taken pretty seriously over there. Getting a German hunter's license requires two years of training, apprenticeship, and overcoming bureaucratic hurdles that would drive an American libertarian to the brink of insanity. As such, most Germans who hunt are of the upper class. They are the ones who can afford expensive game tags and memberships at state-regulated game preserves. The result is an orderly and safe community of hunters and conservationists, well-trained outdoorsmen who are capable of not only surviving but thriving in the natural world and of preserving it.

America is not Germany. And if Ohio is any indicator of national rigidity when it comes to laws and preparedness, it never could be. Reading through the regulations, I discovered that all an Ohioan needs in order to set to the field, gun in hand and pocket full of shells, is a short course in safety—taken either as a home study or a two-day seminar—and $19 for a general license. I know people who've spent more time training to operate a dolly in a warehouse. I made some notes about possible dates to take hunter's safety and downloaded an electronic version of the course manual to Rebecca's iPad for late-night study. I also browsed through the sections of the site that detailed the kinds of animals available in the state for hunting. These fit into a few neat categories: small game and upland birds, which included pheasant, quail, grouse, rabbits, squirrels, woodchuck, and all manner of other wee beasts winged and not; deer; waterfowl like ducks and geese; turkey; and other animals like red fox, feral hogs, and the occasional black bear that makes the news every time one is spotted on the other end of the southern part of the state.

Deer seemed like a natural choice. For the few hunters I do know outside of the family, this is their most likely target. The season is relatively long, broken up by types of weapons—bow, black powder, shotgun, handgun, and rifle—and having eaten my fair share of venison over the years from Dad's hunting trips to Wisconsin, I knew I liked the taste. But I didn't consider it as an option for long. For one, deer hunting is a solitary activity. You may go out with other people, but you are all relegated to your own tree stand or spot in the woods. You sit for long stretches, as I had with Uncle Mark a couple decades before, in the cold, not moving and just waiting. I don't have the attention span to do that. I need a little more action. I also didn't like the idea of camouflage. Bow hunters wear camo head to toe, going so far as to spray themselves with either simulated or real doe urine in order to draw males in close. Camo is for the military and little boys pretending to be in the military, I reasoned. And while sartorial considerations should not have been high on the list of priorities, they were there somewhere. If I was going to invest in clothing and gear, I wanted it to suit my particular idiom, my style, my sense of cool. That was one of the reasons why I gravitated toward fly-fishing. Men in waders casting a line from a bamboo rod and standing up to their asses in ice water just looked a whole lot cooler than some dude sitting on the shore with a coffee can full of worms and, one imagines, a cooler full of cheap beer.

Camo may also have put a dent in the idea of turkey hunting. But there were a few other factors that eliminated it as an option. One, who wants to shoot a Butterball? Don't get me wrong, turkey is without a doubt my favorite meat at the local Subway, but the idea of nestling in close to the ground and calling one close was not appealing. Uncle Mark once told me about going turkey hunting and calling in a gobbler only to hear a shot ring out from the other side of the clearing as another hunter, unable to see him for his camo outfit, nearly blew his head off. I didn't want that to happen. And knowing my luck, it would be exactly what came to pass. And, two, the turkey season in Ohio is in the spring, making it nearly impossible since it was already March, leaving little time for me to get myself in gear and get out into the field for that year's hunt.

Duck and goose hunting had some appeal. Sure, there was camo involved, but remember that scene in Hemingway's *Across the River and into the Trees* where he goes hunting with the Italian noblemen? It seemed like, pardon the pun, such a blast. Plus, I love duck. It's one of my favorite things to eat, and having played golf fairly regularly as a teenager and into my twenties, I have a real disdain for geese. I held that option open for a while, but eventually closed it when I realized learning duck hunting would be something I would do on my own. I don't know any duck hunters. My dad had never really hunted them that I knew of and I wanted this to be something I could share with him.

Bear? Not reliable enough. Dad got one in Canada. So did Uncle Mark. But the idea of trying to find a black bear in Ohio seemed an awful lot like trying to find Bigfoot. Except instead of shooting some grainy footage of the beast with a Super 8 camera, I would have to shoot and, presumably, eat it. Red fox felt too much like shooting a dog. And pigs? Well, the ODNR encouraged any hunter who came across them to shoot feral hogs, so it felt less like sportsmanship than blood sport. I decided to pass.

This left small game and upland birds. After several hours of careful consideration, I decided on pheasant. I remembered going hunting with my dad and uncle and cousin that one time for pheasant, so it fit the family requirement and, since we had done it in a group, it was more social than deer hunting. I knew Uncle Mark and his sons, Will and Tommy, hunted pheasant regularly. Plus, the more I read, the more I realized it was the perfect bird for me. And I remembered the pictures from the L.L.Bean catalogs of upland hunting scenes—men in orange vests and hats, khaki pants, and cool-looking boots walking through fields of tall grass, their English springer spaniels on the scent of birds. I had had a springer named "Quigley." I loved that dog. The pictures were so inviting. They were the hunting equivalent of men in waders fishing for trout. And it's not like you can get pheasant at the local grocery store. It was perfect.

Pheasants Forever, a group devoted to the hunting and preservation of the bird, describes the ringneck pheasant as "America's Favorite Game Bird." It's a bit ironic given that, like nearly all the toys in our house, the pheasant is an import from China. Unlike many game animals, we can trace its introduction to the United States to a shipping manifesto. According to the august UltimatePheasantHunting.com, which seems devoted to all the pheasant news that's fit to print:

> The Ringed-necked Pheasant was imported to America from Asia, and no other game species introduced to this continent has been as successful at flourishing as the pheasant. One of more than 40 species originating in Asia and Asia Minor, these birds from the genus Phasianus are perhaps better known than

*any of the other 15 groups of pheasants in the world. All are related to the partridges, quails, grouse and guinea-fowls which make up the order Galliformes or chicken-like birds.*

*Archaeological evidence suggests that large pheasants lived in southern France in the Miocene period, some 13 million years ago. The Greeks knew the bird in the 10th Century B.C. and we have adopted their name for the species,* Phasianus ornis *(phasian bird), derived from the Phasis River (now Rion) near the Caucasus Mountains. The Chinese knew the pheasant some 3,000 years ago, but the Romans are considered responsible for the spread of pheasants in western Europe. When Julius Caesar invaded England in the first century B.C., the pheasant followed.*

*It wasn't until 1733 that the pheasant appeared in North America, when several pairs of the black-necked strain were introduced in New York. Other pheasant varieties were released in New Hampshire and New Jersey later in the 18th century. Not until 1881, when Judge O.N. Denny released some 100 pairs of Chinese ring-necks in the Willamette Valley of Oregon, did the pheasant really gain a foothold in the United States. Since then, pheasants have been propagated and released by government agencies, clubs, and individuals, and for all practical purposes are established everywhere on the continent that suitable habitat exists.*

Once I had established what I would be hunting, I quickly found myself consumed in the study of the pheasant. I ordered every book I could find on the subject, ranging from a collection of essays recalling individual hunts and lifetime experiences in pursuit of the ringneck to books on butchering and cooking, even husbandry of American pheasant. I hadn't been so devoted to reading about a single topic since college, and my obsession drove me on. Late at night, with my wife and children asleep, I would spend a half hour or forty minutes reviewing the course material for hunter's safety, then an hour or more reading about pheasants—how they prefer to live near brushy fence lines or scrubby woods that provide cover from predator species; how you're more likely to find them in low-lying areas and how they tend to run when threatened as opposed to fly; how, when cooking them, you need to be sure to add plenty of fat since the meat tends to be very, very lean. I studied techniques for hunting and watched video after gruesome video of the proper means of removing entrails from the bird while in the field.

This was the part that scared me the most. I loved the idea of being out in a field with a dog or other people and shooting the bird. That seemed so sporting, so regal. And I liked the idea that I could prepare one to be served. But it was the required action in between that made me nervous. I watched a series of videos in which American hunters of questionable dental stability displayed their preferred means of field dressing a bird, which consisted of standing on the bird's wings, grabbing its feet, and pulling until the head, spine, organs, and other nontasty bits were pulled off like an old sock. The men demonstrating would cackle, then pull out a knife that looked like it had been purchased at a truck stop, and cut off the wings, leaving just the pinkish breast of the bird. I'll hand it to these men, it was efficient. The whole process took less than a minute, but turning an animal inside out didn't exactly inspire hunger or desire.

There was another method I found equally repugnant, involving a device called the Bird Hitch. Essentially, it's a hook that fits onto the trailer hitch of your hunting truck. You jam the hook through the bird's neck, grab it by the wings and pull. It's dismembered in seconds, leaving the hunter with nothing but breast meat and wings. I threw up a little when I first saw it. Not a full upchuck, but one of those ones that rise up into your esophagus like Scooby-Doo peeking into a dark attic. Yet, I couldn't stop watching because the video was not just one guy in a field, but several in several different settings using the Bird Hitch on several species. Pheasant, geese, ducks. All came apart with equal and apparent ease. It was an infomercial for drawing and quartering, an obvious attempt to drum up sales of the device, which made me wonder—who came up with this thing?

I imagined a group of semidrunk hunters sipping on Old Milwaukee and tediously going about cleaning the day's haul around a campfire with knives.

"Boy," says one, "field dressing birds is just such a pain."

"I know," says another. "I spend all day in the duck blind shooting only to come back to camp and have to spend hours dismantling these geese."

"If only there was another way," the first says.

Then, as if from the clouds, a baritone announcer chimes in: "Now there is an easier way!"

"There is?" the two befuddled hunters say in unison.

"That's right! Never take the time to properly care for your prey again, thanks to the Bird Hitch!"

"The Bird Hitch? What is it?"

"It's only the greatest thing to happen to evisceration since the Spanish Inquisition. The Bird Hitch makes low-grade mutilation easy and convenient, and it looks good on your truck too."

"Wow!" they say in unison. "Thanks, Bird Hitch!"

I found other videos, mostly done by British sportsmen and chefs. These were decidedly more sedate and somehow more humane. I realize the incongruity of saying that I wanted to treat the birds I would theoretically shoot with a bit of dignity. After all, I would have just forced little bits of lead into them at fourteen hundred feet per second, but it somehow mattered. I wanted to be a hunter, not a killer, and grabbing a bird by its legs and yanking it apart head-through-asshole felt more like something a killer would do than what a gentleman hunter would do.

Soon, it was time to announce my plans, to tell somebody, anybody, what I had been doing on all those late nights. I needed to make my intentions known so that they would become a reality, or else I might content myself with surreptitiously watching videos late at night or reading in spare moments at the office. Sneaking off for private moments of hunting research was beginning to feel illicit, sneaky, like a preteen boy sneaking off for a few moments of vigorous self-exploration. I needed to tell somebody so that it didn't feel quite so dirty.

At a dinner party for our wives' moms' group, I pulled John aside and told him my plan.

"I'm going to learn to hunt," I told him.

"Oh yeah?" he said. "What are you going to hunt?"

"Pheasant."

"That's cool," he said. "You got a gun? A license? Anything?"

"Got a gun, but nothing else."

I told him what I knew about the license process and gave him a rough outline of what I wanted to do. I'd make my way out to Iowa in the fall with my dad, telling him I wanted to go hunting. I'd tell him I wanted him to take me pheasant hunting with Uncle Mark and some cousins. They wouldn't expect much, given that I had never been before. But I'd spend the next six months preparing, learning everything I possibly could about hunting so that when I showed up, I would already be as close to an expert as possible.

"They'll be surprised," I told him, "because they won't need to teach me a thing."

"Sounds pretty cool," he said. "What's Rebecca say about it?"

"I haven't told her yet."

"Well, good luck with that one. You gonna write a book?"

"To be honest," I said, "I hadn't thought about it."

He went off to get a couple more beers and I felt more excited than I ever had about the prospect of hunting. It felt like I had passed some sort of initial test. And I couldn't wait to see the look on my dad's and Uncle Mark's faces when I showed up and kicked some pheasant ass.

I told Rebecca a couple of days later about my plan to become a hunter and, to my great surprise, she was fine with it.

"Knock yourself out," she said. "Just don't shoot your eye out."

That may be one of the things I love most about my wife, her ability to be completely unironic. And, to be honest, I had expected a good deal more resistance to the whole thing. I realized later that I may have needed more resistance. Instead, her approval meant the only obstacles I had to becoming a hunter were the ones I would create in my own head. There were plenty of those, not the least of which was the simple question of why I would want to do such a thing.

I think in the very early stages, it's because I was grasping for something. I was looking for something that would make me feel more like a man. But a month or two after my late-night revelation, I realized learning how to hunt would do little to improve my feelings of masculinity. Becoming a hunter wouldn't undo the uncertainties I felt about my career choice; it wouldn't fill my bank account and suddenly put us in a position to buy a house and settle into the life that had for so long surrounded us but that we had not been able to live. I had been desperate in thinking that it would.

So what was it then? Why was I even more determined than ever before to do such a thing? It was because I felt like an outsider, a pretender, a faux adventurer content to live through other people's exploits. When I was in a room or at a party and someone would tell a hunting story, I would tell one of my dad's or recite something I had read in Hemingway. But I didn't know what it was like to walk off into the woods in pursuit of dinner. I didn't really understand what my dad and uncles and cousins got from being out there. You tell your grandpa's war stories when you're in high school and they somehow feel like your own. But, at some point, it's time to stop telling other people's stories and simply enlist. I have told a few of my dad's army stories dozens of times. I've told other people about the day he shot a bear in Canada. I've done it at parties. I've done it in meetings. And I've been crushed by the shadow of legacy, of having to tell my father's stories because I had none of my own. I'm too old to join the army, too entrenched in my life that I was beginning to realize was only half lived. I realized it was no longer good enough to have his stories, because I could not have a perspective built on his experiences. I needed a perspective of my own, to live my own stories, to tell my own stories.

There was also the curiosity. I wanted to know what it felt like to be out there, in the woods or on the field with purpose. I wanted to understand why highly unromantic people like my dad and family seemed so romantically drawn to the pursuit. I wanted to know what it was like to carry a gun, to listen to the sounds of the woods, to taste protein I had procured. I was well beyond the notion that learning to hunt would somehow make me feel more like a man. I was beyond the Hemingway code. Instead, I was driven by curiosity and a desire to once and for all feel what it meant to have stories of my own.

I had so few, particularly ones that were so grown-up, so adult. There were stories from my beat on the paper in Virginia, from college, and from life with Rebecca. There was our engagement and marriage, but those seemed like the last vestiges of youth, not the full-blown tales of adulthood. We had some. The birth of our kids, for example, or the child we lost to miscarriage, surviving soul-crushing debt and coming out better for it, but these aren't the stories you tell around a bonfire. These are stories you tell yourself when you're alone and in rush-hour traffic, the ones you tell no one.

I remained devoted to the idea that I could learn to hunt not because people were expecting me to do it, not because I had told a hundred people and they were watching me closely, but because they weren't. Because it was unexpected. Because I wanted to do something disruptive and to understand better what hunting was about. And hunting was, at that time, the most disruptive thing I could do.

Plus, I wanted to carry a gun into the woods and maybe stop somewhere along the way to pee on a tree.

That would be a story worth telling.

# PART II
# SPRING

# 6

## LONG ROAD TO IOWA

I checked my mirror three or four times, hoping not to see lights. I don't know that what I was doing was illegal, but I imagined it would be, at least, frowned upon. No cops. No cars. Nothing behind me but miles of highway rolling out like a ribbon, much closer than it appears. The cruise was set at seventyish and I was trying to adjust the zoom on my iPhone camera while maintaining control of the steering wheel. I wanted the photo that I could see out ahead of me, but it was hard to balance driving, paranoia, and my Ansel Adams vision for landscape photography. I'm just glad my wife wasn't with me. I can't imagine what she would say about me taking pictures while driving. True, it's not texting, but it's not exactly safe either.

I love driving through the Midwest. I love the farms, the wide-open spaces, the mild shock of coming to a city or town with multiple exits. It's like finding treasure in the sand at the beach. And on this drive, western Illinois is something to behold. It was only April, so the corn wasn't up and most of the trees were still without leaves. There's just something about being alone in a car surrounded by that much space, that much all-over nothingness. It's completely different from driving alone in other places. In the Virginia Blue Ridge or the Oregon Cascades, you're not really alone. You're never alone in city traffic; there's always other motorists, pedestrians, stoplights. Out here, on Interstate 74 west of Peoria, you can check out for a while.

I snap a couple of pictures of the road rising in front of me. A truck in the distance, farm fields creeping up to the edge of the blacktop like strangers. I'm on my way to my uncle's funeral. He died suddenly, without warning. In some sense, the best way to go. No hospice, no dreary hospital beds, nothing pending or lurking in the future. He just went upstairs to the bathroom and never came back down. I decided the moment I heard that I would make the trip. In the Midwest, in a family like mine, you don't miss these kinds of things. Miss a wedding, maybe. A baptism, that's understandable. But a funeral, you go. My cousin Chris was flying in from his home in Kazakhstan. He's an oil field engineer. My parents, sister, brother, and niece were driving in from Cleveland. They, at the moment I snapped the photo, were somewhere north of me—west of Chicago, but not yet to the line.

With eleven hours to myself, I did a lot of thinking. I thought about my uncle—the oldest of my grandparents' nine children. Third brother up from my dad. He was the family historian. The know-it-all, but in a good way. He was the kind of guy who talked to everyone he met. He was the kind of guy who got endless enjoyment from an old farm implement catalog. He was never fancy. I remember seeing him in a suit just a couple of times—my cousin's wedding, my grandmother's funeral. He wore funny-looking suspenders, and his beard looked like the hide of a mange-ridden dog. He was serious, in his way, but also not. At his oldest child's wedding—which was held in the

pasture a hundred feet from his front door—he built a big bonfire by way of a rehearsal dinner. After the sun went down, he
brought out a mason jar filled with clear liquid and a moldy-
looking peach. A little white lightning someone had given him
as a thank-you gift for some unknown favor. Uncle Don embodied all that Iowa has come to represent to me.

I thought about him as the miles ticked by. I thought about
the way he told stories, how he took me to the Surf Ballroom
when I was in college so I could see where Buddy Holly, Richie
Valens, and the Big Bopper played their last concert. He never
forgot about the Big Bopper, even though history generally does.
Once, when visiting with my wife and kids, he tried to convince
me to take my sons to see the World's Largest Tractor. He spoke
of it as transformative, as if seeing it would cure all the wrongs
my suburban life had foisted upon me, my sons, and my conception of manhood. I didn't go. I should have gone.

And thinking about him got me thinking about other midwestern men. My dad, my uncles, those I am related to and
those I have come to know. Their stoicism. Their ability to stand
up and face a fight. The way they talk about doing what's right
and what's good. They don't like taxes, they shoot guns. They
are patriots. They liked Ike. How many other great men have
called the Middle of America home? Well, off the top of my
head: Henry Ford, Frank Lloyd Wright, the Wright Brothers.
Ted Nugent is from Michigan. John Wayne. I'm reminded of
Herbert Hoover as I pass his memorial highway just east of
Iowa City. Bob Feller and Jim Thome. Warren Buffet, Ulysses
S. Grant, Warren Harding, Abraham Lincoln for God's sake.
Harry Truman was from Missouri, I think that counts. Ronald
Reagan. Charles Shultz. Walt Disney and Ray Krock. Michael
Jackson was from Indiana, though I'm not sure he counts.

But Larry Bird and Magic Johnson—Indiana and Michigan, respectively—certainly do. Harry Houdini claimed to be from Wisconsin, though he was born in Hungary. Miles Davis, Ely Lilly.

The writers alone who called the Midwest home make for a staggering list: Hemingway, F. Scott Fitzgerald, Elmore Leonard, Mark Twain, Carl Sandburg, Kurt Vonnegut, Saul Bellow. Jonathan Franzen is from Illinois. Two of my personal heroes, Bill Bryson and Garrison Keillor, are from Iowa and Minnesota. The lists go on and on.

All my life, I thought I needed to be from somewhere else in order to be the person I wanted to be, but the more I drove, the more I realized I was already from somewhere. As the miles wore on, past Waterloo and on the home stretch to Mason City, I contemplated the men of the Midwest. I thought about all their accomplishments that, inevitably, led to a critique of my own. I'm in my thirties, a husband and a father, and, yet, I don't feel like a man. I feel like a watered-down version of a man. I certainly don't feel like any of the men listed above and don't even feel like a Heimbuch man. I feel like my life is too much about compromise. That's not to say that being a man means living without compromise, but I do feel too ready to give in, too willing to cower, to hide from problems, and to shy away in the face of opportunity. I realize that, if I am ever to become the man, the husband, the father, the writer I want to become, I need to learn how to face life standing up.

I spent two days in Iowa for the funeral. I shot about five hundred rounds with my brother and cousin at the shooting range my uncle Mark has built on his property. I slept in his basement and listened as he explained the finer points of gun mechanics, hunting laws, and the latest thing that has him pissed. I realized I don't allow myself to get pissed. I don't roar the way he does. Uncle Mark has kind of a famous temper. When he witnesses something that he feels isn't right, he speaks his mind. When his kids do something stupid, he'll yell himself hoarse about it. But, inevitably, he hugs them and helps them out of the jam they've gotten into. He told me stories about the jams he's been in. He told me about getting in trouble in college, about my dad getting in trouble. He embraces his failures. I've never been in trouble— not really—and yet, I tend to run at the first sign that I might be wrong—cover it up, silence it. It makes me feel weak, to hear someone talking about how they've been wrong. Because I could never do that, could never admit it.

Hours were spent in small conversations. My dad and his cousins told hunting stories. My cousin told me about the time he did something that got him in hot water, something brave and unthinkable for me. My dad told the story about the first time he went deer hunting. He was younger than I am and already married with two children. He was so scared he shot the same buck three times. "They told me to keep firing until it went down," he said, laughing. I tried to relate to the story, but, really, I couldn't. I don't know what that feels like. I don't know the nerves, the twitching hands. I don't know what a real adrenaline rush feels like. I don't know the thrill of the hunt. My best adrenaline story involves working up the nerve to ride a roller coaster that was particularly tall. What kind of a man am I when I don't know what it means to tell someone off when they have it coming? When I have no idea how it feels to be in the wilderness possessing the power of life and death?

I chided myself for not understanding what the other men were talking about when discussing their guns. I berated myself for not disagreeing with Uncle Mark when he said something about President Obama and "those damned Democrats who won't leave Bush alone." I wanted to tell him that the Republicans were still blaming Clinton seven years after he left office and that the fact that we're still paying for two wars in Iraq and Afghanistan—not to mention tax cuts—just three years after President Bush left office is worthy of disdain. But I demurred. I chickened out. I tried to tell myself that it's about respecting my elders, about blending in, and that discretion is the better part of valor, but I am not brave enough for valor, so I say nothing.

I mentioned to my cousin Tommy that I was thinking about coming out for a pheasant hunt in the fall. We were sitting in the basement at Mark and Linette's house. I was staying in the spare bedroom down there, and neither Tommy nor I could sleep all that well. I think after a couple of days of potlucks and receiving lines, we were both a little tired of nodding reverently and accepting or giving condolences. So we played video games.

Strange that in my midthirties, Tommy, then sixteen, is the one I feel the most comfortable hanging out with. I guess in some ways you just never leave the kids' table.

"I'm thinking about coming out in the fall to go pheasant hunting," I told him during a particularly quiet game of video football. He didn't exactly drop his controller in amazement, but he didn't say anything either.

"Cool," he said after a pregnant pause.

"Do you think you could help me figure out what I need and schedule the thing?"

"Hell yeah," he said. And I tried to imagine what my reaction would have been had one of my older cousins asked me to help him or her, had they taken an interest like that. I would have been flabbergasted. I look at old photos of family gatherings and can never remember what circumstances led up to them being taken. Even now, all grown up with a family of my own, I think about how separated I feel from my generation on my dad's side. My mom's side? Well, I don't even know all their names, let alone have a private memory of a time spent together with them.

But Tommy and his brother, Will, are different. Will is thirteen years younger than I am, Tommy another three years younger than that. But they've always felt more like siblings separated by distance than cousins. Maybe it's because Uncle Mark has always felt like more than an uncle and Aunt Linette more than an aunt. Maybe it's because they are the people in the family my parents are closest with, but I've always loved being with them.

Once, when Jack was small, Rebecca and I went to visit Mark's brood in Iowa for a long weekend. We spent long days just chatting, letting Will and Tommy play with Jack in the massive yard and listening to Mark tell stories about a family that was mine and yet something so unfamiliar. That tends to happen in big families. There tends to be one or two siblings who move away and their children are raised apart from the rest. We were those children, my sisters and I, and my dad was one of those siblings who left. Mark never left. He remained, an epicenter in a family bound for a quake. He and Linette built a house on the property where my grandmother had spent nearly her entire life. They did it to help her, to be there, and to give their boys an upbringing they could never get living in town or in another state. I listened for hours as Linette told me about my grandmother's favorite recipes, how she liked to can blackberries from her garden near the back of the seven-acre property, right next to the shooting range.

We'd have a bonfire in the yard in the evening and after Jack had gone down and Mark and Linette had gone to bed, Rebecca, Will, Tommy, and I would stay up late playing cards and singing silly songs. Here were two boys in the throes of adolescence, on the cusp of the independence that comes with driver's licenses and high school football, yet it seemed like there was no place they would rather be than with us, playing canasta and cracking each other up with falsetto versions of Stevie Nicks, singing about the white-winged dove.

Still, for all this familial bonding, there were reminders that in addition to being great hosts and kids cool beyond their years, Will and Tommy were still brothers. Will has always been the quiet one. The brainy one who loved to get his little brother's goat. And at that point, he was probably fifteen and developing that cockiness that comes with pubescence. But while Will's confidence was growing, Tommy's temper was inherited from his dad and was already in full blossom. Most of the time, it was pretty simple. Little jabs from Will, big demonstrative lashes from Tommy. Will would tell Tommy he was an idiot, Tommy would tell him to go to hell. But on the second-to-last day of our trip, I witnessed something truly amazing, something that astounded me as the much younger brother of two sisters, a man so afraid of conflict that I refuse to send back food when given the wrong order.

Will and Tommy were helping out a neighbor across the street. Apparently the neighbor was out west and the boys had agreed to take care of his dogs. This involved crossing the road a couple of times a day, getting the dogs out of their pen, feeding them, changing their water, and tossing a ball for a bit. Will had been riding Tommy's tail for a good bit of the morning and since the afternoon sun was getting pretty hot, we had decided to take Jack inside and lay him down for a nap. While we were doing that, Will and Tommy had gone across the road to perform their duties. I went back outside and was wandering about the property under the cool shadows of the ancient oak trees when I looked toward the road and saw Tommy coming back. I would say he was walking, but it actually seemed more like the stride of a man on his way to murder his wife's lover and he was muttering under his breath like a deranged homeless person.

"Tommy," I called and he looked up, veering toward me. I could hear him muttering, absolutely spitting mad and noticed that his T-shirt was wet. It took me a second to realize that Will wasn't with him and judging by Tommy's gait, I wondered if he had murdered him and fed him to the dogs. It turned out I wasn't far off. "Where's Will?" I asked as my twelve-year-old cousin drew closer.

He looked me straight in the eye and spat, "I can't get any Goddamn respect around here."

"Tommy, where's Will?"

"Son of a bitch."

"Where's Will?" I asked, feeling a sense of genuine concern by this point.

"He sprayed me with the hose, so I locked his ass in the kennel," he said and walked past me into the house. Even now, just remembering the moment, makes me chuckle. Partly it's because I love the idea of the much smaller younger brother succumbing to his own fury and managing to throw the older brother into a dog kennel and partly it's because I know this is going to be Jack and Dylan someday. The age difference is about the same, and so are the personalities.

I doubled over laughing and went inside to tell Rebecca and

Linette what had happened. Rebecca had the same reaction as I did, a combination of mortification, admiration, and hysterical laughter. This was, sadly, not Linette's first rodeo when it came to refereeing the boys, and it wouldn't be her last.

"Thomas, you march back over there and let your brother out of that kennel," she snapped. And Tommy, a good son at heart, did as he was told, but the moment he left the house, she laughed so hard she cried. We all did that night. We all laughed about it. Even Will. Then we played a few games of canasta.

Ever since that particular moment of that particular trip, I've looked at Tommy as my coconspirator. He's been my point of contact with the Iowa relatives and the person I turn to when I need a good laugh.

He gave me some advice about clothes and equipment, reminded me about the things I would need to do in order to hunt legally, and even recommended a book about the ringneck, one I had not seen on Amazon or in Barnes and Noble. He even agreed to go with me and offered to let me use one of his shotguns if I needed.

The next day the drive back to Cincinnati was dull and gray. A freak spring snowstorm had blanketed much of Iowa in white, and the sky—cloudless and pristine on the drive over—was hung low with clouds. I couldn't stop thinking about my dad, my uncles, the great men of the Midwest. And the more I thought, the more I felt this weight of unmet expectation on my shoulders.

I looked around as I drove, at the farms, the fields, the wide-open spaces and was, somehow, cut raw by the nobility of it. I imagined the farmer working the land, tirelessly putting forth effort to make things grow. I was enamored by this place, these people. The Midwest, which for so long was nothing and nowhere to me, had me intimidated. And I began to wonder if I can ever rise to meet its gaze.

The thoughts came like raindrops—individual and constant. I needed to pull off, to take a break. I stopped at a truck stop to stretch my legs. I went inside and walked around the food court. I was thinking simultaneously about my uncle Don—whose funeral was a reminder of the power a man derives from being honorable, decent, and interested in other people's lives, as he must have been to the five hundred or so people who came to the visitation. I'm thinking about my own funeral and what people will say—

"He was pretty funny."

"He was punctual."

"He was very tall."

"He really liked to read."

"He was a pretty good guy, but his dad was better."

*Jesus, what's wrong with me?* I wondered.

And then I heard something that brought everything back into perspective, that immediately put an end to my self-flagellation. Three people were sitting at a table in the food court, wrapped in heated conversation. Two men, about my age, were arguing with a woman who was maybe a little older. The men looked like truck stop sophisticates—cheap, pseudodesigner jeans adorned by custom leather cell-phone/chaw cases. One had a hands-free microphone in his ear. It wasn't the kind you see on urbanites, but, rather, the kind you see on drive-through attendants. The content of their discussion reminded me that not all midwesterners are great:

**Man 1:** "No, no, you're wrong. He's not your first cousin."

**Woman:** "Yes, he is."

**Man 2:** "No, he's not."

**Woman:** "How do you figure?"

**Man 1:** "Because he's not the oldest."

**Man 2:** "His older brother is your first cousin because he's oldest."

**Man 1:** "David is your second cousin because he's the second oldest."

**Woman:** "Wait, so what's Karen?"

**Man 2:** "She's your fourth cousin."

**Woman:** "Because she's the fourth oldest?"

**Man 1:** "Yeah. Don't you get it? You can't be this stupid."

**Woman:** "No, I get it now."

**Man 2:** "Good."

**Woman:** "Nobody ever explained it to me before."

**Man 1:** "Glad to be of assistance."

A few minutes later, another overheard conversation reminded me yet again that I'm not as bad off as I sometimes think myself to be. I was standing in line to prepay for some gas. Toward the front of the line was a woman in her early twenties. She had bleach-blond hair arranged in a trailer park version of dreadlocks, a pierced eyebrow, and a bolt through her nose. She was holding a case of Budweiser, waiting her turn, and I couldn't help but notice how she was dressed. Tight jeans and white loafers like the ones Cousin Eddy wore in *Christmas Vacation*. She was wearing a tight, low-cut T-shirt, the kind popular among loose coeds, only this one revealed all the wrong things. Rather than flattering her figure, it revealed her midsection—like ice cream melting over the edges of a cone. She turned to the man behind her—maybe forty—in a flannel shirt and thick spectacles.

"Johnny, you want to come over and have a couple beers with me?" she asked in a tone three steps beyond coquettish.

"Yeah, maybe," said Johnny. He motioned to a little girl standing next to him. She was around twelve, round in every way and, oddly, dirty. "I've got to help her buy some cigarettes first."

The woman didn't blink at this, just flirted a little more, then turned to pay for her beer. At this point, Johnny turned to the girl standing next to him and said, "So how come your momma doesn't buy your grandma's cigarettes?"

"She didn't want to leave the house," said the girl. "It's my fault, I guess."

"How's that?" asked Johnny.

"I shouldn't have showed her that I have five dollars. Soon as I showed her my money, she sent me over here to get Grandma's smokes."

Johnny helped the little girl, waved lasciviously at the bleach-blond ice cream cone, and then offered them both a ride home. They jumped into the back of his truck and turned into a trailer park across the street.

I got a call a couple of days later from my dad. I was at work, between meetings, when my cell phone rang.

"Hello?"

"Hey, Scoop," he said. "I've got a little reporting project for you." My dad has called me "Scoop" since I took my first job at my hometown weekly newspaper, just days after I told him

I had changed my major from marketing to journalism. Well, not so much told as blurted in fear and frustration. It was the summer after my freshman year in college. That spring semester, I had toiled, slogging my way through calculus, which was a prerequisite class for all business majors. I had known early on that I wasn't going to be an engineer like him. I simply didn't have it in me. I was too dreamy, too in love with Kerouac and Yeats. But, like many dutiful sons of German fathers, I wanted to do something that would please him, so I went off to school to study marketing. Which lasted until midway through second semester when I found myself unable to understand a single thing my professor was saying during my eight A.M., five-days-a-week calculus class. Then there was economics, equally as mystifying to my poor brain. The only class I was doing well in was freshman English. Really well. I loved going to that class, loved reading the books by feminist authors I would never really understand, then writing lengthy term papers about them. I was under the spell of my professor, a doctoral student named Dair. To this day, I don't know if that was her real name or not, but she encouraged my writing, encouraged me to pursue it. There's something about being away from home for the first time. You fall prey to the strangest things.

I met with Dair to review my midterm paper. I had gotten an "A," but that was only because she was required to give grades. If it were up to her, I'm sure my paper would have earned a rainbow sticker and my efforts would have been rewarded with a drum circle and dance around a tribal fire. But, either way, she asked me about what I was going to do with my life. I told her that I would probably end up working in a cubicle, figuring out a way to improve sales of industrial solvent, and she convinced me that doing so would be a waste of my talent, that I belonged in the English program. Visions of tweed jackets with leather elbow patches, of long nights spent reading by a crackling fire danced in my head, and I went straight to the registrar's office to change my declared major from marketing, "MKT," to creative writing, "ENG."

Dad didn't ask me about the "D" next to economics or "D-" next to calculus—the final for which I wrote an essay laying out an argument why it would be bad for the professor's chance at tenure and, thus, citizenship to fail me—on my report card that summer. He asked me why it said "ENG" next to the word *Major*. I knew I couldn't convince him that I was now an engineering student, but I realized in that moment that changing my major to creative writing was a silly and futile thing to do.

"I changed my major to um, um, journalism," I told him. Not so much a declaration as an excuse, like what you tell your mom after you get home late from making out with your girlfriend—"we, um, fell asleep?"

He stared at me, and my mouth began moving on its own. It didn't matter that I wasn't sure if my university had a journalism major. It only mattered that in that moment I believed it did. I told him about how I had a plan to write for free for the local paper to get experience, about grad school, about wanting to cover business rather than be a part of it. He looked at me a bit longer, before relenting under the pressure of my verbal onslaught. It was good enough. I went that afternoon to the paper down the street and made good on my bullshit. The first time he read my byline above a story about a local school board meeting, he started calling me "Scoop" and it's stuck ever since. (My university did, it turned out, offer a journalism major, in which I enrolled, but I kept the creative writing major and, just to ensure that I would never make much money, declared a minor in American history, with an emphasis on the South from Revolution to Reconstruction. I guess I decided early on that being rich would never be a priority.)

"What kind of journalistic project did you have in mind?" I asked him.

"Well, Uncle Mark called and he and I are going to the NRA show in Pittsburgh and we think it would be cool if you got a press pass and came with us."

The show was two weeks later and I had no idea how I would go about getting a pass on relatively late notice, but I decided to take the challenge anyway. I thought it would be a good opportunity to tell them both that I wanted to come to Iowa in the fall to go pheasant hunting. I also figured that I could impress them a bit with my ability to nose my way into the show without paying for admittance. That would be pretty cool. Cooler than calculus anyway.

# 7

## INTO THE LION'S DEN

I got up at 4:31, hit snooze once, and, after washing my face and getting dressed, I kissed my wife on the head and lit out into the predawn darkness bound for the National Rifle Association's Rivers to Freedom convention—sort of the ultimate gun show and a gathering of gun-loving, Second-Amendment-defending sportsmen, collectors, and enthusiasts. Okay, so maybe it's not quite as noble as that. Maybe it's a hundred thousand people getting together for the common purpose of touching thousands of firearms and complaining about Presidents Obama, Clinton, Carter, Johnson, and Roosevelt. Kennedy gets off the hook because, you know, he was assassinated and got us into Vietnam and, also, because he was a lifelong member of the NRA. Either way, there's bound to be a lot of guns for me to touch and mount as if I know what I'm doing.

The plan was for me to meet my dad and Uncle Mark at the media registration area at nine. Pittsburgh is usually about a four-hour drive from where we live in southwest Ohio, so I thought leaving by five would be fine. And, to be honest, for most of the way it was. I was on the outskirts of Columbus by the time the sun started to warm the eastern sky and east of the city, cruising unmolested by traffic on I-70, by the time the pinkish-gray morphed into a sunny orange. Overhead and stretching into the distant east were low-hanging clouds that reminded me of sand in the shallow waters of the beach—rippled and undulating as if washed by an ebbing tide. I put my Pontiac on cruise and listened to Brad Weiner read his *The Geography of Bliss,* which recounts his search for the happiest place on Earth. I imagined, based upon how excited Uncle Mark sounded on the phone the night before, that he was going to his happiest place. Pittsburgh, as the site of the convention, had little to do with his bliss. As a lifetime Benefactor member of the NRA, Uncle Mark is not only a supporter, but also an enthusiast. He speaks of previous conventions as if he had seen heaven and only wished to go back. I was excited too, but it had more to do with a road trip and spending a little time with him and Dad—basking in their enthusiasm—than anything to do with the conference itself.

I was just west of Zanesville—named after Ebenezer Zane, an ancestor of its most famous native son, the western writer Zane Grey—the town that would become infamous later in the year when amateur animal keeper Terry Thompson would release more than fifty wild animals from his backyard cages before killing himself. The police would spend hours hunting down the lions, tigers, bears, and wolves and find Thompson's body serving as a buffet for a lioness. But that was months later. I was passing Zanesville when I realized I needed gas and, from the rumbling in my stomach, a bathroom. I found a gas station off to the side of the road. It was one of those megastations that cater to truckers, with lockers, pay phones, and DVDs of movies that were bad when they were released in the '70s. I like these places. The coffee is usually strong, the snacks are terrible for you, and the CD stand is bound to feature at least two versions of Conway Twitty's greatest hits. I pumped my gas, then pulled forward to a spot near the door. I always do this and it usually makes my wife mad. "Why move the car?" she asks and I tell her that I have a phobia of making other people wait—particularly little old ladies—for me. She doesn't get it, but she also doesn't understand why, at the mall, I intentionally choose a spot far from the door. Same logic applies. Save the close spots for the gray hairs and asswipes, I always say. So I pulled into a spot away from the pumps and stepped out. Right into a pile of, what is that? Oh God, gross. It's about two and a half gallons of discarded chewing tobacco and associated juices. I slipped in it. It squished, oozed even. I thought I was going to vomit, but with my stomach still rumbling, I thought it best to wipe the nastiness off my boot and move on.

The bathroom wasn't much better. I walked in and was overrun by a stink that was not quite human, but also too bad for a beast. The stall next to mine was overflowing, putrid brown mostly water pooling in the drain below the divider. Noisy trucker gurgling was coming from elsewhere in the bathroom. I watched as the water encroached on my personal space and decided I needed to get the hell out of there. On the way out, the woman behind the counter—a toothless hillbilly who had probably done unspeakable things in pursuit of meth—said she hoped I enjoyed my stop and asked me how my day was going.

"It just got shitty," I said, admiring my own pun.

"I'm sorry to hear that," she said, friendly and guarded.

"You might want to have someone take a look at the stall in the men's room," I said.

"Is it actin' up again?"

Acting up? What is it? A petulant child? No, it's not acting up; it's deluging shit. On to the floor. On to my boots. I wanted to complain, about the stall, about the chaw I stepped in, but thought better of it. "Yup, sure is," I said, managing a smile.

I was determined not to let the truck stop incident deter my fun. I was a man on a mission, after all, and should not be deterred—not even for turd. I returned to my driver's seat and my book on happiness and continued blithely on my route. Less than an hour later, my GPS dinged to announce an upcoming turn. I merged onto a northbound interstate, then, almost immediately, was directed to take an exit onto a two-lane highway. This pleased me greatly. I love back roads, and Highway 23 through southeastern Ohio was no disappointment. Bendy, winding its way up and down hills with a fifty-five-mile-per-hour speed limit, it was like bombing around the track with Jeremy Clarkson. I feel like a driver—up and down, left, right, on the brake, on the gas. A smile plants itself on my face. The sun is rising, the rain has stopped, and I'm cruising through a landscape redolent of Wales—lush green pastures undulating over hills and amid stands of oak. I saw a white horse galloping along the ridge of a hill and knew, instinctively, what it was feeling. I pass a sign for DEERASSIC PARK WHITETAIL EDUCATION CENTER and begin considering how I'm going to tell my wife that we're moving to the middle of nowhere in the sparse corner of Ohio.

Weiner was reading a passage about his time in an Indian ashram when I saw it, up on the left. It was a white, single-wide trailer with two outbuildings, one a garage, the other a shed. And in the front yard was a flagpole with a large American flag flapping in the light breeze. Just below it was a Confederate battle flag, equal in size and flapping right along with the one on top. The message was clear: We don't take kindly to black people, Catholics, Jews, or anyone else. My euphoria was immediately and irrevocably dashed. I was shaken from my automotive bliss, which was completely spoiled a few miles up the road when I rejoined the interstate, crossed through the northern spit of West Virginia, and found myself sitting completely still on the outskirts of Pittsburgh.

I'd been sitting still for more than an hour. Two or three hundred yards behind me is a sign along I-376 announcing that the city's convention center is just five miles ahead, on the other side of a tunnel and bridge. I passed that sign at 8:47 A.M. It was now 9:52 and the overhead sign warned me that the aforementioned tunnel is still three miles ahead. Every direction I looked—ahead, to the left and right, behind me in my rearview mirror—are cars, trucks, and semis. All just sitting here on a gloomy Friday morning. The light drizzle on my windshield is a reminder of just how badly I have to pee and the thought of reaching a restroom burns in my soul, wrapped in a thick larder of hatred for this place.

Finally, after more than seven hours in the car, I found a parking spot in a garage on top of an organic grocery store and join the march of camo-clad men making their way toward the convention center. Dad and Uncle Mark have beaten me there, but only by forty-five minutes or so, and our predetermined meeting time of 9:00 becomes 11:45. I reset the pedometer on my iPod as I step from the garage and 1,913 strides later arrive at the registration booth to ask where I can pick up my press credentials and am greeted with a dumbstruck look.

I should explain that getting media credentials was no small feat. The NRA convention is free for any member and I wanted to avoid joining, so I sent an e-mail to the media contact person on both the NRA site and the site set up for the convention. A week passed. Then two. I sent another e-mail. Then another. Then, three days before I was going to Pittsburgh, I decided I couldn't wait any longer. Uncle Mark, in particular, really wanted me to be there and I had already agreed to go, so I needed to be able to get in the door. So I coughed up $35 for a one-year membership, the benefits of which include, I was immediately informed by an automatically generated e-mail, 24/7 protection of my Second Amendment rights, discounted life insurance, and a one-year subscription to a magazine of my choice—I went for *The American Hunter* because *American Rifleman* and *America's 1st Freedom* both sort of scared me—among other things.

Okay, not a bad deal. Not a great one, but not bad. At least the magazine came with it and I would be able to get into the show, which was the most important need I had at the moment. Such is my luck that I finally heard back from the NRA the next day, informing me that my press credentials had been approved. I half considered asking for my membership dues back, but thought better of it. I have always been a little afraid of an organization devoted to arming citizens, especially one with such high esteem for Charlton Heston. It's not that I disliked the man, but he did have a tendency to overact, that's all I'm saying. Plus, as a newspaper reporter, I was discouraged to join any organization with a lobby. And what a lobby the NRA has. According to a website I found that details the lobbying budgets and spending of organizations with a presence on K Street, the NRA was, as of 2001, one of the most powerful lobbying organizations in the country, as rated by *Forbes* magazine. At that time, it had a war chest of $200 million and maintained "its own $35 million lobbying machine" for the sole purpose of fighting any move to enact gun control laws in this country.

That's a lot of dough.

I felt a little strange giving $35 to an organization that thinks the answer to street crime involving guns is not to disarm the criminals, but to arm the victims. It's not that I have a problem with gun ownership. Lord knows, I understand the joys of shooting tin cans for hours, but the paranoia. I was once driving across Illinois and passed a series of small, roadside signs about the size of two Scrabble boxes stacked end to end. The message was this:

"Thugs won't wait"

"For cops to arrive"

"So you better pack heat"

" 'Cause guns save lives."

Apart from the childlike meter and simplistic rhyme structure, the signs reflect a certain degree of apocalyptic mistrust for which the implied remedy is to be armed at all times, day and night. The signs, and there were several of these series across Illinois, were paid for by the Champaign Country Rifle Association, a satellite group that, on its homepage (www.gunssavelife. com), encourages joining the NRA.

What was I getting myself into? I really did wonder. But, no matter, the money was spent, and I could always fall back upon my membership if my credentials fell through for one reason or another.

The problem is, of course, the people at the ticket booth have no idea where I should go to pick up my credentials. They point me to a woman working the door, a different one from the first one I spoke with, and she, too, denies my entry, telling me I can't get in without a green-and-white sticker. Those stickers are only given to members.

"But I have a press pass waiting for me inside," I say.

"But I won't let you inside without a sticker," she replies.

I point out that her logic makes no sense. I ask how I can get a pass if I am required to pay. I point out that she is a complete moron and should be smote by the gods of all things decent and holy. I tell her I want to speak to her manager, accuse her of extortion. I release all my passive-aggressive rage—the traffic, the racists, the chewing tobacco and shit on my boots. It's all her fault, damn it, and it's time that she pays.

Or at least that's what I do in my mind. I think, in reality, I grumbled something unintelligible and sulked back to the ticket booth. It had, after all, been a long day in the car already.

This time, the man at the ticket booth understood my dilemma. I told him about the press pass and the moron working the door and he nodded empathetically. There wasn't much he could do to get me past Brumhilda, but if I was a member, he could give me a sticker.

*Wait a minute,* I thought. *I am a member! Paid in full for an entire year!* I told him this and congratulated my good thinking as he looked up my name and address.

"Um, I'm sorry," he said. "You're not in the system."

"But I am a member," I said and pulled out my iPhone to show him the receipt still in my e-mail inbox from the transaction earlier in the week. "See? I've already paid."

"Yeah, I see," he said hesitatingly. "It's just that you're not in the system, and you have to be in the system in order to get the free pass. You didn't join long enough ago to have made it in the system."

I must have appeared both bewildered and crestfallen at this news, because the man, who seemed to genuinely care, quickly made me an offer.

"I'll tell you what," he said. "We're offering one-year memberships for $25 today. I can sign you up and then add that membership on to the one you've already paid for, so you'll get two years for the sixty bucks instead of $70. And you'll get another magazine subscription."

For some reason, I thought he was making me a deal. I filled out the card he gave me, handed him my MasterCard and marked the box indicating that I would like a one-year subscription to *American Rifleman*. I walked away feeling grateful for the man and made it past my nemesis at the door—who, I might add, gave me a smug, satisfied grin when she saw my green-and-white sticker—and was halfway up the escalator before I realized: I am an idiot. In the last three days I have paid $60 for a two-year membership into a group I had no interest in joining, just to get into a show I had free media credentials to attend.

Fuck.

I suddenly began to see the merits of being armed.

I checked in with the press office on the third floor of the convention center. I didn't, technically speaking, need the pass anymore, but I knew Uncle Mark might be impressed that I could get one, and it's not often that I can impress a member of my family. I met him and Dad in front of the NRA Store—an ad hoc retail area selling everything from T-shirts to shot glasses, all emblazoned with the NRA logo. My dad was wearing a freshly acquired "NRA Rivers to Freedom" hat, and both he and Mark were carrying large yellow bags with—and I'm not kidding here—at least ten pounds of catalogs and pamphlets each.

"That looks heavy," I said. "You guys only got here an hour before me. How'd you get that much stuff?"

"Well," said Dad, as we made our way into the crowded

convention center hall, "it wasn't this busy before you got here."

We walked into the hall, which was packed with booths and displays like any other convention, all being attended to and milled about by thousands of enthusiastic gawkers. A billboard outside the city had promised "Acres of Guns and Gear," but I hadn't taken it to be literal until I stepped onto the convention floor. There were so many guns—all made safe by the removal of their firing pins, I was assured by Uncle Mark—and so many people, I felt like I was in an old western movie or a military garrison.

Most of the men and women in attendance looked like people anywhere, people you'd meet at the grocery store or Rotary Club. They were a mix of, from what I could gather visually, white collar and blue. Veterans wearing the patches of their fighting groups; some people in shooting vests or hunting shirts, a fair number who looked like they had just left the country club in order to pop over and look at guns for a bit. The people watching was great. I, for one, had been concerned about my sartorial choice for the day. I tend to dress like a paunchy, preppy, slightly disheveled tourist, as if I am perpetually late for a clambake. I wanted to fit in, to blend, so I wore a fishing shirt with some aggressively sized pockets and a canvas cap, blue jeans, and a pair of Timberland boots. I hoped to pass for a hunter, rather than an imposter. My attempted ruse only made me more self-conscious, so I tried to focus on other people.

After hours of careful study, I come to the conclusion that there are five types of people who attend the NRA convention.

1. The Sportsmen—These are the guys who hunt a couple of times a year, maybe a bit more frequently.

They go after turkey in the spring, deer and upland birds in the fall. They're normal guys, not prone to fits of political outrage. You find them looking at the more pedestrian guns—shotguns, deer rifles, the occasional pistol. This is my dad. He enjoys hunting, enjoys guns, but they are certainly not the center of his world.

2. The Period Purists—I like these people very much, especially the cowboys. One, in a black hat, black jeans, and black boots with a white-and-black western shirt, black holsters bearing pearl-handled silver pistols, and a black mustache so perfect it looks as if it was torn from a poster for the movie *Tombstone*, walks with an affected swagger, a genuine mosey. There are other purists—the Prohibition Tommy Gunners with pinstripe suits and delusions of Johnny Depp grandeur; the WWII guy in the basement with the fedora and working replicas of the disposable Liberator pistols, which were manufactured by General Motors and dropped from planes to the French Resistance; the Kentucky Riflemen with their enormous muzzle-loading rifles and coonskin caps. The list goes on. I like the role playing, the sense of propriety. For these people, it's about authenticity, not necessarily firepower. I like that.

3. The English Shootists—Not surprisingly, these people had a relatively small footprint at the NRA

show. English-style or English-manufactured shotguns are elaborate, handcrafted affairs. The wood is furniture quality, the steel perfect and often ornately decorated. These guns start in the tens of thousands of dollars, and English shooting is often as formal as a Royal wedding. For pheasant hunting, the men don knickers, vests, ties, tattersall shirts, and tweed blazers. Their hats are elaborately pinned and their boots are hand-sewn brogue-style. They are gentlemen and, also, snobs. They're fun to look at, but try to talk to them and you quickly get the sense that these men are, pardon the language, douche bags.

4. The Bulletheads—Car enthusiasts and campers have gearheads, the kind of individuals who obsess over the performance of products. These are the high-performance people, the ones endlessly fascinated by the details, passionately devoted to the potential of guns. Uncle Mark probably fits into this camp. He loves to handle guns, to examine the exact machining of their parts. He loves to learn about tweaks and customizations. He fawns in the presence of those champions who have so seamlessly melded man and machine—the three-gun shooters who switch from pistol to rifle to shotgun with speed and capability, the quick-draw pistoleers, the riflemen able to split a hair from a hundred feet, in the dark, after a few beers. In the same way racing drivers appreciate someone like F1 Champion Mi-

chael Schumacher, so too does Uncle Mark appreciate someone like thirty-two-time champion shooter Jerry Miculek. We even stop to get his autograph. I get one and Mark gets one for each of his sons.

5. The Pseudoparamilitarists—These are the guys who scare me. These are the ones who keep automatic rifles buried in their backyards. They seem transfixed studying the details of tactical vests, awed by knives, fascinated by near-military-grade anything. The irony, of course, is that most of the people wandering the floor with telltale signs of actual military service—desert camo backpacks with their name patches on them, worn military boots, and so on—did not fall into this group. They were more the Bullethead or the Sportsmen. No, these Pseudoparamilitary guys were straight pretenders. These are the people who warn of the impending race war, the people who believe the best defense is a good offense. They care, seemingly, about destruction; and they terrify me. A pair of these guys walked past me with a dead stare in their eyes, and all I could think of was Columbine. One imagines these guys storing fifty years' worth of canned peaches in their basement in advance of the Millennium, stockpiling munitions for 2012 and reading books about James Earl Ray with eagerness and avidity. I'm not saying these people are violent. Most, I would imagine, are actually far from it. But they are a little too interested in violence for my own comfort level. I do take

some comfort in the notion that, should an apocalyptic war break out in Pittsburgh, at this moment, I am probably in the safest possible place.

What the hell am *I* doing here?

We walked from booth to booth. We didn't talk, not as much as I would have thought anyway. Uncle Mark studied the menagerie of guns with the eyes of a medieval monk transcribing a bible, pausing occasionally to point out the CEO of this gun manufacturer, the designer director of that one. He and Dad explored the hundreds of versions of the Model 1911 .45-caliber pistol. It's the one-hundredth anniversary of the design, and dozens of manufacturers presented dozens of designs of the gun. Dad was interested. He thought maybe he was in the market. It was the sidearm he carried in the army and, now that he's close to retirement, I get the sense that he's interested more for the nostalgia than the owning. To that end, we handled perhaps a hundred versions, Dad asking questions that I find to be insightful and targeted to the manufacturers' representatives. Uncle Mark poked fun at him, chiding his big brother for asking "dumb questions." Dad laughed.

I snapped a surreptitious photo of the actor R. Lee Ermey, who was signing autographs at the Glock booth. He played "Gunny" in *Full Metal Jacket* and seems to show up on the History Channel every time weapons are the topic. He wore a sergeant's cap, pressed shirt, and pressed pants—all military grade—and a dazzlingly undazzling pair of cowboy boots. It was a pop-culture touchstone, something I could relate to and I was grateful. I picked up a couple of catalogs and a few tchotchkes. I was particularly fond of the miniature pistol key rings. I couldn't wait to walk into the offices of, say, the cable company to dispute a bill. When the clerk tried to blow me off, I would put my keys on the desk and say "there's a bigger one where that came from," at which point I would get free cable for a year. My imagination, as you can see, has a way of wandering.

After a couple of hours of meandering and gun handling, we took a break for lunch. In the outer corridor of the convention center, food vendors were offering hearty, meaty meals. We settled on BBQ and sat at a table overlooking the river, eating silently. I was tired—much more tired than I had thought—and the food was helping to revive my gun-addled mind. I was impressed by the enormity of the event. One representative at the Smith & Wesson booth said they were expecting more than a hundred thousand people to come through over the course of the three-day convention. I ate my convention-grade pulled pork and beans and was lost somewhere between thought and a nap when Uncle Mark snapped me out of it.

"So what do you think?" he asked.

"It's . . . amazing," I said. I wanted to be enthused, but also convey a sense of bewilderment.

"Pretty cool, huh?"

"Yes, very," I agreed.

"So what would you buy if money was not a limitation? What's your lottery gun?" he asked.

Shit. I realized that in all the people watching, I hadn't paid attention to a single gun I had handled. That was sort of the point of my being there, to learn about the guns, figure out what kind I would want to buy for my first hunting adventure. That was part of why he wanted me to join them here, for the spectacle, yes, but also the education.

"Gosh, I'm just not sure," I said. "I sort of liked that . . ." Here, I fumbled for the name, any name of any of the guns I had held. "That, uh, Stoeger side-by-side." I remembered seeing those words on a sign, but I hadn't the faintest recollection of the gun itself. I knew side-by-side meant two barrels next to each other, but I couldn't place the actual gun. It was like trying to pick a needle out of a stack of needles. I saw the whole, not the individuals. So I did what comes naturally to any reporter—I diverted.

"What about you?" I asked. "What would you buy if money were no object?"

"I haven't found it yet," he came back. "Jim?"

"I liked that 1911 with the rounded grip," my dad said. "But I'm a dirty old man; I'd probably go with the calendar girl."

This stunned me for a couple of reasons. One, I have never in my life heard my dad talk about a pretty girl. Yes, once I saw him get a lap dance at my brother-in-law's bachelor party, but he looked as uncomfortable with the situation as I did—like he was trying hard to be one of the guys. Second, my dad is anything but a dirty old man. If anything, he's the consummate gentleman. He always drops my mom off at the door at church so that she doesn't have to walk across the parking lot. He holds doors. He looks people in the eye. He's no letch. So, to hear him say something like this—and in front of me no less—was astounding.

However, he did have a point. If you are not an avid collector, the NRA convention floor can be daunting, and any diversion— whether it's an obscure actor or a moderately pretty blonde signing copies of her firearms calendar—can be welcome.

We walked for several more hours and I took notes about specific guns—a tiny, pink, .22-caliber rifle designed for little girls, a pink-and-white assault rifle for when they grow up. By

God, am I glad someone thought of my daughter. I shouldered several shotguns and aimed a few pistols at nothing in particular. Uncle Mark helped me understand fit and function. He seemed genuinely happy to be, at long last, helping me understand guns and hunting. He pointed out the things I needed to look for, recommended price ranges—new or used—and warned me against brands that have lagged in quality in recent years or those that inflate their prices for no good reason at all. It was like having a personal shopper, and I learned that I should expect to pay between $1,100 and $1,500 for my first shotgun. I want to pay that much, he explained.

"If you go cheap, you won't hit anything and you won't have a good time. It's all about personal preference."

I began to see him in a different light. When I was young and would visit him, I felt uncomfortable with the piles of gun catalogs and old copies of *Guns & Ammo* lying around. I was uncomfortable with the violence, the vigilance. I liked being suburban and blithely unaware of such things and found his seeming obsession disquieting. However, after seeing Mark in his element, I came to appreciate his passion. He wasn't a gun nut; he was an enthusiast and a man with something more than a hobby but slightly less than an obsession. And he shared his lifetime of knowledge freely. All my misgivings, my hesitations and apprehension, melted away as we discussed the merits of an all-wood stock versus those of a polyvinyl, his preference for over-under-style shotguns versus semiautos (I admit a similar preference and it has everything to do with looks, though semiautos are better all around). And I learned—a lot.

We explained to Dad who Ted Nugent was as we passed a booth where Uncle Ted was signing autographs, and we fingered untold dozens of Model 1911s—so many in fact that I was able to distinguish quality from crap, good design from bad—when suddenly Mark snapped to attention.

"That's it," he said and began bird-dogging a booth an aisle or two over.

"What?" I asked, trying to keep up. I was carrying both my bag and my dad's. His weighed every bit of twenty pounds by now and he was getting a little tired, so I offered to help.

"That's my lottery gun."

Among shooters, there are cults. And of these cults, none are quite so interesting as .50-caliber rifle owners. Unlike the distinguished gentlemen of the English persuasion, these guys own a very specific weapon: the Barrett rifle. If you've ever seen the awesomely bad Charlie Sheen movie *Navy SEALs,* then you'll remember the character "God." He was the sniper, the guy who could see through walls and shoot through buildings thanks to his trusty Barrett rifle.

When I say that Barrett owners are an enthusiast cult, I mean it quite literally. Owning and firing a Barrett requires a sort of religious fervor. In part, this is because the weapon has absolutely no practical use. It fires a round designed to inflict a ridiculous amount of damage from marathon distances. No, not exactly marathon, but I've seen plenty of TV shows featuring the gun being fired accurately around a mile from the target. Barrett rifles weigh so much that they have to be fired while lying down, with a bipod beneath the barrel and a monopod beneath the shoulder stock. They are bulky and absolutely wicked looking. Not to mention, expensive. A base-model Barrett .50-cal will run you $5,000. The semiautomatic versions are twice that. And, unlike the fine English shotguns, they lack almost any sign of fineness. No hand-carved wood, no neatly etched steel. These are brutes, the Hummer of the gun world. The rounds they fire are more than twice the size of anything I have ever shot, and each bullet will cost you a dollar or more every time you pull the trigger.

I can't say I was surprised that the Barrett was Uncle Mark's lottery gun. After all, he's the gun owner who has owned just about everything else, so the .50-cal was his Everest. What I was surprised by was the gun itself. What the hell would someone need one of these things for anyway? I suppose if there was a building up the road that was leering menacingly at your begonias you might want one, or if, say, a race of superaliens invaded Earth in fifty-foot-tall spaceships that stayed conspicuously far away—then, it might come in handy. But this thing would turn a deer to dust. It would vaporize a woodchuck, and one has a hard time imagining a situation in which it would be practical in defending your home from thugs prior to the arrival of the police. But I digress.

We each took a turn trying to lift the Barrett, each letting out a little grunt. I felt the early onset of a hernia when I gave it a lift. Mark's eyes lit up like my wife's when she sees a new preview for the next installment of the *Twilight* movie series. In both cases, I have to say, I just don't get it.

We perused the booths for another couple of hours before it was time to go. I took a few photos of manufacturers and hunting guides' signs offering discounts "For NRA members and Tea Party Supporters." You know, just for keepsakes. We walked outside and Dad and Mark looked visibly disturbed by the notion that they might have to walk a dozen blocks to their car carrying their heavily larded brochure bags. I spotted an opportunity to assume the role of teacher, putting my city-slicker upbringing to good use by hailing a pedicab. They were very pleased indeed. Before I could trudge the 1,913 steps to my own car, my phone rang. It was Dad, promising me the coldest gin and tonic of all time the next time I visited. "That pedicab was awesome," he said. "You're a lifesaver."

"Sure," I said. "No problem."

"Did you have fun?" Mark asked. They were on the speaker phone in Dad's car.

"Yeah, it was great," I told them. "I never knew there were so many kinds of guns."

"There's a whole lot more than that," Mark said. "Listen, it was just awesome that you were able to come out for this. I really appreciate you driving over."

"No problem," I said. "I was thinking about coming out this fall to hunt some pheasant. Would you mind going with me?"

"Absolutely," Mark said. "I thought you'd never ask."

"What do you mean?"

"Well, I thought you'd never want to go hunting with me."

Was he serious? Had he actually considered it?

"I guess I'm just curious," I said. "I think I'd like to give it a try."

"You bet," he said. "You name the time and the place. I'll be there."

"What about you, Dad? Would you want to go?"

"Uh, sure. If I can make it work with my schedule." I was a little deflated at this. Here the three of us had spent the day bonding, and I was, although thoroughly tired and overwhelmed, on an odd high. I was picturing all kinds of hunting trips with Dad and Mark—elk out west, moose in Canada, maybe even a bear. But it's not like my dad to be romantic or swept away. Mark and I may have been momentary bosom buddies, but my ever-practical dad needed to check his calendar first.

The drive home was another morass of traffic. Though my GPS app claimed four hours, it took me more than six and I finally arrived home, dead tired and gun worn, well after midnight. Twenty hours, six hundred odd miles, more than twelve hours in the car and eight spent on a convention floor. I had learned a lot about guns, handled perhaps a hundred of them, and heard, for the first time ever, my dad refer to me as a "lifesaver" and himself as "a dirty old man."

It was never about the guns, though I could still feel the oiled steel on my hands. I didn't go because I was looking for something. I went for Dad. I went for Uncle Mark. I went because if I am to understand these men and others in my family, I need to understand their interests, their passions. And while there were certainly frustrations, I felt—as I dragged myself to bed—like the whole day had been worth it . . .

Even if it was spent in Pittsburgh.

# 8

## CONSIDER THE McRIB

There's a story my mom likes to tell when she wants to embarrass me. Mostly around my sisters, my wife, the kind of people who know me and accept my foibles out of love or those who are involuntarily related to me and can, thus, go nowhere—theoretically anyway. It involves an incident from when I was around thirteen years old.

I was at that age, and I suspect many readers will know it well, when I tried desperately to spend as little time among the members of my family as possible. For some, this means spending time with friends, out among the throng. For these people, this is the age when juvenile delinquency kicks in. But, being relatively awkward among my peers and classmates, I spent a majority of this time by myself, watching television or doing other unproductive things in my parents' finished basement. There was a couch. A television. A pool table and enough aloneness to be quite appealing to my adolescent desire for time by myself.

It should be pointed out that I have always been, well, a bit fluffy. From my earliest memories, I was always among the tallest in my class. But, unlike other tall kids, I was never of the beanpole thinness—hollow of chest, slight of shoulder—that is often the case. I was more proportionate. Broad shouldered, thick legged, a slight paunch hanging above the Velcro closure of my Bugle Boy trousers. I wasn't fat, but it was evident to anyone that I had seldom missed a meal and, those I did have the misfortune of being tardy or absent for, I made up for with vigorous snacking.

I was an awkward tween with a snacking habit and penchant for solitude. The story that gives my mom so much delight stems from a day when she decided to clean the basement. I was off at school or spending the night at a friend's house or wandering aimlessly through the woods near our house or otherwise engaged in something benign and not noteworthy. The basement was usually my domain. It was rarely cleaned thoroughly, just regularly dusted and vacuumed, but one day Mom evidently decided, in addition to her usual cleaning tasks, a rearrangement of the furniture was in order. She had moved the chair, the small coffee table that acted as a TV stand, and a few lamps, but she was having a hard time making the room work without moving the couch. Mom is not a large woman. In fact she's quite petite, so I still have a hard time imagining her moving a full-size sleeper sofa on her own. But apparently she did just that. And when she did, she found something that would tickle her funny bone even twenty years later.

"I went to go vacuum behind the couch," Mom usually says, "and I found two-dozen wrappers from Swiss Cake Rolls."

How did they get there? Well, I put them there, of course. I adored Swiss Cake Rolls. Snappy chocolate covering on top of chocolate cake with spirals of fluffy yet tasteless white cream. They were heaven. But what I loved most about them was my ability to cram entire rolls in my mouth, chew a couple of times, and swallow the things in one mushy clump. I didn't eat Swiss Cake Rolls—or any snack food—for the pleasure of taste. I ate them for mass and to prove that I could get away with it. It was not at all uncommon for me to eat an entire box in one sitting. According to the Little Debbie website, each package of two Swiss Cake Rolls contains 270 calories (110 from fat) as well as 9 percent of daily fat; 5 percent of daily cholesterol; 6 percent of sodium; 13 percent of carbohydrates; and 4 percent of protein. That's for one package. I ate entire boxes. At a dozen packages per box, that's a whopping 3,240 calories—more than 150 percent of the 2,000 calories used as the basis for those daily percentages. It might be one thing if that was all I ate. But it certainly never was. Those boxes of Swiss Cake Rolls were pilfered, late at night, after eating three square meals and, more than likely, a couple of snacks.

It's pretty safe to say that I have had—for a considerable portion of my life—a complicated and destructive relationship with food. I didn't eat out of necessity or, even, a real interest in taste, texture, complexity, or preparation. I didn't eat because I had any good reason to eat. I ate out of boredom. I ate out of spite. I ate because I was uncomfortable with myself. Worry, anxiety, self-doubt, a need for comfort or to punish myself—these were and, to an extent, are my aperitifs. At the risk of sounding like an after-school special or a Lifetime original movie, food was a sort of drug to me; eating, an odd sort of coping mechanism, something I depended on.

I ate rather continuously through high school—offset by a couple hours of tennis six days a week—but in college, on my own for the first time with an abundance of food (pizza, the dining hall buffet, Chinese food for hangovers and lots and lots of beer), my eating began catching up with me. I came home for my first Christmas break and Mom saw me take my shirt off. My midsection was covered in red lines, like worms. She was horrified, which had me worried. Mom has spent most of my life working in doctors' offices, so when she gets concerned, it's enough to strike worry in the lightest of hearts. We went to the doctor expecting to hear about a strange skin disease, perhaps some sort of infestation. After a thorough examination, blood tests, and, I believe, a stool sample, the doctor returned with the results—stretch marks. She asked me if I had gained a significant amount of weight recently and I said no. After all, I was wearing the same pants I had been when I left for college, albeit increasingly lower on my hips, and I couldn't for the life of me imagine what would contribute to such a prodigious and rapid ballooning.

Then it hit me—chicken nuggets.

I ate chicken nuggets perhaps nine times a week. They were my favorite item at the dining hall. I ate them for lunch, for dinner, for appetizers and as side dishes, blissfully unaware of caloric content or fat grams.

And, if I was getting larger, I wasn't alone.

According to the Centers for Disease Control and Prevention, obesity hit its stride in the years I was scarfing Little Debbies and pounding chicken nuggets. A regional overview of obesity statistics—in which obesity is defined as being thirty pounds overweight with a body mass index of 30 or greater—shows America was significantly fitter twenty years ago than it is today. In 1991, the percentage of obese American adults ranged from 9.6 percent in the Mountain Region (made up of Arizona, Colorado, Idaho, Montana, New Mexico, Utah, and Wyoming) to 14.1 percent in the East North Central Region

(Illinois, Indiana, Michigan, Ohio—where I grew up—and Wisconsin—where I was born). Seven years later, in 1998 (my third year in college), that range moved from 11.4 percent in New England to 20 percent in the South and West South Central (Arkansas, Louisiana, Oklahoma, and Texas). Three years beyond that, there was not a single region of the United States with a percentage of obese people lower than the 1991 high. And, now in the second decade of the millennium, the CDC estimates that 32.2 percent of American adults can be classified as obese.

The United States is a growing nation. It is unfortunate, however, that it is our collective midsection that is growing the fastest.

So I wasn't alone in my growth, and we only had ourselves to blame. We ate more processed food, more fast food, and less and less healthy protein and vegetables—unless you count the lettuce on our Triple Bacon Deluxes from Wendy's. Food became more fake, fatness more inevitable. I know I speak for myself when I say that I was—and in some small way am still—more likely to put fake food into my mouth than real. Indeed, the very definition of food changed dramatically in a generation. My dad grew up on or around farms and farming. He slaughtered pet cows and processed them into ground chuck, steaks, and all manner of tasty, meaty treats. He hunted for game and grew vegetables. In his lifetime, McDonald's, Burger King, Wendy's, and every other fast-food chain on the planet were invented and became billion-dollar companies.

But this is not about fast food, and I am not a crusading food writer. Michael Pollan and Eric Schlosser, I am not. Food has become so effortlessly available to Americans that it's no wonder we are expanding at such an alarming rate. We take for granted how easy it is to get nearly anything we want at nearly any time of day. It's become so easy that we are inventing ways of making food scarcity once again novel. There are many ways to illustrate this, but for the purposes of this chapter, let's look at one example in particular: The McRib sandwich from Mc-Donald's.

Unlike other items on the fast-food giant's menu—the cheeseburger, the McChicken, et al.—the McRib is not a regular offering. Instead, it makes an occasional appearance and, in so doing, whips up what amounts to a national frenzy. Media outlets have reported customers crossing state lines just to get at the sandwich, which, in its construction, is shockingly simple. A pork patty on a bun with onions and pickles. So why do people go crazy for this foodstuff? Novelty, of course. It makes people feel like they are eating real food, slow-cooked pork ribs lovingly prepared, from the convenience of their cars. But the McRib frenzy would never have been possible were it not for the work of a midwestern academic.

In 1972, the exquisitely named University of Nebraska professor Roger Mandingo—I could say that name all day if given the opportunity, Mandingo, Man-ding-go—was awarded a grant from the National Pork Producers Council to work on a process to create something called "restructured meats." The good Professor Mandingo worked what I imagine was tirelessly to find a means of binding pieces of meat together in different shapes using salt and mechanical action. He was successful, of course, and the resulting technology is what enabled such memorable meat products as chicken nuggets and the McRib, which is a pork patty shaped to give the rough look of rib meat on bone. Only there are no bones, just jutty bits of processed meat that are slathered in barbecue sauce.

One has to wonder why it is so important to form ground pork into pig-shaped patties in the first place? Authenticity, one has to imagine. Give eaters the opportunity to think they are eating a pig. In the October 2010 issue of *Esquire* magazine, Dan Coudreaut, the executive chef for McDonald's, tried to explain the sandwich's origin and its rampant popularity, even the need for shaped meat. *Esquire* writer Mark Mikin questioned Chef Dan about the design of the sandwich in the following exchange:

"It's a process called 'chopped and formed,' " he told the magazine. "So they take these big cuts of meat, they chop them up into smaller pieces, and then they press it together and put it into a mold that looks like that rib shape. It's frozen very quickly, then when it goes to the restaurant, it's put into our clamshell grills and cooked, and then helped with the sauce in the restaurant, and then voila."

When—pardon the pun here—pressed about the presence of faux-rib-shaped ridges in the meat when they are not, in fact, real, Chef Dan said, "They are. They are real in our hearts. I hope I have a legacy like that someday."

At the risk of coming across as hypocritically snobbish, I have to say—what the fuck? I have a dysfunctional relationship with food, but the McRib inspires examination. Let me get this straight. We kill a pig and strip the meat from its body. Once that meat is stripped, we chop and mash it until it bears positively no resemblance to a pig, only to then stuff it into forms in order to give it the appearance as once having been a part of a pig? I see.

Add to this the realization that I eat unhealthy food in quantities large enough to lead to obesity despite burning nearly 50 percent more calories than the government recommends and

I come to the conclusion that it's high time I reconcile my relationship to food, eating, and the whole business of putting things in my mouth for the express purpose of mastication and ingestion.

Me, fat boy, need go on diet.

It was something Steven Rinella had said about the relationship between hunting and food that had gotten me thinking. It was in an episode of his show *The Wild Within* when he was hunting wild hogs with dogs among native Hawaiian people. The dogs had a hog cornered in a stream and the animal began attacking the dogs, making a lunge at Rinella. A second of hesitation passed before Steven killed the hog with a knife. In the moments following the kill, he looked at the camera and ad-libbed this line: "Everyone likes bacon; it's just that no one wants to kill the pig."

That line stuck with me for some reason, and I began to see a secondary purpose to my hunting project: to change my relationship to food. Everywhere I turned that summer, food seemed to be the topic of conversation. There was an undercurrent of postmodern foodieism at the NRA show as salesmen hocked meat curing and flavoring products from their booths and implored sportsmen to feed their families right. Michael Pollan, the author and food guru, was on television news programs and Dr. Oz's show. A friend gave me a copy of Eric Schlosser's *Fast Food Nation*, which was turned into a movie and was available on cable. The First Lady, Michelle Obama, was offering tours of her organic vegetable garden on the White House lawn. America's youngest billionaire, media darling, and freakishly genius founder of Facebook, Mark Zuckerberg, had made a public proclamation to eat only food that he himself hunted.

I read with a keen interest the first story about Zuckerberg's project in the *New York Times*. He had killed a chicken by snapping its neck and butchered it in his backyard. He made headlines again a couple of months later when he announced that he had killed a bison for the meat. I thought it was interesting that the story made no mention of hunting the bison, just killing it, which led me to believe that he had called up fellow media mogul Ted Turner and asked if he could come over to shoot one of his. Turner, in addition to being the sire of CNN, is one of America's largest private land owners and possesses one of the biggest private stocks of bison, which he uses to supply his restaurant chain, Ted's Montana Grill.

"Hello, Ted? Hi, it's Mark Zuckerberg."

"Who?"

"Mark Zuckerberg. I created Facebook."

"Look, if this is one of them cults or Amway or some other foolish thing, I don't want any and Jane don't live here no more."

"No, it's Mark Zuckerberg. I created a social networking site that is slowly putting CNN out of business."

"Oh, you're the guy from that movie with Justin Timberlake in it."

"Well, yes sir. There was a movie inspired by an unauthorized biography of how I created the single most important site on the Internet that costarred Justin Timberlake."

"I love me some Justin Timblerlake."

"Me too. Say, I'm working on a project in which I eat only what I kill myself and I was wondering—"

"You ever see him dance?"

"Who?"

"Justin Timberlake. Who the hell are you talking about?"

"You see, I was just wondering if I could come over and shoot one of your bison."

"He brought sexy back, you know."

"Yes, sir. He sure did. Now, about that bison."

"Bison?"

"Yes, sir. I was hoping to kill one of your bison. You own the world's largest herd and I was hoping I might be able to kill one of them."

"Oh, hell, I don't care, them things like alley cats to me. You ever see Timberlake on *Saturday Night Live*?"

"Yes, sir, he's very funny. So Saturday then?"

"For what?"

"Can I come over Saturday and kill a bison?"

"Fine. I love that 'Dick in a Box' song. That is funny as hell."

"Great," says Zuckerberg. "I'll see you then." He hangs up the phone then makes a call to his accountant to begin the proceedings of buying Ted Turner's brain.

I didn't want to go that far. Zealotry is not strong in me. But I was looking forward to the idea of eating something that I had procured. Of course, I've done this lots of times over the course of my life, but up until now procurement had always required a drive-through window or a trip to the grocery store. This was different. This felt historically appropriate, like the uncomfortable shoes worn by employees in Colonial Williamsburg. Learning to hunt was not just about bonding with my relatives or feeling like an adult. It was about feeling like a provider, a member of a tribe old as the millennia and dying out fast.

A 2006 study of hunters found that the number of American hunters sixteen and over dropped 10 percent in the preceding decade. That's not because hunters in midlife suddenly decided to quit. It's because hunting is not being carried on as family tradition in the numbers it once was. Despite more than 75 percent of Americans saying they support legal hunting, just 6 percent in 2006 claimed to actually do it.

Moreover, the line in the sand between hunters and non-hunters is growing wider and deeper. When Vice President Cheney famously shot a friend on a quail-hunting trip in 2006, nonhunters derided the practice as dangerous and Neanderthal. And yet, the work of Michael Pollan and the locavore, grow-your-own food movement has exploded at the same time. It's a troubling dichotomy.

To be fair, many hunters have only exacerbated the problem. Rinella told me that he believes the insular and defensive posture hunters (and gun owners) take makes the sport inaccessible to the curious. They are defensive about their sport and are thus not letting people like me, who may want to try it at an older age, into their club. He believes hunting is losing out on potential participants—and advocates—because the most vocal hunters come across as clannish and paranoid. Indeed, one only need read the headlines stirred up by the NRA to get a sense of the militancy its leaders promote in the name of defending their Second Amendment rights. It's a sign of the polarizing times we live in when former NRA president Charlton Heston stood before a gathered group claiming that the government could take his gun away when "they pry it from my cold, dead hands"; that polarized stance probably doesn't do that much to encourage those with a passing curiosity to try the shooting sports.

But I wasn't curious about shooting. I'd done quite a bit, as you'll see in the next chapter. I was curious about what it would feel like to roast, boil, fry, or fricassee something that had, until

I put an end to it, been alive and blissfully unaware that I was on its tail.

In relative terms I didn't know anything about food. But I wanted to. I began reading books about game preparation and even went so far as to call a chef I had once interviewed looking for advice.

"Don't overcook it, use plenty of fat, and be sure not to break your teeth on a pellet from your shotgun," he told me. "Game like pheasant can be a real pain to cook, but you do it right and you won't have anything better."

I was months away from my first hunting trip and already my stomach was rumbling. I wanted to try it, to practice. I went down to my local Whole Foods and asked if they could order me a pheasant. They could not, but they could offer me a deal on free-range, hand-fed turkey that was bathed in angel tears and educated at the Sorbonne. I tried to find a farmer's market and even called a pheasant club in the next county wondering if I could buy one of the birds they stocked their hunting fields with.

"You can't keep them as pets," said the woman on the phone.

"I'm not interested in a pet," I said. "I'd like to eat one."

"Well, they're a bit small right now, but if you call back in the fall, I may be able to sell you one."

Alas, it appeared I was out of options. I would just have to wait for my opportunity to shoot a pheasant in Iowa, but I would never look at Swiss Cake Rolls the same way again.

# PART III
# SUMMER

# 9

## COMFORT BREEDS CARELESSNESS

I love the smell of nitrocellulose. Metallic, but sweetly earthy, it hangs in the midsummer air like fog on San Francisco Bay. It's heavy and lingers on your fingers and in your clothes for a couple of hours, leaving a tang on your tongue and setting up shop in your nasal passages, like a reminder of the thing you have just done: the rounds you've sent downrange, the targets you've more than likely missed.

My left hand starts to tremble a little as the weight of the gun becomes noticeable. Is it possible I am really that weak? The boxy earmuffs block out almost all sound, leaving me with the sensation of my own breathing and an odd, unexpected sense of congestion—like a bad cold—though I feel perfectly fine. The sun coming through the branches of the old hemlock trees on the back of the property and the humidity rising from the deep Iowa soil creates a bluish camouflage of air separating me from my target. I close my left eye and rest my cheek on the stock of the old Winchester lever-action rifle, trying to line up the notch between the two rear posts of the site with the post at the muzzle of the gun. You want the post out front to fill the space between the two back posts, the tops of all three lining up to form a straight line. That's how you know the gun is level. Then, you want all three to line up with your target, twenty-five or thirty yards away.

At its best, it's an effortless dance. At its worst, something you become mildly obsessed with, this perfection. You begin to overthink things. You concentrate too hard. You begin to notice the sweat on the palm of your trigger hand, on your cheek, the lid of your closed left eye. Your left hand begins to waver. The gun starts feeling heavy and you wobble. You're thinking too long. Just pull the damned trigger.

Miss.

The eight-inch steel plate does not fall, its freshly spray-painted front, unblemished. I pull my cheek off the stock and cycle the lever action, the way I've seen thousands of cowboys do it in those great movies. They make it look effortless. It's not hard, but there is some resistance. Halfway down, the spent cartridge flings off and to the right. Pull the lever back up and I can feel a new one being rammed into the action in its place. The whole process starts over again—the closed eye, the cheek to stock, lining up the posts, the sweaty palm, the quavering hand. The whole thing takes just seconds, but it can feel like hours. Whole days seem to pass in the time it takes to shoot off ten rounds. It's the strange silence, the complete concentration. It might be and can be fun to come out here and burp off rounds like a tommy gun, but that's not important to me now. Nothing else is. Be safe, shoot clean. Knock that little white steel disc off its base. Teach it who's boss. Pull the fucking trigger.

*Blam*. A puff of smoke, a distant *ding*, the swoop and pull of another round loaded, another chance to shoot. That sweet smell of powder filling my nose. My breath coming quicker with the excitement of having hit the target. Shouldering the gun, I take aim again. Close my eye, rest my cheek, focus on the poles and the target downrange, this time a smaller steel circle, this one mounted on a hinge next to a plate fabricated in the shape of a squirrel. Squeeze the trigger, don't jerk it. *Blam.* Miss. I rushed it. Jack the lever and rack a new round.

And so it goes for hours.

I don't want to give anyone the impression that I have never been around guns before. I have. Spend enough summers and vacations at my grandma's house and sooner or later Uncle Mark is going to have you on the back acre—out past the old barn where the pigs used to be and the garden where Grandma kept vegetables, wildflowers, and red raspberries—at his shooting range. When you're young—maybe ten or so, depending upon the permissiveness of your parents—you're shooting the Chipmunk, a single-shot .22-caliber rifle about two-thirds the length of an adult arm. It weighs a couple of pounds, you have to pull back a knob on the action to make it fire, and, when you squeeze the trigger, you get pretty much the greatest thrill and surprise of your young life. It's a starter gun, a kid's gun, the kind you hear octogenarian former Boy Scouts talk about using to terrorize the local woodchuck population back in those golden, more permissive days. As an adult, the Chipmunk—and here I have no idea if that's the brand name of the gun or just a pet name given by Uncle Mark to the trainer we all used—feels comically, toyishly unsubstantial. It's lighter than a Super Soaker, shorter than a T-ball bat, and leaves you with the impression that it would shatter at the slightest touch. But I can't count the number of rounds I put through that gun barrel.

It was also the gun Uncle Mark and Dad used to teach me gun safety. Never point it at anyone or anything you didn't want to shoot, maim, or kill. Never look down the barrel. Keep it pointed up in the air or downrange at all times. Check the action to make sure it is loaded or unloaded—depending upon which you want—and keep the safety on until everyone is clear, you have it pointed at your target, and you are ready to shoot. Guns are not toys. I repeat GUNS ARE NOT TOYS. I can't tell you how many times I heard that and other admonitions for safety as a kid—so many that, despite shooting nearly every time I was in Iowa (and that is a lot of times), I never became comfortable around guns. That's a good thing. Comfort breeds carelessness. If you are at least afraid enough to never take your mind off the fact that the thing in your hand is designed to kill, then you'll probably be inclined to follow the safety protocol. If, however, you stop thinking of a gun as something designed to impart destructive forces on that which is unfortunate enough to be directly in front of it—well, that's how people get hurt.

I cried the first time I shot a gun.

I was six years old, maybe seven, and we were standing in the back garden at my grandma's house outside of Mason City, Iowa. My dad and Uncle Mark were standing next to me, just behind and to the right. Uncle Mark had loaded the Chipmunk and given me some basic instructions. Hold the stock tight against your shoulder, and keep your face pressed firmly against the wood. Squeeze the trigger; don't jerk it. Remember that even if the safety is on, the gun can still go off. Take deep, smooth breaths and pull the trigger as you exhale. It was a lot to take in, a lot of instructions.

I had never wanted to fire a gun, but my dad and his brother had decided it was time for me to learn. My cousins had all learned at my age. The ones who lived in Iowa had learned even younger. This was my time, my rite of passage into this family of hunters. This was supposed to be my first step toward becoming a Heimbuch man. Of course, they didn't say it at the time, but they had been looking forward to showing me how with the hopes of sharing a whole lot more. Bigger guns, different guns. Shotguns. Deer hunting, bird hunting. Maybe someday there would be an elk or a moose. Dad had always wanted a bear.

That's why I pulled the trigger, because Dad and Uncle Mark were standing next to me, encouraging me. They weren't cheering me on, exactly. Cheering is too gregarious. But every time I told them I couldn't do it, every time I tried to hand the small rifle back to them, Uncle Mark put it back in my hands, and Dad told me not to be scared and to just try it.

I tried to settle my nerves, to calm my shaking hands. A hot tear formed in the corner of my left eye that quickly got cold in the crisp winter air. I tried to line up the sights the way Uncle Mark had taught me—center the front sight between the two rear posts; line up the tops and see the target in the background. I had heard them shooting before, that day and during other visits to Grandma's house, but the noise, the concussive snap when I pulled the trigger, startled me and I jumped a little. The force of the recoil, which could not have been harder than a friendly chuck on the shoulder from a family friend, hurt me and I let out a little yelp. My cousin Kevin was standing behind me to the left and he laughed when I quickly handed the gun to Uncle Mark and turned to run back to the house. Dad tried to call me back, but I choked out that I had to go to the bathroom. I ran into the steamy warmth of Grandma's house and into the bathroom near the mudroom door. My breath stuttered and I felt tears run down my face. I removed some layers of clothes only to realize I had wet my pants. Not all the way, not a full soaking, but enough to reinforce my embarrassment.

I tried to tell Mom that I didn't feel good, but she shooed me back outside. Walking the hundred yards back to where Uncle Mark and Dad were standing with Kevin, I made a decision to mask my fear, the sheer horror I had experienced firing that weapon. I wanted them to be proud of me, to embrace me into their world. Even at a young age, I had an instinct to diffuse discomfort with humor. Dad asked if I was okay as I crunched back through the thin layer of snow back to the shooting range.

"I guess," I said, "it scared the pee out of me."

He and Mark laughed; Kevin gave me an evil smirk and returned to shooting. Mark warned him several times to keep the gun pointed downrange as I leaned into Dad's side. He put his arm around my shoulder and asked if I wanted another turn. "Yeah, sure," I told him and felt that empty sense of numb that follows a good scare, a cry, and a few drops of urine in your Superman Fruit of the Looms.

From the Chipmunk, you move to a shotgun. A .410—light ammo and enough kick to make you a little afraid. Then it's back to the pistols and more rifles. My dad has a .22-caliber Ruger sport pistol that I remember fondly from my early teen years. Bigger .22-cal rifles, more powerful handguns and shotguns. If you spend enough time and express enough curiosity, chances are pretty good Uncle Mark will have you handling, shooting, and understanding every kind of gun there is. I, of course, being the carpetbagging suburban kid from up north or back east, never got all the way through the armory. I never shot a black powder muzzleloader, never tried an assault rifle. But, whenever I visited Iowa—before kids, marriage, or other such distractions—I used to love shooting on that range.

When I was old enough, Mark would give me a brick of .22 bullets and my choice of armaments. "These better be gone before you leave," he'd say. And I would make, what I thought was, a rather heroic effort to do just that. I would shoot until my fingers hurt from reloading, until I could smell nothing but the chemicals of the powder—the brass from the shells on my fingers. Unfortunately, I never shot quite enough to be able to hit anything.

I was in college when Dad and I went out to Iowa on our way to a fishing trip in Canada. Dad and Mark are competitive in the way older and younger siblings are. My dad, who is the fourth of the nine kids, is a pretty good shot, especially for a guy who doesn't get to shoot all that much. Uncle Mark, the youngest and something slightly more than a devotee of the sport, likes to try and show up his older brother. At times, I find myself in the middle of their armed pissing contests, taking shots between them. On this particular trip, we were shooting pistols—something of a specialty for Mark and also something my grandfather, a man I never got to know all that well, would have considered strictly verboten. "Pistols are for gangsters and crooks," he might have muttered. And, it turns out, for his youngest son.

Mark's a great shot, especially with a pistol. Growing up, I used to think he was the best in the world, not that I had anyone to compare him to. So he was knocking his targets down pretty well. My dad is the kind of guy who can do just about anything if he puts his mind to it and, when it comes to beating his little brother at his own game, his mind gets put to things. When the time came for me to take a clip's worth of shots, I was lucky my rounds hit the backstop—stacked railroad ties—behind the targets, let alone the targets themselves. This caused Mark to chuckle and grin that childlike grin he gets at moments of pure mirth. You see, Mark may lose to my dad, but his kids—more than ten years younger than me—were already better shots and he could take rest in the fact that, if nothing else, he was a better teacher than my dad (if not one with better facilities, more access, and a more receptive student body).

"What's the matter, city boy?" he asked. "Got to be hanging out of a car window, going forty miles an hour in order to hit anything?"

Yes, Uncle Mark, growing up in the pressed khaki suburbs I am indeed more comfortable doing a drive-by than shooting at some secondhand bowling pins in Grandma's backyard. You get an idea of the relationship.

I love Uncle Mark and his wife, Linette, for a lot of reasons, not least of which is their hospitality. Whenever I come to Iowa for a visit, they always offer up their downstairs guest room and their home to my family and me. And we appreciate them for it. I had already had children before I made my first adult visit out there without the rest of my family—Mom, Dad, sisters, brother, and so on—and I was surprised by how at home I felt. On that particular side trip to Iowa with my dad, after a day or two of eating and loafing and walking the grounds of my grandma's place—where Mark and Linette had built a home to be nearer to her—I got up the nerve to ask if I could shoot. It was something, I gather, Mark had been waiting for me to ask all along. He ushered me into the basement, where I had my pick of a few weapons stored there. I went with the .22, then something a bit bigger and more exotic and, over the course of the next few days, managed to cure my jones for firing weapons—even if I didn't hit anything.

We followed a similar ritual two summers later when we visited again, saving the shotguns for the last day. This trip, Mark introduced me to cowboy guns—Winchester rifle models from the era of Reconstruction, old Colt revolvers with their eccentric loading requirements—and I ate it up. I shot the heart out of the Queen of Hearts from twenty paces and grew to love the *chick-chick blam* sound of the lever-action rifles.

Guns and shooting have long been a big part of Uncle Mark's life, but they were only a means to an end. It's hunting that seems to make him tick. The experience of being out in the field, among the elements in pursuit of one of God's creatures and food for his family table—these things are sacred to him. And I know that the best thing I can ever do, the best gift I can ever give him is to worship at the same altar.

To this point, my shooting experience, my time handling guns has been akin to spending years at the driving range without ever playing nine holes or reading the *Joy of Cooking* cover to cover without making a meal. There's no substance, no pudding to bare the proof—pistols are still, by the way, completely a loss to me—but, for what?

I'm not trying to say that the only reason a person picks up a gun is to kill something, but in our family, it does go hand in hand. And the idea that I have gone this long, these three and a third decades without ever becoming a part of that family tradition seems a little ridiculous. We don't talk about the definition of manliness among the family. We don't stand around discussing a man's role in the world. There's no Charlton Heston–like monologues about a man doing what a man's got to do. But, standing on the outside, being separate from something that seems so central to the other men in the family's lives, I feel like I'm not a part of the conversation. An outsider. I mean, what's the big deal? I love to shoot, love being outside, love to eat.

# 10

## EDUCATION

The Fairfield Sportsmen's Association is tucked into the extreme southwest corner of Ohio, just a dozen miles or less from the Indiana and Kentucky borders. It's a rural section of Hamilton County, one of Ohio's most urban areas. Driving down the narrow, two-lane road in search of the club's entrance, I was surrounded on either side by lush, dense forest, broken only by the occasional single-wide trailer set back fifty or sixty feet with rusty cars in the yard and, inevitably, a large American flag tacked directly to the siding.

This kind of landscape—an up-from-the-holler warren of feral dogs, unbiblical sex, and, one assumes, methamphetamine production—always gives me the creeps. In its way, it's beautiful, verdant. But it's also the kind of place that sets my often overactive imagination off in unsavory meanderings. Once, in college while working as a delivery boy for a pizza restaurant, I spent an hour searching for an address in a place that looked very much like this, only to be greeted at the door by an indignant man in a stained white undershirt and wearing a pistol in a leather holster on his hip. I was terrified, more terrified than I had ever been to that point in my life, and when he said, rather blandly, "You're late," I took it to mean that I was about to die. I thrust the pizza in his hand and ran away without taking his money. I covered the hundred feet from the door to my still-running car in giant bounds and backed down the long, narrow gravel driveway at a speed that might have qualified me for a poll position in a NASCAR race. I hit the tarmac and backed across two lanes without pausing for oncoming traffic, threw the stick shift into gear, and hardly slowed down until I arrived back in the delivery bay of the restaurant. It was only once inside that I realized I had not waited for payment, so, wanting to avoid discussing my own cowardice, I paid for his pizza out of my tips. This was only to find out weeks later that the armed customer had sensed my fear and called my manager, offering to pay by credit card. They apparently had a good laugh at my expense and the manager didn't make him pay, telling the armed and disheveled man that I had "taken care of it."

It's not as if I've ever really been harmed by anyone who lives in these places. Yet every time I find myself in an unfamiliar, not-quite-rural place with deeply shadowed woods and unkempt homes, I somehow assume death is imminent. Add in my general discomfort with not knowing precisely where I am at every moment and you can begin to imagine the sense of nervous dread, the clenching stomach nerves that washed over me when I circled back for the third time, instinctively knowing I had missed the entrance to the Fairfield Sportsmen's Association but having no real idea where it was.

Plus, I was worried about being late. For one thing, I hate being late. But I also felt much the same way about attending this weekend hunter's safety course as I did on every first day of school. I didn't want to be the center of attention. I didn't want to be the brainiac or the jock, the stoner or the princess. I didn't want to fit any *Breakfast Club* stereotype. I just wanted to be completely forgettable, which wouldn't work if I were the last person to walk in.

When I realized I must have missed the turnoff for a fourth time, I saw the clock on my dashboard read 8:58. Two minutes to find where I was going and slip silently into class. My nerves frayed a bit more, and a bead of nervous sweat formed on my temple. Finally, I saw a road leading off into the woods—one that had definitely *not* been there moments before—between two mobile homes that had seen better days and decided to give it a shot. There was no sign that I could see, and pulling down the winding path, I began losing faith that I had found the right road until, crossing a small stream, I saw a small collection of cinder-block buildings and heard the distant pop of guns being fired on an unseen range.

I parked in the middle of the lot between the two largest buildings and, not exactly sure where I was supposed to be, began walking toward one. An older gentleman, dressed in head-to-toe khaki with a shotgun slung across his arm, pointed to the other without saying a word.

I must have stood out rather boldly from what the man—obviously a member of the club—was used to seeing around the facility. While most of the people I saw darting in and out of buildings or lingering around the shotgun ranges were dressed in some form of khaki, camouflage, or denim, with thick-looking boots and masculine hats, I was wearing the loudest pair of madras shorts I own—all yellows and reds—a T-shirt with a cartoon piece of smoked pork and the slogan BACON IS MEAT CANDY screen-printed in a flourished font, and flip-flops.

You'd think I would have known better after my experience

at the NRA convention. I had seen firsthand how costume and tradition dovetail with safety and a shooter's particular sense of identity. Hunting and shooting are sports in which people who participate often look the part, and, at that moment—running late and ill-clad—I certainly did not. So, somewhat sheepishly, I waved at the older gentleman and received his nod before stepping into the tan cinder-block building that would be my home for twelve hours over the next two days.

Relative to the sport, hunter's safety courses are a new development. The first was organized in 1944 in Frankfurt, Kentucky, and the first volunteer course in Ohio was taught in 1961. They weren't made mandatory for hunters seeking a license until more than two decades after that. Prior to the introduction of the courses, hunting and trapping were learned pastimes, something a father passed on to his son or, historically less likely, daughter. In the days before the supermarket, suburbs, or refrigeration, hunting was less about recreation than survival. Old dad would teach his young son to hunt so that he could pull his weight, literally helping to put food on the table. That's not to say that hunting's sporting roots do not run deep. Indeed, the English have been hunting for sport and recreation since the seventeenth century. But in frontier America, hunting tended to have less to do with ornate costumes and gun handlers than it did survival and provision.

This was truer later in the Middle American states than almost anywhere else. I once spoke to a World War II U.S. Army veteran who said that recruits from the Midwest and Deep South were taken for granted as having rifle-handling abilities and were thus subject to two weeks' less firearms training than their more urbane and coastal brethren. I've never been able to confirm the man's story, but it makes sense, really—certainly the idea that hunting for sustenance was more common in agrarian cultures than in coastal or urban communities follows my own family's experiences. My dad and his five brothers were taught to shoot by my grandfather while growing up in rural Iowa. This wasn't for sport: shooting a pheasant or a deer was a nice way to balance out the larder.

My dad was never forced to take a class like the one I was about to, though once when I was in my midteens, I mentioned that I might like to go with him on an upcoming deer-hunting trip. He immediately told me that in order to do so, I needed hunter's education and left for that trip without me. Neither of us ever brought it up again. However, he did enroll my younger brother, Kosta, in the class when he was seventeen, and when I told Kosta that I was taking the class, he was quick to point out that he had scored a 98 out of a possible 100 on the written final exam.

"Beat that, bro," he taunted.

As brothers, we are not Cain and Abel, but I have always felt a bit of a rivalry with Kosta. My parents adopted him from Russia just as I—their youngest—was getting ready to graduate from college. And from the start, Kosta took a much greater interest in the outdoors than I ever did. He barely spoke English by the time he shot his first deer with Dad. Soon, he'll be off to the army, an organization my dad credits with making him a man—and one, like hunting, that I never showed much interest in.

So, for three months leading up to my arrival at the Fairfield Sportsmen's Association, I had a voice in the back of my head. *Beat Kosta on the test*, it said. *Your manhood and possibly your inheritance depend on it.*

I became fixated on achieving a perfect score. I downloaded the course book to my iPad and spent hours trying to commit it to memory. Never before had I experienced such a keen sense of competition. I was not a great athlete growing up. The only sport I played in high school was tennis. Most of my time was spent practicing for the marching band or singing in choral ensembles. On paper, I was the definition of a geek, and Kosta, a closed-mouth football player who bears a striking resemblance to the actor Daniel Craig (only my brother has bigger muscles), could not have been more opposite.

We have only ever lived under the same roof for a couple of months and yet it is as if we grew up together. He sleeps in my old room. Uses my old furniture. Hangs his dashing clothes in my old closet. Beating him on this test was not only a matter of personal pride, but of reclaiming my territory. It was, in an odd way, like the movie *Can't Buy Me Love,* in which Patrick Dempsey plays an industrious geek who, by fate and a set of circumstances involving wine-stained suede, has an opportunity to run with the cool kids. When he gets there, he doesn't just want to fit in, he wants to be the coolest of them all.

That's very much how I felt about becoming a hunter. I didn't just want to participate, I wanted to excel if for no other reason than to make up for years of being left out. And it all started with beating Kosta's near-perfect score on the safety exam.

Safety is something hunters talk a lot about and with good reason. Unlike, say, basketball, in which a bad day might involve a sprained ankle or jammed finger, the consequences of a misstep while hunting may include death or dismemberment. So it is understandable why hunters (good ones anyway) pay so much attention to safety, and why, as a person interested in the sport, you are forced to learn proper procedure and precaution before being allowed to participate.

Over more than half of a century, 35 million students from the United States and Canada have completed the courses, and every year, another 750,000 enroll, according to the International Hunter Education Association. An impressive number to be sure, but perhaps even more impressive is that every course is taught by volunteers—70,000 of them to be precise. That's roughly the same number of people who work as volunteer firefighters in the United States. And the courses are free to anyone who wants to learn.

In 1937, Congress passed the Pittman-Robinson Act, which is essentially an excise tax on hunting and outdoor equipment. Every time someone buys an article of hunting apparel, a rifle, a shotgun, or a bow and arrow, they are charged an 11 percent tax (10 percent for all handguns, lower because, one assumes, they may be used for hunting but also nonhunting activities like scaring lost pizza delivery boys). That money is earmarked for conservation and hunter education. It's a remarkably smart system. Hunters pay for future generations of hunters not only to learn how to do it safely, but to have areas where they can hunt.

And it seems to be working. One thousand hunters are injured in accidental shootings every year in the United States, according to the IHEA, and 10 percent of those are fatal—a relatively small percentage, given that, according to the 2001 National Survey of Fishing, Hunting and Wildlife-Related Recreation, there were upward of forty-five million hunters in the United States alone.

Although a hundred deaths from hunting-related accidents are tragic, consider the relative safety of hunting to another sport popular in America—golf. There are roughly the same number of people who identify themselves as golfers and yet, curiously, the American Orthopedic Society of Sports Medicine reports that 40 percent of amateur golfers report golf-related injuries every year. These injuries range from repeated stress injuries, strains, pulls, and those related to carrying a heavy bag full of clubs to, more dramatically, lightning strikes. Factor in the odd heart attack suffered by an elated older player, and other injuries—perhaps sustained while drunkenly driving a motorized cart—and you get a figure of around twelve million annual golfing injuries.

So, comparatively, hunting seems downright safe.

Today, a hunter's education course is required for obtaining a hunter's license. Doesn't matter the species you're going after, states will not issue a permit to hunt unless you have completed the course. However, the states are forward thinking enough to allow hunters who complete the training in their home state to get a license in another, as long as they can prove that they have completed the course. Since my plan is to hunt in Iowa, I was relieved to know I could complete the course in Ohio and still get credit.

While I liked everything about the system in theory, I became a bit disconcerted when I looked in to the particulars of the program. I've never put a lot of stock in the academic rigidity of state-sponsored teaching—after all, I know how hard I worked in order to get a driver's license, and that was not very hard at all. Answer a few almost insultingly easy questions and drive home with a learner's permit. Watch *Blood on the Asphalt* and *Green Means Go* in a classroom above a pottery shop and walk away legally permitted to operate a two-ton, two-hundred-horsepower killing machine.

I'm not sure why I expected more rigorous instruction when it came to an activity that by its nature involves some sort of weapon, but I did.

*  *  *

I entered the classroom, which bore a strong resemblance to the cafeteria at the Lutheran church camp I attended for a week during the summer between seventh and eighth grades. It was slightly rectangular—say forty feet by thirty-five feet—with bare painted concrete walls, wide banks of windows that opened by turning a handle and angling them out, and dull, flaccid overhead lighting that usually gives me a headache. Closing my eyes, I could almost smell the prepubescent odor of unwashed and creek-trodding boys and half expected, based on the room, to be asked to join in on a chorus of "Kumbaya."

Perhaps fifteen rows of rectangular tables sat on either side of a central aisle. At the front of the class hung a large American flag, and just in front of it were four lunch tables covered with rifles, pistols, shotguns, bows and arrows, and, to my surprise, a crossbow. I don't think I had ever seen a crossbow in person before that moment.

There are roughly 280 million legally owned firearms in the United States, according to the American Firearms Institute. And the Institute boldly states on its website that this equates to nearly eight of every ten Americans being a gun owner, before sheepishly mentioning that more than 50 percent of all people who own guns own more than one. When I realized that all of the twenty or so firearms on the front tables—including the crossbow—were from the private collection of one of the instructors, it became clear that the 80-percent-of-the-populace-as-gun-owners assertion was, perhaps, a bit skewed. I don't know a single gun owner who owns less than three.

Still, I understand why the AFI wants to make it seem like everyone owns a gun. It's good for advocacy. And though it's hard to nail down the exact number of gun owners in America, a commonly repeated statistic is around 80 million. In a country of roughly 320 million people, that's closer to one in four as opposed to eight in ten. But the exact proportion of the gun-owning populace to non-gun-owning is less important than the idea that people who own guns are often collectors. Judging by the collection presented on the table at the front of the room, I guessed at least one of my instructors was very serious when it came to guns.

I had no idea how serious until the class began.

A middle-aged gentleman with close-cropped hair and a Boy Scout–style shirt (tucked neatly into matching cargo pants, which were, in turn, tucked into the type of boots you might expect a SWAT team member to wear) handed me the course book, a supplemental course book, a pocket guide for identifying Ohio game animals, a sticker bearing the Ohio Division of Wildlife emblem, and three unsharpened pencils the color orange you associate with hunting—garish and bright. Before I could ask him anything, he shooed me up the aisle and attended to his distribution duties with the person behind me.

At that moment, a huge wave of relief washed over me, for while I may have been a few minutes late, I wasn't the only one. There were at least ten people who shuffled in behind me. So I actually had time to debate seating arrangements. Sitting in the back might leave me unnoticed, which suited my desire for anonymity, but I worried about accidentally nodding off or letting my mind wander while staring out one of the windows. The middle section of the room was filled with fathers and young sons and grandfathers with their grandsons, and I felt out of place being on my own. It goes against my personality to sit near the front, but on this particular morning my desire to beat Kosta was more powerful than my ego. I chose a seat in the front row and waited for the course to begin.

Because I never actually made my presence as a writer known, I'll call my instructors Matt, Tim, and Arthur (not their real names). Each brought his own particular expertise and teaching style, and they would alternate teaching the nine chapters in the *Hunter's Safety* book.

Matt was the man who handed me materials when I first walked in. In his introduction, Arthur described Matt as a lifetime hunter and Scout with more than fifty years of experience "in the field." He seemed nice enough, if serious, and carried himself with the poise and posture of a man who had never quite left the military despite decades living as a civilian.

Tim was tall and thin, with a thick white mustache and hair parted so sharply as to imply the use of a gas-powered implement—an edge trimmer or weed whacker, maybe—who reminded me of a teacher I had in junior high named Mr. Dunkle. Mr. Dunkle taught woodshop and mechanical drawing. He was easygoing in a way most teachers who deal with preteens can't bring themselves to be, and I often imagined him sitting on his porch at night, listening to bluegrass music and whittling a snack bowl out of a piece of driftwood. *Happy* isn't quite the word to describe him, maybe *content*.

Tim seemed content. He was the friendliest of the bunch and struck me as possibly an engineer in real life outside the classroom. He taught the most technical aspects of the course and made clear from the start that he felt his job was to tell us exactly what questions we might expect on the multiple-choice test and how to answer them. He seemed to be the instructor to take follow-up questions to, the most eager to help.

And then there was Arthur. If forced to guess, I'd say Arthur was slightly younger than Dwight Eisenhower, but older than Dick Cheney. The guns sitting on the front tables were his, and he was quick to warn us "not to touch them unless given express permission, which you're not likely to get." Of the three, he was the instructor who spent the least amount of time looking at the course materials in favor of editorializing on media conspiracy and left-wing lunacy.

I felt immediately uncomfortable around Arthur, not only because I have spent most of my professional life working as a journalist and have voted Democrat in, say, 70 percent of the elections in which I have participated, but because he didn't seem to be all there. I imagined he lived in a house in the woods with a false basement floor, beneath which lay a cache of rocket-propelled grenades and assault rifles that he keeps "just in case." Not particularly scary physically—he stood with the slight stoop of a man in his eighties—there was a certain degree of menace in his smile. I knew to pay attention to him, but to discard half of everything he said.

After an initial diatribe about how the media wants to take guns out of American hands, and a strong suggestion that everyone in the room should join the NRA (he just happened to be a recruiter and took cash, check, or plastic), Arthur launched into the first chapter, which explained the construction, uses, and safe handling of shotguns.

There are four basic safety rules when it comes to hunting:

- Always keep the muzzle of the gun pointed in a safe direction.

- Treat every gun as if it were loaded.

- Be sure of your target and what's beyond it.

- Keep your finger off the trigger until you are ready to shoot.

These rules are emphasized at the beginning of every chapter in the book, drilled by rote into the minds of every student. They are good rules. If you follow them, it's very hard to have an accident. And being simple enough to remember means that, with a little bit of experience, they can form the basis of good safety habits. Uncle Mark, who is a hunter's education instructor in Iowa, hammered them into my head as a boy on the range in Grandma's backyard.

Arthur read them verbatim, and as he was midway through rule three, Tim piped up with a "this is on the test" from the corner of the room, like a choir director in one of those lively Southern churches shouting "Amen!" to a preacher. I can't say I completely understand the segue, but for some reason Tim's approbation took Arthur down a completely different subject track all together.

"They don't want you to know this," he said with a bit of devious mischief, "but there's something called a Class 3 license that lets you hunt with machine guns. There are thirty thousand of these licenses in the United States. The people who have them pay $200 a year and not one of them has been used in the commission of a crime. Think about that."

And so it went for the shotgun portion of the class. Arthur would read a sentence or two from the book, then make a comment on them. For instance, he described the procedure for safe handling of a shotgun while crossing a fence line, then retreated to his table of guns and picked up a torn and twisted hunk of metal.

"This is what happens when you don't handle your shotgun

correctly while crossing a fence line," he said. He held what had once been a shotgun barrel in the air for all of us to see. It was completely destroyed, looking very much like Elmer Fudd's gun after Bugs Bunny put a finger in the barrel. "This was given to me by a former student who didn't check his gun after he crossed a fence. There was snow in the barrel, so when he fired it blew up. He lost two fingers and had a chunk torn out of his face. Don't let that happen to you."

The terror-by-example method of teaching has been highly effective with me ever since an elementary school art teacher warned me that mishandling the drying racks would result in our eyes being "turned into hamburger." So I made a note to always check my gun barrel after crossing a fence line and underlined it in my notebook three times.

Matt taught the second section on rifles in approximately a quarter of the time it took Arthur to get through the equally long first chapter. He read verbatim from the text, highlighted the information that would likely show up on the test, and kept the editorializing to a minimum.

Arthur was back for pistols, and over the course of ninety minutes, managed to cover exactly four pages of heavily illustrated text. Though the materials strictly covered the basics of how handguns are made and their safe operation, Arthur proselytized his views on why Americans are better off being armed at all times and just how ridiculous it is that carrying a gun into an elementary school is illegal in most states.

*Damn Democrats,* one imagines his inner monologue going, *always trying to ruin a guy's good time.*

It might seem hyperbolic to describe Arthur's teaching as brainwashing, but with so many young impressionable people in the room, it's hard to come up with a more tactful description.

He was prattling on about his favorite junkyard—where hand-gun carriage is actually encouraged—when my mind began to wander and I started examining my fellow classmates.

I was among the very few students attending the class alone. By and large, they were there in pairs, and most looked like relatives. There was a man who was obviously an avid hunter and excited to bring his son, perhaps twelve, into the fold. He laughed at Arthur's jokes, flipped the occasional affirmation into the lesson, and was positively atwitter with excitement as the discussion moved into the mechanics of felling large game with an old-fashioned six-shooter. I mean it: his legs were bouncing and arms shaking with excitement. If talking about the proper way to brace your handgun for more accurate shoot-ing had him this excited, imagine what this guy must have been like the first time he went all the way. It's surprising his head hadn't exploded.

On the other side of the room, a well-groomed grandfather beamed with pride as his eager and articulate grandson—again probably around twelve—raised his hand to answer every ques-tion asked by Tim, Matt, and Arthur. The way he spoke, his poise, this young man had the promise of a career in politics. Of the fifty or so questions asked over the two-day class, he raised his hand for forty-nine of them and answered forty-seven correctly. I wanted to be in the woods with this kid—at least you'd know you were safe, even if you were overcome by the uncontrollable urge to give him an atomic wedgie and stuff him into a locker.

Trust me, I know what I'm talking about. I was this boy. I was the eager beaver in my class. While I have always hesitated to be noticed, I've also had to deal with impulse control, or, more specifically, the lack thereof when it comes to knowing something. There was, let's just say, an incident my freshman year of high school. I was in English class and doing my best to play it cool because a girl I liked very much was sitting next to me, passing me notes about how boring the class was and how much she hated poetry. I gave her knowing nods, as if to say, "You bet, babe. I'm with you." The problem arose when the teacher asked the class who the author was of one of my favorite poems. No one's hand went up, and I could feel something inside of me begin to boil. The right answer was there, in the pit of my stomach, just waiting to burst free. I tried to resist and hoped the teacher would eventually get tired of waiting and simply reveal the answer, but she didn't. And the longer she waited, the more I felt I had to speak and the harder it became to suppress the impulse. I wanted to be cool, I really did. I wanted this girl to be impressed by my swaggering remove. But it's like trying to get dogs to sit when you hold a cookie in front of them. They can resist for a while, but eventually their instincts take over. My instincts took over and I burst. "William Butler Yeats," I said. Shouted really. Needless to say, that particular girl and I never dated. When I saw her recently at a high school reunion, she asked if I was still into poetry. I told her no. "That's funny," she said, "because I remember you really liked it in high school."

Hang your head in shame, you big geek. Hang it in shame.

I understood this kid. I ran into him as he was coming out of the bathroom on a break. "Please, pardon me, sir," he said earnestly, if a bit too formally, then held the door for me as I went in. I wanted to shake his hand, take him aside, and let him know that everything, no matter what, would be okay. I wanted to tell him to never resist the urge to answer no matter what his peers tell him and that being smart would, eventually, get him far in life. But I didn't. Instead, I touched the brim of my baseball cap and said, "No trouble at all," then continued inside.

The rest of the people in the class fit somewhere between obligated teenager and mentoring parent. Except for the two girls in the back of the room. I could not figure out what they were doing there. Every fifteen minutes or so, they would push back loudly from their table and step outside. They were teenagers, dressed in too-short shorts and T-shirts, and had the attention spans of fourth-graders at a real-estate conference. I gathered being there was not their idea, but I wondered who they were trying to impress. Boys? Their fathers? Was hunter's safety some sort of elaborate goof? Something told me that they didn't share my burning desire to ace the final.

We took a break for lunch and proceeded en masse across the parking lot to the club building, where a woman named Clara sold very reasonably priced sandwiches, hot dogs, and cheeseburgers. I took my cheeseburger out onto a covered porch overlooking a trapshooting range. There were two four-man teams shooting expensive-looking shotguns at blaze-orange clay targets, which were fired from a launcher hidden in a structure beneath their feet. It was fun to watch—the orange disks gliding gently toward an open field in graceful arcs, the percussive snap as the men took turns shooting at the targets in a highly organized succession.

The men shooting at the range, just twenty or so yards from where I stood eating my delicious and cheap cheeseburger, moved with a sort of wordless efficiency. Each was thrown two targets and each had two shells in his gun. The clay pigeons went up, then *bang! bang!* and that man lowered his gun, broke the breech, and reloaded while the next man took his shots. When the fourth man in line was done shooting, he turned and followed a path to the other end of the line, and the other shooters moved one station to their right. It happened in continuous flow, each man shooting, reloading, and moving on, like a well-choreographed dance.

I watched the men, all of whom appeared to be middle-aged or older, decked out in khaki shooting vests, wide-brimmed caps, and rose-colored glasses, until I finished eating, then decided to use the remaining ten minutes of the lunch break to have a look around the facility.

The main building, where I got my lunch, consisted of two central dining rooms roughly the size of a suburban family room. There was a large stone fireplace, above which hung the Fairfield Sportsmen's Association crest—the name carved in a circle around two crossed shotguns, two crossed six-shooter pistols, and a concentric-circled target. It wasn't a particularly attractive crest, not the kind you'd expect to find in a Scottish castle. It kind of looked like it had been designed as an afterthought or as a placeholder and before they could have a new one made, a member had whittled one and someone in a leadership position decided, "Well, we've got it—might as well have it hung above the fireplace." And all around the walls hung pictures of illustrious former members—two Olympic trapshooting champions, the founders, and prestigious guests. There was a large corkboard covered in notices very much like the one that hung in the student union in college, where students offered rides or advertised for roommates. I found homemade fliers with notices of guns for sale, offerings of private concealed carry licenses (which are required in Ohio for anyone who wishes to pack heat when they go to, say, the grocery store), and a couple announcing planned hunting expeditions to Wyoming, Colorado, and New Mexico for which space was still available. Just call Steve on his cell phone and he'll give you the details.

The whole place felt less like a retreat or the kind of facilities you'd find at a country club than a clubhouse, like the one on *Little Rascals,* but housing more weapons. The furniture was worn, almost shabby, and the sodas were served in Styrofoam cups. The more time I spent lingering, the more I could see myself spending Saturday afternoons at a place like this, chewing the fat with other sportsmen over burgers and shooting a few rounds of skeet before heading home to mow the lawn or take the kids to baseball practice.

I then wandered across the large central parking lot to the pistol range. The club encompassed perhaps eighty heavily wooded acres running along the Great Miami River, and clearings were cut to facilitate different shooting sports. The shotgun ranges were the central feature, but leafing through the brochure I picked up from Clara's counter, I saw there were also facilities for pistol and bow shooting.

The pistol range was perhaps a quarter the size of the main shotgun ranges and off to one end of the property. I kept my distance as I walked up and watched as a half-dozen men, clad in blue jeans and the kind of button-down sporting shirts that feature a tab that fastened just below the shoulder to keep the cuffs out of the way when you roll up the sleeves. And straps on the shoulders. I liked those, the hunter's epaulettes. They all had holsters strapped to their legs and were taking turns moving through an obstacle course of some kind. Each would move from one wooden frame to the next, taking two shots from each and reloading at every other one.

I stopped a man as he was walking away and asked him what they were doing.

"Urban combat," he said. "That's the club pistol team."

Urban combat? In a small clearing in the midst of a dense

wood? There was nothing urban about it. Not even suburban. Not even exurban. And pardon my literal sensibilities, but wouldn't combat require some sort of returned fire? Sometimes, I guess, men never outgrow playing army like they did when they were eight.

"The targets are set up to simulate a hostage situation," he explained and as he did, he pointed out the cardboard targets. They were roughly the size and shape of a human torso and every station had two of them. One represented a terrorist, the other a hostage. The person who shot the most accurately, without hitting a civilian, in the shortest amount of time won. It was like a video game, but with real guns.

It was a contradiction, in a way, from the shotgun shooting I had just watched. On one hand, the shotgun shooting was venerable, graceful, and steeped in a rich shooting tradition. With the pistols, it was tactical, aggressive, and based on a decidedly modern premise. Both were shooting and both were games, but they seemed to be worlds apart. Aged steak versus MREs; leather and deeply stained walnut versus tactical nylon and aluminum.

I was intrigued by the pistol shooting, but I was drawn more toward the clay pigeons and wide-brimmed hats. I've never been all that good at video games, and the extent to which I exhibit aggressive behavior is pretty limited. Plus, I like the way the clay pigeons exploded when they were hit and turned into a mist of orange dust. It seemed satisfying in a way shooting a paper terrorist never could be. Call me old-fashioned, I guess.

The rest of the afternoon went much the same as the morning—one of the instructors stood at the front of the class and read, talked about, or segued from a chapter, then provided verbatim answers to the review questions in the back of each section. In total, we covered six of the nine chapters in the book that day, learning everything from the component parts of a crossbow to how to behave at game check-in centers on the off chance that a news camera happens to be present (the hunting community, apparently, is very media conscious).

Tim covered in great technical detail the proper way to load a musket—"This is on the test," he admonished, though it plainly was not—and the complicated mechanics of a compound bow and arrow. Matt was efficient with his instruction on the "attitude of safety" every hunter must adopt, and Arthur continued to frighten me. I think it had something to do with the relish with which he recounted tales of limbs lost due to improper cleaning of a gun.

I wouldn't say Arthur particularly enjoyed gore—more that the idea of putting the fear of God into us made him feel somehow important. Given that he would be the one grading our tests and signing our certificate of completion, I felt obligated to not only listen but nod along in reverence with every one of his haunting anecdotes.

The class ended just after three, and I drove the forty-five minutes back home, where I was greeted by my wife and kids. They asked how the day had gone and I told them all about Tim, Matt, and Arthur; about the exploded shotgun barrel and the training I had received on dealing with the media. I told my wife about watching the men shoot clay pigeons and paper terrorists and admitted to her that, foreign as the world of hunting and shooting had been, I was getting excited about it. I told her that I could imagine joining a club like the Fairfield Sportsmen's Association one day and prattled on a bit about my romantic visions of becoming a crack shot and respected member.

"Arthur scared me," I said, "but I really liked the people I met, and I think I'm starting to get comfortable with the idea of hunting."

"That's nice, dear," she said dismissively. "I'm glad you had fun at your class, but we need to be over at Anne and John's in twenty minutes for a cookout."

A tad deflated, I realized then that learning to hunt was my thing, not hers. She may have accepted that I was committed to seeing this thing through, but I shouldn't expect her to share my enthusiasm. Plus, she hadn't been there and, even if she had been, I don't think she would have found the concrete walls, worn furniture, and exploded clay pigeons quite as romantic as I did. In fact, I would wager that if she had been with me and seen the clubhouse, she might have been mortified and begun to clean. Hunting was my thing, but organizing? Well, that's hers.

I didn't sleep well that night. I kept imagining myself accidentally shooting off a toe, because I could not remember the proper method of installing a tree stand. Or finding myself staring down a charging grizzly and not being able to properly identify the frizzen on my muzzle-loading rifle. I was still thinking about Kosta and beating him, but the more I tried to remember every detail of what had been covered, the more I worried about just *passing* the test.

I tossed and turned in bed for a while before getting up around two and going out to the living room, retrieving my iPad and reviewing chapters one through six until I nodded off.

I woke up the next morning and discovered I had fallen asleep sitting up on the couch. The iPad was off, but still in my lap and when I turned it on, the last page of chapter six was on the screen though I had no conscious recollection of having read all the way through it.

I had a moment's pause—Was it really worth going back? Was this really me? Perhaps Rebecca's response to my dreamy excitement was a sign that I was doing something I shouldn't be. For months I had been fixated on the idea that learning to hunt would somehow make me feel like more of a man, more like my dad. But maybe I was already a man, the man she had married. Maybe this whole hunting thing was me trying force some sense of identity, to shoehorn myself into a greater sense of comfort with who I am. But was it really me?

I thought about the first day objectively. It had basically been a drawn-out and tedious retelling of course material I could have read in less than an hour. Granted, I would have missed out on all the interesting bonus material, such as the mechanical differences between military-grade triggers and those used on civilian weapons. Or how, if fallen upon at just the right angle, an arrow with a broadhead tip can bifurcate a man's torso without the slightest bit of pain.

But, after a lifetime of not hunting, of not being the sort to find himself enamored by a gun club, I wondered if I was trying too hard to change, to become something I never had been and never wanted to become. It wasn't just the pressure of the test—it was the questions about who I am and who I want to be as a man that created the doubt.

I thought long and hard in the shower and over a cup of coffee as I got dressed—this time in a pair of jeans and a nondescript polo shirt. I sat back on the couch to check my e-mail before heading out the door and noticed I had a new message on Facebook from Kosta.

It read: "98. Beat that, sucka."

That did it. Suddenly, my neurotic ennui lifted and I was once again steeled in my resolve to beat that little bastard, no matter what. The mere possibility of being able to hold that over his head—at the Thanksgiving table, say, or when he receives the Medal of Honor for heroism in the army—had me so excited I skipped my usual second cup of coffee. I kissed my wife and kids, all of whom were asleep in their beds and headed out for my second day of training and, ultimately, the final exam.

This time, I found the path to the club with ease, having re-membered the particularly grimy and dilapidated trailer home situated near the entrance, and walked into class fifteen minutes early, resuming my place at the front of room. Although I had kept largely to myself the first day, the delirious anticipation with which I awaited the test overcame my desire to not be noticed. Whenever a question was asked, I found myself in competition with the articulate kid on the other side of the room—shooting my hand into the air with the enthusiasm of a second grader in need of a bathroom break.

I was like Ken Jennings, the greatest champion *Jeopardy!* has ever known, on an amphetamine bender:

*Who can tell me the difference between a conservationist and a preservationist?*

My hand is the first one up.

"A conservationist advocates the responsible usage of natural resources and a preservationist insists they not be used at all."

*Why is it important to store ammunition of different types separately?*

Again, my hand.

"In order to avoid accidental usage of the wrong ammu-nition in the wrong gun, which could result in damage to the weapon and serious injury, perhaps even death."

Had I not been so focused on acing the test, I might have

considered my actions with a bit more remove and given myself a wet willy for being such a brownnoser. But, as it was, I didn't care. Not even in the slightest. I was in the know-it-all zone. It was freshman English all over again, only this time there was no girl to impress. I was letting my inner geek out and he was tearing up the course. I couldn't wait for the test, but unfortunately I had to. We had three chapters to cover that second morning and were told that a guest would be visiting the class. Every bit of me wanted to skip ahead, but I couldn't. I liked this newfound competitive edge and wanted to take a crack at the test before the adrenaline wore off.

The Hamilton County wildlife officer, a pleasantly officious man, showed up midmorning to give a little talk about what he does and how hunters should interact with game wardens in the field. He was dressed all in green and wore a tactical belt complete with a telescopic club, handcuffs, and a .9-millimeter semiautomatic pistol (which, incidentally, differs from a rifle only by length and, thanks to a rifled barrel, creates spin on the bullet as it leaves the muzzle—not the barrel—to ensure in-flight stability and greater accuracy).

"Don't do anything if I walk up," he said. "Most of the time I'm just there to check in with you and see how you're doing."

I can't say I was really engaged in his lecture, as I was thinking only of how this tiny little man was further delaying my taking the damned test.

I read ahead through the final chapter of the book—a real page-turner about bag limits and habitat reconstitution—and was finished with the review questions before Arthur had finished covering the review of the four tenets of hunter safety. I couldn't stop my fingers tapping as I waited impatiently for the old man to finish his duties and was crestfallen when he announced that we would take the test after lunch. It was like waking up early on Christmas morning and being told you couldn't open your presents until after Great-Aunt Sylvia put on her face.

When it finally came time to take the test, Arthur took his sweet time reading the one paragraph of instructions on the cover of the test, telling us three mildly disturbing stories about accidental dismemberment, and admonishing anyone who dared use a pen.

I was prepared. I had my number two pencils sharpened. I was locked, cocked, and ready to rock. I tore into the exam with such eagerness, I nearly grunted marking my first answer.

The test itself is composed of one hundred multiple-choice questions. Perhaps thirty-five of these questions are true or false. The rest cover everything from naming parts of particular weapons to short situational paragraphs in which a hunting tragedy has occurred and the test taker must identify the likely cause.

A passing grade is 80 percent or greater. Matt made himself available to read the questions to those who had difficulty with reading comprehension—mostly younger children, though not exclusively. The instructors also had the authority to retest those who scored between 70 and 79 on the spot, but they would only ask those questions which the people missed.

Did I mention that a significant portion of the questions were true or false? This reinforced my doubt about the rigorous standards that these tests measure. As I understood it, for anyone scoring in the "C" range, an instructor might pass a person through by asking them a question they know they got wrong the first time, but for which there were only two possible answers.

Forgive my incredulity here, but seriously? It's possible for someone to be sanctioned by the State of Ohio to carry a lethal weapon into the wilderness with the intent of taking a life, and they only need be smart enough not to get a true or false question wrong twice on the same day?

All that is neither here nor there. I was not going to need any retesting. I could feel the knowledge coursing through my veins and into my pencil as I completed the first two pages of questions—nineteen in all—in slightly under three minutes.

The next page was true or false, and I managed to get through those in about thirty seconds before coming to a series of questions related to situational awareness. There were four or five of them, and though Tim had been careful to point out every sentence of the course book that would appear on the test—from the structural difference between a flintlock and inline black powder rifle to the distinction between field dressing and dressing out an animal—he never mentioned that there would be questions requiring logic.

I had a moment of panic when reading the instructions, but by the time I was through with the first question, my mind was at ease. I can't recall the exact wording, but it went something like this:

"You are planning a day of pheasant hunting with your friends. You've prepared a hunting plan, and on the day they come to pick you up, you notice empty beer cans on the floor of the truck. When you arrive at the place where you are going to hunt, your friends each take out another beer, chug it, and stuff a few more into the pockets of their hunting vests. What do you do?"

a. Join them and suggest a quick bump of cocaine because you always shoot better when you're drunk *and* stoned.

b. Shoot them both in the face for insulting your honor, then go have your way with a nearby sheep, thus proving you are both noble and mighty.

c. Cancel the hunting trip and call another friend for a ride home.

You can see why I was not terribly worried about this small wrinkle, particularly given that this question was the most nuanced and tricky.

In total, I spent a hair over fifteen minutes completing my test and was, by a margin of more than ten minutes, the first one done in the class. This, in and of itself, was reason for concern. Had I missed something? A second booklet of questions perhaps? Had I gone too fast and skipped some?

I made a quick scan of my answer sheet and checked that all hundred blanks had been filled in, then handed my completed test to Arthur for grading and returned to my seat in nervous anticipation.

What would have taken any reasonably competent teacher fifteen seconds to grade required fifteen minutes of Arthur's careful study, and the more I sat there, the more I questioned my answers. I only had a 2 percent margin to beat my brother, so if I missed more than two questions, I would forever bear the shame of having failed at this manly undertaking. I might as well join a nunnery to escape the relentless mockery from my younger sibling.

I was on the very edge of a panic attack when I heard Arthur call a name: "Chris Hindburge?"

Given that I had been done first, I figure he was simply misreading my sometimes-sloppy handwriting. I stepped to the table and awaited the verdict.

"Chris?" asked Arthur.

"Actually, it's Craig, Craig Heimbuch."

He looked down at the registration form and exam in front of him and shook his head with an "oh, yeah, right."

"Congratulations, Kyle, you passed." He handed me my registration card.

"By how much?" I asked.

He took a moment to process this, not because he was particularly slow, but because I'm not sure a student had ever spoken directly to him before. He consulted the answer sheet and appeared to do a little math in his head before returning his gaze to me.

"One hundred," he said. "You got a hundred. Congratulations."

I shook Arthur's, Matt's, and Tim's hands furiously, thanking them all for an enlightening weekend. I was skipping out the door when Arthur called after me.

"We're having an NRA info session afterward if you want to stick around," he said.

"Not a chance," I replied. "But thanks anyway."

I ran to my car and got out my phone to call Kosta.

This just couldn't wait until Thanksgiving.

# 11

## THE INTERSTITIAL TIME

Though I was now a licensed hunter, hunting season was still months off, which left me with a good bit of time to dally and daydream, but little in terms of opportunity to put to practice my theoretical knowledge. It is hard to picture yourself on a cool fall morning dressed in warm clothes and intently following your hunting dog toward an unseen pheasant when the temperature is roughly that of the surface of the sun and the humidity is enough to turn your skin into a spigot of sweat. Summers in southwest Ohio are my least favorite time of year. It is awfully, almost unbearably hot, and the air is thick with moisture, pollution, and, to my great and constant chagrin, allergens. The summer weather in Cleveland was very similar, but there we had relief in the form of Lake Erie. One could always take a dip, provided you were willing to swim amid cast-off syringes and municipal waste. But Greater Cincinnati offers no such recreational relief. I may be brave enough and even enjoy submersion in the lake, but swimming in the Ohio River is an act of pure madness. Rebecca and the kids spent their days at the community pool or the amusement park near where we lived while I perspired my way through twice-daily commutes and long hours trying to find a cool spot in the offices where I work to take advantage of purloined moments of Internet research on the topic of hunting and sportsmanship.

In mid-July, we did something we had never done as a family, had not done, in fact, as a couple since our honeymoon. We took a vacation. No parents or siblings. Just Rebecca, the kids, and me and our closest friends, Anne, John, and their three kids. We all rented a house in coastal North Carolina and had what was for me, the trip of a lifetime. Born in northern Wisconsin and raised in northern Ohio, I was culturally trained to hate the beach. For that matter, I've never much enjoyed the sun because it seems to hate me and my pasty epidermis. But an entire week spent sipping coozie-wrapped beers and bobbing up and down in the waves with Jack and Dylan turned out to be an ideal I could never have imagined. Each night we ate as if the next day were our last and every morning began with a cocktail. We didn't drive anywhere, apart from a trip to a nearby seafood purveyor to pick up some crabs and an ill-advised trip to discover that Myrtle Beach is, in fact, the missing ring from Dante's vision of hell. We didn't have anywhere to be and, because we were in a house and not a hotel, I found myself perfectly content to do nothing more than sit on the couch or sit on the porch and sip scotch. I was amazed how quickly I fell into the habit of taking long showers in the outdoor stall before bed and how good the warm water and cool night air felt on my freshly pinked skin. I felt, well, free and, judging from the constant smiles on the faces of my children and wife, like a real man, a father, a family provider in a way I had never felt before.

Our trip was halfway over before I got a chance to sit for an extended period on the beach, beer hidden from sight and buried in the sand next to me, to read. I had made a promise to myself that I would finish the volume of Hemingway's *The Nick Adams Stories* that had sat on my bedside table for more than four years. It felt somehow appropriate and important. My parents were in the midst of buying their retirement home in northern Michigan, less than fifty miles from the place where Hemingway spent his summers and where his most famous (and some argue autobiographical) character, Nick, was born and raised.

I'll admit that I have for a long time been enamored by the Hemingway mystique. In my younger years and in college, this feeling was something I would never admit; certainly not to my friends or the liberal feminists in my English classes. Hemingway represented the stoic old misogynism, the drunken depressive chauvinist we've all worked so hard to move past. And when one of my professors or classmates would launch into an anti-Ernest tirade, I would find myself nodding and making polite sounds that indicated at least tacit agreement. But I loved Hemingway, or at least I loved the idea of him.

I first came across his work in high school. I was a junior and already a fan of Henry Miller and some of the other American expats (though I wouldn't admit that either since Miller's books were all very graphic and sexual and not something I was willing to discuss with anyone) and was assigned a project in English class to read and report on Hemingway's last and unfinished-by-him novel, *Islands in the Stream*. There had been a list of books to choose from—*The Adventures of Tom Sawyer, Canterbury Tales,* and others, the random selection of which probably says something about the quality of a public school education at the time—and the title sounded familiar. Of course, I was disappointed later when I realized the book had nothing obvious to do with the Kenny Rogers, Dolly Parton song. I procrastinated like all good high school students do, so long in fact that two nights before the paper was due I had yet to even locate a copy, let alone begin reading. I panicked. I began calling libraries in the area looking for a copy of the book and ended up driving more than forty-five minutes—halfway to Toledo—to get an audio recording of the book and drove around town for more than three hours trying to listen to it in a single sitting.

I believe I got a C- on the paper.

So my introduction to Hemingway was inauspicious at best, but it did plant a seed. In college, I picked up a used copy of his collected short stories—"Hills Like White Elephants" and "The Short Happy Life of Francis Macomber" quickly became favorites—and even skipped studying for a history exam because I made the mistake of beginning to read *The Sun Also Rises* and didn't stop until I was done. After graduation, I bought a copy of *The Old Man and the Sea* for a dollar and have read it every March since. But I had never read the Nick Adams stories, not all the way through anyway, so I sat on the beach for a couple of hours, not noticing the severe sunburn rouging my shoulders or the fact that a tiny, spiderlike crab had taken refuge in the hole left by my long-empty beer, and read.

I couldn't stop turning the pages. The writing was so dense and heavy, so serious and without a trace of whimsy, not exactly your typical beach reading, but I wasn't in the frame of mind to plow through a mindless novel. Vacation had relaxed me, but that relaxation only clarified my focus on learning to hunt. When I came to the last story in the collection, "Fathers and Sons," it was as if this long-dead and personally denied writer were speaking to me directly, laying out the ideal of a youth I had never had but was now picturing as if it were a fond memory. Nick is driving with his young son, returning to the Michigan of his youth and remembering what it was like to grow up there with his own father, a doctor and outdoorsman. It's only a few lines, but Hemingway writes about how Nick learned to hunt pheasant from his father, how to shoot and how to be a sportsman. I began to feel a pang of regret. My own dad would have loved to have taught me all those things, but I was too unwilling to learn. I began to wonder what I had missed out on, but more than that, what I had denied him by not taking any interest in what he wanted to show me. And I understood that his random gift of a gun, his encouragement when I told him about my plans to learn to hunt, all of it, was him feeling like he might get to make up for lost time and there was still a chance to have those kinds of experiences together.

I hoped there was.

Regret quickly morphed into renewed vigor, but not before I put down the book, grabbed a fresh beer from the cooler, and, after a long slug, ran into the ocean to play with my sons. What had started off as an inkling, an experiment—learning to hunt— was now a multigenerational pact and I needed to keep it.

We spent a few days in Iowa before July was over—a family reunion—and I finalized my plans with Mark and Tommy to come out at the beginning of November. We did some shooting and Mark began to pressure me to get in the game.

"How are you going to do all this and not buy a gun?" he asked.

"Well, Dad gave me one to use," I told him.

"Yeah, sure, but are you really gonna get into this using your old man's gun?"

"Um, yes?" I said.

"Well, you seemed to like that Buckmark (a semiautomatic pistol) at the NRA show."

"I did," I said, though in that moment I was having a hard time figuring out what the hell he was referring to.

"I got one I'll sell you," he said. "Why don't you come out tomorrow and we'll shoot some guns and see what you like."

I was, of course, in no way prepared to buy a gun. The thought had not really occurred to me, not since Dad gave me one of his. But, at the same time, I knew he was right. I did need to buy a gun. I needed to make that investment, but more important, that commitment if I was going to not just play at being a hunter and sportsman, but actually become one.

The next day, he, my uncle Roger, and I shot together at the range in the back end of the property, the same place where I fired my first gun and the place I have always associated with guns. I tried a couple different models and wanted so badly to be able to shoot the sleek and sophisticated semiautomatic Browning Mark had referred to the day before. But the truth is that I could not have hit the broad side of a barn with that thing if I ever found myself in a situation that required me to shoot the widest part of a storage building in order to, say, save a busload of orphans from a fire. Okay, it is admittedly hard to imagine that situation, but you take my meaning. Plus, the way I hold a pistol, the position of my arms and the angle of my elbows were not what Mark described as "a strong enough base" to facilitate the semiautomatic action. These kinds of weapons require resisting force in order to reload properly and my arms, hands, and upper body simply gave too much with every shot. I was, in other words, too much of a weakling to fire a small-caliber weapon and make it work. He recommended I try out a couple of revolvers.

"Roger and I prefer revolvers," Mark said. "We just think they're cool."

"Yup," acknowledged the seemingly always quiet Roger. "We're old school."

I felt like an old-time Chicago cop stepping up to the line with the nine-shot Taurus .22-caliber revolver, like I should have an Irish accent and be on the lookout for whiskey runners. Sort of ridiculous actually. But I cocked the hammer and pulled the trigger and it felt good. I emptied all the chambers and walked down to the paper target to discover I had shot a nice grouping. It was love at first shot. I couldn't buy the gun at that moment, but I made a weak promise to Mark that I would buy it someday.

Getting back to Cincinnati, we quickly fell back into real life after our vacations and more than three thousand miles driven. Rebecca and the kids made the most of the last days of summer and I settled back in at work, a little tanner and a whole lot less stressed. I continued to look for opportunities to improve my essential hunting skills, and though they were few and far between, I managed to find some.

One night, Rebecca was tired and didn't feel like cooking or ordering a pizza, so she called me on my way home and asked me to stop at the grocery store to pick something up.

"What do you want?" I asked.

"Oh, whatever, just bring it home quick. We're starving."

I was walking through aisles of frozen food and couldn't help but think of what I had learned about the McRib, which made every single scrap of it repelling to the point of revulsion. I didn't feel like grilling since the idea of standing over flames on the hottest day of the year was as appealing as a tax audit during a community theater performance of *The Lord of the Dance,* and I was just about to give up and order Chinese when a smell came to me like a smoke signal from God. I followed my nose and soon found myself in front of a warmer oven chock-full of rotisserie chickens. And they looked as good as they smelled, all wrapped up in cellophane and paper bags, dripping with their own juices and glistening under the heat bulbs. I quickly grabbed one and the makings for a salad and went home to surprise the family.

The directions on the package said to remove the bird from the bag and place it breast up in a pan, heating it for twenty minutes or so. And as I was situating the carcass in the foil-lined pan, I realized something—this looked familiar. Very familiar. I had seen this before and not just under these circumstances. I wiped chicken grease off my fingers and went to the bookshelf in the living room to retrieve my copy of *Field Dressing and Butchering Upland Birds, Waterfowl, and Wild Turkeys* by the exquisitely named Monte Burch. I flipped to a dog-eared page that contained step-by-step line drawings demonstrating how to remove meat from bone on a pheasant. It looked about the same as the chicken, so when the timer went off and the pan came out of the oven, I held the book open with a salt cellar and a bottle of gin and followed the directions. I felt so smart, so innovative, so much like a surgeon practicing on a cadaver.

"What are you doing?" Rebecca asked me as I slowly slid my knife between the breast meat and wishbone. "Hurry up, we're starving."

I tried to hurry, but I wanted to make sure I got it right. I felt like I had an opportunity and didn't want to waste it. It took me nearly as long to carve the bird as it did to cook, but when I was done I admired my serving dish of moist, succulent chunks of chicken and my trash bag full of neatly and near-completely cleaned bones.

Take that, hunting season. Who's the man now?

There was something else I wanted to do before the summer was over, another source I wanted to turn to. I've mentioned my childhood obsession with the L.L.Bean catalog. What if, I thought, I called up L.L.Bean and asked if they would teach me how to hunt?

I knew I wouldn't know everything by the time I went to Iowa. There is, after all, only so much you can learn from reading books and dissecting rotisserie chickens. But I wanted to be more prepared than someone who had never done this kind of thing before. I wanted to close the gap between the twelve-year-old me who didn't know anything and the thirty-three-year-old me who should know something by now, and I had a hunch that L.L.Bean could help me.

To my pleasure and everlasting gratitude, I was right.

I sent an e-mail to the general inquiry inbox listed on their website explaining that I am an author and the editor of an online magazine, outlining my goals and asking whether they could point me in the right direction to get some advice, either over the phone or through content—books, videos, websites— that Bean may have prepared. Less than two hours later, I had an e-mail in my inbox from a man named Mac McKeever. He was a hunting and fishing public relations specialist for Bean and he asked if I would call him to discuss how he could help. I was stunned to say the least. I hadn't expected a response, let alone a personal one and so quickly. I wrote the number down on my hand and stepped out of the office and into the enormous parking lot to make my call. I work in a creative environment full of young hipsters and didn't want to be discussing my desire to learn how to hunt in front of them for fear of recoil or, worse, attention.

"This is Mac," he said.

"Hi, Mac, this is Craig Heimbuch. I just got your e-mail about . . ."

"You're the guy who wants to learn how to hunt," he said. "Was it pheasant in Nebraska?"

"Iowa, actually," I said, impressed that he had actually paid attention.

"Iowa pheasant, that's legendary," he said. "How can we help?"

"Well," I said and tried to fight my voice from sounding too much like a groupie, "I've never done it before. I've shot guns, but not a ton and I've always loved Bean and I thought maybe you had a guide or somebody I could talk to for some advice."

"I'll do you one better," said Mac, and he told me about the company's Outdoor Discovery Schools program, which is basically a series of workshops in Maine teaching skills from kayaking to dogsled racing. "You've got to take one of our Wingshooting classes. I'll comp you the admission. I just think it would be perfect for what you're trying to do."

I thanked him aggressively and hung up. Had I just been invited to Maine by L.L.Bean so they could help me learn how to hunt in order to impress my Iowa relatives and feel like a man? I believe they just had. We set a date over e-mail for early October, and I went back upstairs to begin looking for flights.

Look out, Maine, here I come.

# 12

## INSTRUCTION

It had been a rough week. Late on a late September Monday night, a severe rainstorm weaved its way through a gap in the bushing around a vent on the roof and opened up a backwater creek down the plaster of our vaulted (and mercifully sloped) living room ceiling. This prompted a call to the landlord, who we'd been trying to get to come out for weeks to take a look at the cracking linoleum floor in the kitchen and a strange gap in the padding beneath the carpet. Or, more accurately, it prompted several calls. Rebecca would call me, I would step out of a meeting or interrupt my writing to call the landlord who would not answer. I would then call Rebecca to tell her that no one had answered and she would call me back twenty minutes later to see if anyone had called back and ask me if I thought it was strange that no one would return our calls. I would tell her that, yes, I thought it was strange and the whole process would repeat again, seemingly ad infinitum.

I finally got a call from the maintenance guy who said he would come Wednesday or Thursday, though what a three-day wait for service did for a leaky roof, I could not be sure. I told him I needed to confer with my wife on the schedule and call him back. I called Rebecca and we agreed that Wednesday would work just fine. She had some things to do with the kids, but I had a relatively meeting-free morning and could stay home for a couple of hours. I called him back and left a message saying as much, satisfied with my manly handling of this precarious situation.

That Monday at work had been a blur. Meetings forgotten, deadlines missed, and the constant interaction with my phone. It seemed I could do no right. Tuesday wasn't much better. There were too many places to be, too many commitments with the kids. I found myself alone on the high school track just before midnight, huffing and puffing my way through a three-mile run listening to a podcast about the various techniques of fitting a gun to a larger-framed man without hearing a word. I had hoped the run, the fresh air, the podcast would help me relax, help me sleep, help me let go of the stress at home and the stress at work.

It did not.

The next day was Dylan's birthday and I barely got to see him. I put Jack on the school bus and walked back to the condo to wait for the maintenance man. Rebecca had made plans to take Dylan and Molly to meet some friends at one of those indoor inflatable gyms, the kind with air-filled slides and bounce houses that serve the dual purpose of entertaining children and serving as host to dozens of flesh-eating communicable diseases.

When I had spoken to Joel, the Kentucky-mumbling oddly dusty maintenance man, on Monday, he had told me he would be out between 9:30 and 11. So having the rare opportunity to be home alone on a weekday morning, I did what any self-respecting husband and father would do, namely drank coffee and watched *SportsCenter* in my underwear, waiting until 9:29 to pull on a pair of jeans and a sweater. One must always be presentable for guests after all. By ten, I'm getting restless, so I do the breakfast dishes, vacuum the carpets, and fold some laundry. At eleven, having cleaned the bathrooms, checked my e-mail, made all the beds, and refolded all the T-shirts in my middle dresser drawer, I call Joel and get his voice mail. I call Rebecca and get hers. I have a meeting at noon, one I assumed I would be able to make given the times Joel had laid out. I'm beginning to dread what was to happen next—namely, Rebecca getting mad at me for somehow failing to make this all come to fruition—when just before 11:30, Joel calls.

"Yeah, it's Joel," he said. "You called me?"

"Yeah, Joel, hi," I said. I've never been the kind of person to seek confrontation. I've never sent back the wrong order. I've never asked to speak to a manager—except under the direst of circumstances and only then over the phone with a customer service representative whom I assumed was based somewhere closer to Kuala Lumpur than Cleveland, and only then if something was actually on fire. I've always subscribed to the distinctly Lutheran precept that you get more friends with tuna hot dish than you do by shooting their dogs. (Okay, maybe it loses something in translation, but if you say it with an Upper Wisconsin accent it sounds much less menacing.) So I go the nice route. "Joel, it's Craig, the guy with the leaky roof? Just wondering how long you were going to be?"

"Huh?" he says, and I could hear his confused mouth-breathing through the phone.

"We had an appointment," I demurred. "You said you could come out between 9:30 and 11 and I took the morning off work. You remember?"

"I never did got no call back from you," he said.

"I called back within five minutes of hanging up," I entreated. "I left you a voice mail."

"No, you didn't," he said.

"I'm pretty sure I did," I said.

"No, you didn't."

I don't know if it's because I generally have a guilty conscience or if it's because my first instinct in almost any situation is to apologize, but I've always been amazed by some people's knack for delusional deniability. Had I been on the other end of this call, my first instinct would probably have been to apologize profusely then begin immediately trying to make amends. But not Joel. No sir. It had to be my fault. No way had he not missed a phone call. No way was it his fault. I could feel my blood pressure rising like the thermometer in one of those old Saturday-morning cartoons when an ill-meaning and inept cat is goaded into eating a hot pepper by his intended prey—a small, sarcastic bird with a superiority complex and questionable sexual predilections. It was genuine anger, true, but also a sense of dread, a feeling that I had actually somehow screwed up. I wanted to reach through the phone and grab Joel's tongue and say something to the effect of:

"Listen you cousin-loving bastard of an excuse for adulthood, I absolutely did call you and you damn well know that you got the message. And if you don't get your drop-out ass up here in the next five minutes to fix my ceiling and floors, my wife is going to have hell to pay for me which can only mean that I will be well within my rights to come to your single-wide, tear up your collection of White Snake and Lynard Skynard commemorative beer coozies and use your syphilitic three-legged dog as target practice before setting the whole thing up in flames in a vengeful conflagration against you and all the other dim-witted self-absorbed jackasses who have ever screwed me over. Believe me you, buster."

Of course I actually said none of that. What I said was something much more benign and in keeping with my long history of timidity in time of conflict. Something like, "Gosh, this is a real pickle. Any chance we can schedule something when it's convenient for you?"

"Let me check my messages to see if you called and I'll call you back," he said.

"Okey-dokey."

Had I thought about it, I might have realized the evidence of Joel's lying that he had just presented. He was going to check and be sure that I had called on Monday? Hadn't he just returned my message from earlier that morning? He called back moments later.

"Well, I still didn't get no message, but I suppose I can squeeze you in tomorrow," he said in that way that the self-satisfied have, as if he were doing me a favor at great personal expense and expenditure of effort. I could not believe he was acting like he was doing me a favor. This was not our first issue with Joel, who had done a subpar job recaulking our bathtub once and had sent my wife off into a near-apoplectic rage. She yelled at me to yell at him. Clearly she is more comfortable with confrontation, but when it comes to dealing with Joel and our landlords, she prefers confrontation by proxy. I did my best to get answers from Joel, but all I managed was a weak-tea apology and the implication that my time would be better spent by engaging in a vigorous—if not physically challenging—sexual act elsewhere. I ended up recaulking the tub myself and while I wouldn't say I did a better job, it was certainly no worse.

All this—the caulking memory, the tongue lashing, and Joel's behavior—was in the back of my head when I accepted his offer to come out the next day, then took off for work in such a frenzy and with such rapidity it was almost therapeutic.

That night, traffic on my evening commute was worse than normal. The twenty-seven-mile drive usually takes just over an hour in the evening, but took nearly twice that because of a couple of accidents. I was late getting to Dylan's birthday dinner, which earned me a doleful look from my loving wife, who took me aside to complain—not at me but to me—about the situation with Joel. It was her position that I needed to be stronger with him and if I really cared about my family and the condition of the home they are living in, I would have no problem finding that strength. I kissed her head and hugged Dylan, sang Happy Birthday, then grabbed Jack, went home and changed, and took him to a Cub Scout meeting.

I share the den leader responsibilities with another dad in the group, which meant that after the meeting I took Jack home and made sure everyone was in bed before heading out to meet with the other leader to plan out our meeting schedule. I had quickly earned the ire of the type-A suburban moms in our den by not having a full and comprehensive schedule prepared by our first meeting. How could they manage the next nine to eleven months of their sons' lives properly with such an imbecile at the switch? I had sensed an impending mutiny—after just a single meeting—and my wife said an e-mail campaign had been launched demanding greater accountability. She recommended that I plan through May, just to get the ladies off my back.

I couldn't sleep that night. I kept having these terrifying visions of being late for work, hearing a clap of thunder and looking up to see the ceiling collapse and hundreds of blond crows in Dolce & Gabanna sunglasses flying through the hole to peck away at my flesh, with my wife standing by telling me that if I had just cared more, none of this would have happened. I went out onto the couch and flipped through the nine-hundred-odd channels of our cable service, finding nothing but infomercials and reruns of bad shows from the 1990s—and just who exactly wants to watch old episodes of *Blossom* at two in the morning? I turned off the TV and sat quietly in the dark for ten minutes before I saw a flash out the window and heard the patter of rain on the roof, at which point I fell right to sleep.

Thursday came early, with Dylan tugging on my shoulder a half hour before dawn. The hole in the ceiling had gotten worse overnight. I got out of bed, put some coffee on, and situated our biggest sauce pans under the ceiling so they would catch a majority of the still-dripping water. I made breakfast, got everyone ready and out the door, and even dropped Dylan off at school. Joel and the woman from our landlord's office showed up within fifteen minutes of on-time and Rebecca stayed in the bathroom while they scanned the floor and ceiling, the screen door we had told them needed to be fixed four years earlier, and pretty much everything else we have ever complained about in roughly the time it took me to have a sip of coffee. They then spoke in hushed tones as if I weren't standing right in front of them and were gone before I knew what happened.

"What did they say?" asked Rebecca, toweling off her shower wet hair.

"Not much," I said. "Joel said he'd call later."

He did, later that day, and told me that they were going to replace carpet padding but not the carpet itself, put a veneer over the cracked kitchen floor and talk to the condo association about fixing the source of the leaky roof. Not exactly the cure-all we had in mind, but it was a start. I moved all the furniture out of the dining and living rooms, then went to work, promising myself that I was going to do whatever was necessary to get us out of renter's hell and soon.

As you can probably imagine, the repairs were hasty and the process a clusterfuck of incompetence and disappointment. (I'll note here that more than four months later, the hole in the ceiling has not been patched, though the leak did mysteriously stop.)

I needed to leave. I needed some distance. I'd been carrying a lot of extra water at work, taking on side jobs to help make ends meet, and with everything going on with our stupid ceiling, it was just time for me to go. Lucky for me, I was leaving the next day.

The night before I left, I didn't sleep a wink. Too much pressure. Too many frayed nerves.

"What are you doing?" Rebecca has a way of snapping at me when I wake her up late at night.

"I can't sleep," I whispered. "I'm going out on the couch. Just go to sleep."

I don't generally like being awake at four in the morning. My dad does it every day. So does my friend John. Both engineers, both grew up in the rural Midwest. Must be something in all that rusty water that makes them believe this is an appropriate time for a human being to be awake. It patently is not. I flipped on the television in our dark living room and for a moment the light burned my eyes. There is something absurd about television at this time of night. With a thousand channels constantly angling for the most engaging prime-time programming, I wonder why they never consider the early riser or late-night watcher when they force-feed infomercials for the next miracle abdominal exercise machine and the get-rich-quick real estate moguls hawking their wares. I have a hard time imagining my midsection will end up trim if only I make three easy installments of $39.99 and am willing to attach a car battery to my navel. I also have a hard time believing that a man making $25,000 a year was able to pay off his thirty-year mortgage in nine months without robbing a bank.

Had it not been such a bad week, I might have been giddy with anticipation when my plane landed in Portland, Maine, as I arrived for my L.L.Bean workshop. But, as it was, my nerves were fried. I was tired of the stress at home, tired of the hassle of traveling—who wouldn't be with a two-hour layover in Baltimore?—and I found myself getting short with my wife on the phone while I was waiting for my bag to come out of the carousel. It was almost midnight. No sleep. I just wanted to get to my room and go to sleep.

I never sleep all that well on the road. Uncomfortable beds, strange sounds. I was in Freeport, Maine, the place where I proposed to my wife, the place I held up so highly in countless memories from childhood and college road trips. And yet, I woke up to a drizzling sky and a knot in my neck. I worried that my class was going to be canceled, so I grabbed some coffee and headed over to the home of the L.L.Bean Outdoor Discovery Schools, a small farmhouse set on the other side of I-295 called the Fogg House.

I arrived a half hour early and was met by one of my instructors, Amy. She was a ponytailed blonde in a khaki-colored hat, shooting shirt, field khakis, and thick hiking boots. She was younger than I would have assumed—I'd place her in her mid to late twenties—and a third-grade teacher. She also happened to be the Maine state sporting clays champion. Friendly and broad-smiled, she was the very picture of the L.L.Bean woman—happy, outdoorsy, free of makeup and pretense. We made small talk in the front room of the old farmhouse, and she greeted the nine other students in the class as they rolled in and we busied ourselves sipping supplied coffee, signing release forms, and ordering sandwiches for lunch to be delivered to the shooting range later in the day.

We were introduced to the other two instructors. Bernie was a retired field scientist from New Hampshire and a passionate hunter. He spoke with professorial confidence and ease and, with his cargo pants, shooting shirt, Bean boots and jacket, and khaki hat, he looked every bit the wise woodsman. John was tall and oddly symmetrical. Standing around six foot four in the same outfit as Bernie, he was a skyscraper of a man. Salt-and-pepper hair, a Down East accent, and a broad smile. He's a math teacher. Was Amy's math teacher in fact. And between the three of them, they have twelve years' experience teaching this course.

After an introductory safety meeting, we all pile into our cars and drive to the back of the property where, set in a clearing surrounded by thick stands of pine and balsam, is the shooting range. Five small covered stands in a row looking out onto a mud and grass field a hundred yards deep and speckled with blaze-orange specks of broken clay pigeons. The sky is low. Wispy strands of clouds like an artificial ceiling that seems almost close enough to touch. We meet under a tent on picnic tables, where Amy gives us more safety instructions and admonishes us to never, under any circumstances, shoot at an animal that may wander onto the range. Groundhogs, deer, moose, maybe even a bear. They've all found their way onto the live range at one point or another, and L.L.Bean takes its responsibility to conservation very seriously. We get more instruction from Bernie about the proper operation of the school-supplied shotguns and are quickly broken up into two groups of five. My group—composed of myself, a fellow Ohioan named Mike, a recently civilianized navy pilot named Matt, a fourteen-year-old Boy Scout named Ed, and Ed's dad, Tom—heads to the stand on the far right with John. The rest go to the far left with Amy. Bernie, the senior instructor, is going to roam in between, acting like an art teacher who watches his students mold pots, interrupting only to offer experienced advice.

At first, I'm tense. I've never shot in front of people other than my relatives. I'm also still tired and feeling the effects of the previous week. We start with some easy comers—targets launched from the other side of the field at an upward angle. The clay pigeon comes toward you, reaches an apex, and pauses for a moment before falling more or less straight to the ground. I've shot enough that this should be easy. With shotguns, we're told, it's all about the mount. Once you have the gun tucked into the pocket of your shoulder and your cheek is firmly on the comb of the stock, you don't need to aim. Just focus on the target and track its movement with your front arm. Don't look at the end of the gun, just the target. Focus on the target and your body will move in one smooth motion. You pull the trigger when you see the target the best. That moment is the apex, when the clay disc pauses before succumbing to gravity and falls to the ground.

I'm second in line. Matt, the pilot, goes first. He's just been told that he's left-eye dominant. A lifetime as a righty and now the instructors want him to shoot from the left shoulder. He does what they say and misses the first couple of targets before getting the hang of it and breaking two out of the last three. I step up into the stand, and John covers the things Bernie told us about safety and pointing (not aiming) a shotgun. He loads a shell into the bottom barrel of the twelve-gauge over-under I've been assigned (the only one big enough for my outsized frame) and tells me to call the "pull." I call it and am trying to remember everything I've been told all at once. My focus is back and forth. Front of the gun, edge of the target. I'm trying to remember to be smooth, and it only makes me jerky. My left eye blinks uncontrollably as I pull the trigger and I miss. Then I miss again. Then I miss again. And again, and again. All the hours in Grandma's back acres in Iowa amount to nothing. I feel incapable of hitting a clay pigeon and am suddenly struck that it is going to be a very long day.

We try a few different targets as the morning goes on. One that launches from behind us, some that come in from the side, even one shot across the ground that they call a rabbit. I am consistently inconsistent and have hit perhaps 15 percent of those clay pigeons I have called for before lunch. The ones that I did hit were usually the second target of a double—when two pigeons are launched simultaneously. You have time to find the first one and track it, but the second one is already midflight by the time you turn to shoot. The second shot is instinctive. You don't have time to do much thinking or preparing. It's turn your head and shoot. Bernie tells me that most times the second shot of a double is better than the first because you don't get to think. Shotgun shooting is about instinct and trust. It's about blocking out all your thoughts and emotions and concentrating on nothing but the edges of that target.

I am thinking too much. I am too worried I will do something wrong, trying too hard to do it perfectly. And that's why

I'm missing. It is the story of my life. I worry about things I don't need to, analyze things better left unanalyzed, think when I should act.

After lunch, I try to convince myself not to think, which only makes me think harder. As all the other students in my class are demonstrating marked improvement, hitting more targets, I am stalled. I stumble my way through crossing shots and more doubles. I feel comfortable and yet uneasy. Mac had promised me this was fun, but for some reason, I am not having much. It's no fault of the instructors. They are doing a fantastic job, but with every missed target, with every jerky motion or switched focus, I feel an opportunity missed. I feel myself thinking about being away and feeling guilty. I feel the pressure of providing for a family and the need to fix any problems that might be waiting for me at home. And the more I think about this stuff, the more I try to write that narrative in my head, the less clear it becomes.

Finally, we reach the last hour of the class. As a whole, we've done well. I've gotten a little better, but many of my classmates are ten times the shooters than they were at the beginning of the day. As a reward, Bernie offers us a game of five stand.

Now, assuming you have no idea what five stand is—as I did not—here's a primer. Each shooter takes a position at a stand. They are numbered one through five. Hanging to the right of the stand is a metal sign with three lines on it marked "Single," "Report," and "Simo." Each of these lines has one or two numbers next to it corresponding to the number of the launchers that will be used during that particular round. The launchers are spread around the range, each offering a different kind of shot—comers, goers, crossing left-to-right, crossing right-to-left, and a rabbit. There are three rounds at each stand—the aforementioned "single," which is the first round and consists of a single target being launched from the specified launcher; "report," which launches the first target on the shooter's call and the second on the sound of the first shot; and "simo," which launches two targets from two launchers simultaneously. Each stand has a different combination of launchers for every round. When all the shooters have shot from their first stand, they rotate to the right. The one on the far right rotates to the one on the far left. But in every round, the person who started on the far left is the first shooter, regardless of position. So with five targets at each of the five stands, a full game is completed when every shooter has shot at twenty-five targets.

Believe me, it seemed a lot more complicated at the time. Because there were ten people in the class and only five people could participate in the game—one shooter for each of the five stands—we were broken into two groups. I was in the second, which meant I got to sit in the drizzle for a half hour while the first group played the game. I watched as the first shooter called nervously for the first target and joined the cheering as shooters eventually settled into a groove. Tom, the Boy Scout's father, was the first to hit a target and the first to break both clays of a double. The women in the class shot really well, and all earned a hearty whoop from Amy when they broke clay. Watching them, all the people of the first group, I felt a little weight lift from my shoulders. When they hit something, they smiled. When they didn't, a look of determination came over their faces. I found myself smiling for them, becoming determined on their behalf.

Bernie stood behind me when it was my turn to step into the stand. I was second in line, and my first single was a crossing shot from left-to-right. I got myself comfortable on the gun and just before I called for the target, I tried to remember to relax and not think. When I yelled "pull," that clarity went right out the window, and I was back to the nanosecond second-guessing, the shifting of focus back and forth, listening to my own thoughts. Bernie yelled from behind me after I missed. "Stop thinking and shoot!," he said, like a high school wrestling coach. The message was clear: get out of my head and get out of my own way. I took two deep breaths as the shots went down the line, muttered "just focus on the target," and made a conscious effort to do nothing consciously. I hit my first double of the day and the whole world changed. I stopped trying to manage the shooting. I stopped thinking about the carpet and ceiling. I stopped worrying about taking notes in my head and focused on nothing more than the edge of the target. The gun, which had been heavy and unwieldy all day, became an invisible extension of my body, weightless.

I didn't hit all the rest of the twenty-two targets that made up my round of five stand, but I hit enough to more than triple my morning percentage. The ones I hit felt as natural as a flinch, instinct. The ones I missed I forgot about instantly. No berating. No second-guessing. I missed one—whatever. I'll get the next one, and half the time I did. By the time the game ended, I wanted more. I wanted to keep shooting. I felt like a different person—confident, awake, unfazed for the first time in a long time.

John put his hand on my shoulder as I was walking away from the stands and back toward the tent. "Great shooting today," he said. He was right. I may not have hit very many targets, but the shooting was fantastic. I asked an older student to take a picture of me with the instructors, and in it I'm smiling in a way I haven't for a long time. For all the guilt or anxiety I feel about fixing things, about being away, about work, I realized right then how important it is to have an escape, to have something to change your focus. It's pretty easy to get wrapped up in the everyday. A guy like me (and so many others I know) has to go in a lot of different directions, to keep a lot of balls in the air. The constant demand for multilensed focus, the strident pressure to handle so many things—it can break you down, make you lose sleep and a piece of yourself. Sometimes you just need to forget about all those things. To focus on something new— to see the edges of the target and concentrate on nothing else. You need to let your body move without thought, to allow your instincts to take over.

Sometimes you need to stop thinking and just shoot.

I was on a high of sorts as I snapped a few photos on my phone and climbed back into my rental car, having no idea what I was going to do. I had been in Freeport for eighteen hours, the longest I had ever been in that perfect little town without visiting Bean's flagship store, and I was tempted to head straight there. But I was also wet from the persistent drizzle, my feet hurt, and I needed a shower, so I headed back over to my hotel for a fresh set of clothes, a steaming hot rinse, and some Advil for my aching joints. I remembered reading about these classes in the catalogs of my youth and having just completed one, it felt like a circle coming to a close.

The sun was already almost down in the gray New England sky by the time I got back out to my rental car. I always forget how much earlier it gets dark when you're that far east, and the rain had returned, this time in full, big drops that *thwat*ted on my coat as I sprinted across the parking lot. I followed the main road into town and found it awash in the soft glow of store windows. From the outside, Bean seemed to glow like a warm fire and I had a feeling like nostalgia. The last time I had pulled into the parking lot, I was in a spat with the woman who was about to become my fiancée. It had been ten years and four days earlier and a lot had changed. Bean had gone from a single rambling store to a campus of buildings housing individual departments. The town, which had been small and felt like a Main Street, had grown tremendously, if not in size, then in commercial prestige. The old schoolhouse was now an Abercrombie & Fitch. The little shops along the main thoroughfare now bore the emblems of Gucci and Patagonia. It amazed me to think that a hundred years before, the real Leon Leonwood Bean had just wanted to make a better hunting boot and he had spawned a retail destination.

I parked and ran into the closest door I could find, the one leading to the brand-new Hunting and Fishing wing of the old flagship building. I had forgotten that there are no locks on the doors at Bean. The store is open 24/7/365, so there is no need. I don't want to get weepy or overly sentimental, but it felt oddly like a homecoming to return to this place. The last time I had been there, I proposed to my wife. Our life had not even begun yet. There was no Jack, no Dylan, no Molly. There was no credit card and college debt, no years of struggling just to get by and wondering if I would have enough money for gas or if I would have to call in poor to work. I had not yet left Virginia and we had not even considered a move to Cincinnati. So much had changed. So much had gone right and so much had gone wrong. So much had simply gone. It's funny that a store can generate such a feeling of milestone, such a sense of accomplishment and regret, pride and embarrassment. Of course it had nothing to do with the store itself. That was just a building. A rapidly expanding building. But that particular store had represented the dreams I had in my youth, the ideas I had had for my future, visions that did not, could not, and would not come to fruition.

I wandered aimlessly for nearly two hours before I realized I was hungry. Since I had left Cincinnati the previous afternoon, I had only had a few bites of bad airport Chinese food, a few cups of coffee, and the sandwich provided by the class. I wanted something good. I wanted lobster and found it a block away at a place that from the outside looked promising, but inside felt like an old Kentucky Fried Chicken. But they served fresh Maine lobster, local beer, and a chowder that had won a regional competition that very afternoon.

Tucking into my meal, which was brought to my table on a cheap plastic tray and in paper-lined baskets, I fell into listening in on the conversations taking place around me. There was a family I had seen earlier in the boot section. Mom, Dad, and three teenaged kids. It sounded like they were from Boston and were up doing some shopping for clothes. The entire booth next to them was filled with familiar brown Bean bags and the kids were talking about Adderall use among the members of the lacrosse team.

"I don't get what the big deal is," said one of the boys.

"The big deal is that they are prescription drugs and should not be taken without a prescription," said mom.

"I only do it when I have to study," the boy said.

"Or when you want to party," said the girl, who was probably the middle child.

"No," he said.

"Honey?" said the mom. "Are you gonna chime in here?"

"Don't take drugs," said the dad, who seemed much more interested and concerned with the last claw of his twin lobsters than his child's dalliances with prescription drugs. The whole conversation had been so casual, it terrified me. I remember not feeling that comfortable admitting to my parents that I was signing up for marching band, let alone telling them that I had scored some absconded drugs and was taking them to help me study. I had a terrified vision of my future. Would this be our family someday?

I shook my head and turned my attention to a couple from Ohio sitting at the table on the other side of me. They were young, perhaps in their midtwenties, and had gotten married the day before. They were spending their honeymoon in Maine, a place she had never been and he had always loved. They had that dewy gleam of potential about them, and that too felt familiar. I felt like I was having a Scrooge moment, as if I had just been visited by the ghosts of family future and past. For so long, I had assumed my love for Maine and Bean were unique. I had assumed our story of getting engaged there was special. But it could not be. The company would have folded long ago if it had been relying on my sales. I took a certain comfort in the realization though and sort of enjoyed the moment of "Craig Heimbuch, this is your life."

So much to ruminate upon, so much fodder for cogitation, I drank two beers, finished my lobster, and stopped just short of licking the Styrofoam bowl my chowder had been delivered in. It was getting late, around ten, but I wasn't ready to go back to my cheap hotel room and watch *CSI* reruns, so I went back to the store and wandered around, picking up and putting down a million things I wanted to buy. I called Rebecca and over the phone we picked out a fleece jacket for her to replace the one I had bought the night we got engaged. I paid for it and walked around the store until my feet were tired, until after one in the morning, when I finally gave up and went back to my hotel to fall perfectly, comfortably to sleep.

*  *  *

The next morning, I had naively hoped to go for a long hike. Just before leaving the store, I had bought a guide book, a flashlight, a new pair of socks, and a couple of Power Bars. I woke and picked a couple of parks up the coast to check out, but when I went outside, the rain was heavier than it had been the previous day. Thick, deep, soaking rain, and the sky hung low, mingling with the tops of the everywhere pine trees. It was a Sunday and I had nothing to do. I wasn't flying out until Monday evening and I weighed my options. I thought about driving four hours up the coast to Bar Harbor and Acadia National Park and considered the idea of doing nothing but walking around the store again. It was early. I was up and showered, dressed, and in the car by seven, which gave me an entire day of possibility. I stopped for a breakfast sandwich at a little bistro across the street from Bean and decided that even though the weather was cold and wet, I didn't want to be inside. I wanted to drive, just drive, and that's what I did.

I had been dreaming for ten years about having a day with nothing to do in Maine. Down East, on the coast. No schedule, no expectations. All alone with a rental car, limited only by my own willingness.

I drove for an hour and a half before a detour gave me pause to stop. I had driven through Rockland before. A decade ago. Five years before that too. But I can't remember ever having stopped. Hunger, boredom, a general need to get out and move around must have come over me, and I decided to stop and wander the rain-drenched streets of Rockland, Maine.

I looked at the menus hanging in the windows of all the little mom-and-pop shops, the sandwich joints, the corner bars that interrupt the street-side flow of art galleries and curio shops.

Rockland is for the tourists, sure. It's right on US 1 between Portland, where people fly into or where the train from Boston arrives, and Acadia National Park—one of the busiest and most-visited in the country. During the summer, this stretch of road is one long tangled mass of cars with out-of-state plates. Same thing later in the fall when the leaves turn and the "peepers" come out like cockroaches to take pictures, buy maple syrup, and wear their new wool sweaters. But on this rainy day in early October, the leaves are still mostly green and the summer crowds have all but disappeared. So Rockland may be built to accommodate tourists, but the shops, the galleries, and the little restaurants are all still open. They are all still there. A local economy built on people from other places that has retained a semblance of soul, community.

I'm not normally one to scrutinize menus for very long. I'm not all that particular, to be honest. But I looked because I wanted something a little different at a place that accepted American Express. I was nearing the end of the central down-town block when I caught a sign out of the corner of my eye. A small, cottagelike building had a giant wraparound sign that read something like TRY THE CLUB SANDWICH THAT BEAT BOBBY FLAY.

The owners of The Brass Compass Cafe are obviously very proud of the fact that the celebrity chef and host of, among other shows, *Throwdown* came to town one unsuspecting summer day to challenge them to a lobster club sandwich challenge. Even more proud that they won. So proud that the story of the affair is printed in bold type on the cover of their menu. Ordinarily this sort of opportunity to dine two steps from fame wouldn't mean much to me, but there was something about this place that drew me in. Plus, the menu posted on the window had the

AmEx blue shield on the bottom. And the idea of eating a club sandwich piled high with Maine lobster meat while meandering up the coast of that state? Forget about it. I had to try it.

I ordered coffee to warm my chattering bones and told the server I'd have the special—the lobster club and fries. The place was small and cozy with a kitchen that opened into the dining room. It was still Sunday morning, so there were some leftover postchurch diners about and more than a couple of tables filled with the burly, thick-fingered kind of guys who looked like they made their living in the harbor, about two hundred yards to my rear as I sat with my back to the window, eagerly anticipating what was sure to be a unique dining experience.

I watched the cook—*chef* isn't the right word for a guy wearing a T-shirt that read something like IT'S NOT THAT YOU'RE BORING, IT'S JUST THAT I'M AWESOME—grab whole handfuls of precooked bacon and pile them on the homemade wheat bread that was still warm from the oven. A woman used what looked like a soup ladle to pile thick chunks of mayo-drenched lobster on top of that. When the server brought my plate out and set it down on the worn wood table, it made the kind of thump you'd expect to hear as a peg-legged sea captain paces the deck of a ship. It wasn't just that the plate was heavy, but the food—oh God, the food—was rich and thick and filling.

I half considered splitting the sandwich—taking the lobster and bread layer off the bottom bacon, tomato, and lettuce layer—but I decided I must soldier on to gain full appreciation of the pseudofamous sandwich. One messy, ill-executed bite—who hasn't dreamed of lobster raining down onto their plate like delicious manna?—and I understood immediately why this sandwich beat down Bobby Flay. In the story printed on the menu, Flay's recipe is described with derision as having included "exotic spices like cumin" in order to add a flavorful bump. And I thought, why? Why ruin such a perfect thing? The sweet, creamy lobster, the smoky and salty bacon, the savory burst of tomatoes impossibly fresh for the time of year. It was better than almost anything I had ever eaten. That the bread was homemade and delicious, that the portion was beanstalk giant, that the fries were fresh cut and steaming hot—bonuses all. This sandwich could have been served on a month-old hot dog bun with some freezer-burned Ore-Idas and still be wet-dream-inducing good.

After I was finished, I stared for a bit, absorbing the warmth of the small café, the rain clacking on the window behind me, appreciating the moment. I don't get away all that often. Not like this. I travel for work. I travel with my family. But rarely do I fully immerse myself in a sense of escape. I'm usually too hardwired for productivity, too worried about what needs to be done. But that moment, the rain, the coffee, the sated feeling and sense that I really had nothing to do, no better place to be, it was as if I were sitting in a daydream, a completely constructed reality I could never really have imagined.

I went to pay the bill only to find out The Brass Compass does not, in fact, take American Express. *Whatever,* I thought. I handed the woman some of the small stash of cash I carry when traveling, and when she asked me if everything was okay, I told her it was excellent. I say this all the time. I've said it at the cash register at Dunkin' Donuts and, really, has an experience there ever been excellent? But I meant it this time. I really did. I spent the rest of the day driving and wandering. Wandering and driving. Stopping when the notion to stop came to me. Moving on when I felt like moving on.

I felt the most satisfying sense of exploration, the kind of thing you can't do during your daily commute, between getting dinner on the table, the dishes done, and the kids in bed. I needed it. I think most of us do. But we have to be willing to wander, if only for a day. We have to be willing to follow a whim, not a schedule or a to-do list. It makes us better in the long run, better in our daily lives. That sandwich was the best meal I've had in a long time. Not just the food, the meal. It was the kind of thing that can only happen to an open-minded traveler—an experience better than the sum of its succulent parts.

I got as far north as Camden, maybe a little farther on, where I stopped and walked along a pebbly beach, took some pictures, and looked out across the water. The channel islands, the low sky, the lobster boats and sailboats moored in the rolling tide. It was a postcard. So enthralled was I by the whole scene, I hardly noticed that I was soaked and my skin was covered in goose pimples. Or maybe I did, but I just didn't care. I wanted to soak in every moment, every drop, and just before I turned around for my return trip to Freeport, I realized that I wished my family were there with me. I wish my kids were kicking sand on my boots and my wife was there wanting more coffee. I wished they had been there for that sandwich, that drive, the whole experience. But it needed to be this way. I needed to be alone in order to realize how much I appreciated them.

A lot had happened in the decade since the last time I had been in Maine and I had hardly taken the time to notice. That's the way it is with life sometimes. You get so focused on the stuff you need, the things you don't have, the stress, the ambition, the obligation, that you forget to look around. You forget to appreciate what you've got. I know that sounds schlocky and trite, but turning back onto US 1 South, I knew it was true.

# PART IV

# FALL

# 13

## PREPARATION

I returned from Maine more excited than ever to get hunting. In a little less than four weeks, I would set to the field with my relatives in pursuit of my first game, and I still had some things to take care of, namely gearing up. I suppose I have always been a bit of a gear junkie. I love specialized items designed for specific purposes. For many, and here I mean mostly real adventurers and enthusiasts, gear is a means to an end, the accoutrements of a lifestyle. But for me, the gear has always been central to any endeavor.

My mom likes to tell people that when I was a little boy, I loved to play baseball. I loved spending hours and hours in the backyard hitting my dad's pitches or pretending to hit pitches when there was no one around. But I could not simply grab a glove or bat and head out into the street. Even at a young age, I understood the importance of proper attire and would only spend hours playing baseball if I were wearing my baseball shoes, batting glove, uniform, and hat. Not just any hat. It had to be a real baseball hat, which in my youngest days was a Milwaukee Brewers cap Dad had given me for a birthday or some other like occasion. If I were to play make-believe soldiers with my friends, I would only do so if wearing my dad's old army canteen and ammunition belt. I suppose that I would have required full padding and helmet for a toss of the football. It wasn't that I was soft or even particularly attuned to my appearance so much as my imagination would not allow me to undertake anything without the requisite gear.

I see this in my sons, Dylan especially. When he was three, he watched my favorite movie, *The Sandlot,* with Jack and me, and it has changed him ever since. The sweet story of a boy who moves to a new town and tries to fit in with a misfit baseball team seems simple enough. But the movie's hero, Benny "the Jet" Rodriguez, does amazingly athletic things while wearing jeans and Chuck Taylor sneakers, so Dylan requires the same outfit for his everyday life. Every night before bed, he asks me to lay his jeans out on his dresser. At four years old, he has more than a dozen pair of the simple canvas sneakers. It is his uniform and my wife doesn't quite understand it. She thinks he's just too picky. She doesn't understand, as I do from my own youthful experiences, that his devotion to those articles of clothing has much less to do with a sense of personal style than it does a need for fulfillment and preparation. What would happen if he were playing ball with friends and accidentally knocks one over the neighbor's fence? How would he be able to retrieve the ball and evade certain death at the furry paws of a legendarily vicious dog if he weren't wearing jeans and a pair of Chucks? Well, he certainly doesn't want to find out and neither did I. I mean, how would I ever become the first eight-year-old to play for the Brewers if I weren't wearing my official cap when the team's scout peered over our fence to see me hit home runs off my dad? I shudder at the thought.

When I was nine or ten, at about the same time I was beginning to fully absorb the L.L.Bean catalog as my reading material of choice, I came across an article in *Sports Illustrated for Kids* about Phil Knight and Tinker Hatfield, the founder and head designer of Nike and its products. I was simply enthralled. I devoured the article, reading it three times before heading into the basement for some typing paper and colored pencils. Every day for more than four years I sat down and designed a pair of shoes. I'd start with a profile outline and then filled in details, worked through color schemes, and pushed the envelope of design. After about two months of doing this, I swiped a brown mailing envelope from my dad's desk, scribbled a note, and shipped off a package of designs addressed to Hatfield. A few weeks later, I got a note from someone in Nike's public relations department thanking me for my submissions and politely telling me that the company does not accept unsolicited designs. But the person thanked me in that "keep up the good work, slugger" kind of way and included a cheap, neon pink Nike painter's cap for my trouble.

To a lot of kids, this would have spelled the end, the logical outcome of a small social experiment; to me the message was quite different. What I got from all of it was that I could continue to draw shoes and mail them off and, in return for my efforts, I would get free stuff. So I doubled my efforts. I began sending packages to Nike on a monthly basis and expanded my scope to other shoes companies: Reebok, Adidas, New Balance, Converse, even the practical business casual shoemaker Rockport. All told, I probably submitted a hundred packages of hand-drawn shoes over the course of late elementary school and junior high. I would find an advertisement in the Sunday newspapers and trace each company's trademarked logo until I could reproduce it with something resembling accuracy, then set about designing a pair of shoes for that company. Hundreds and hundreds of pairs of shoes. I then expanded further to include tennis rackets, sunglasses, casual sportswear. And the free hats, stickers, and T-shirts began piling up.

It wasn't until I fully discovered girls that my fetishistic devotion to footwear finally abated. But my instinct for gear never really did. And before I had told anyone about my desire to learn how to hunt, I snuck hours late at night to troll the websites of popular hunting outlets like L.L.Bean's, Cabela's, Gander Mountain, and Bass Pro Shops. I made exhaustive comparisons of style, fabric, and cut of hunting boots, coats, shirts, and specialized upland pants that feature reinforced nylon patches on the legs to repel briars, thorns, and other potentially sticky flora while traipsing through fields in pursuit of game. I would have little debates with myself on the relative merits of waxed cotton outerwear versus Gore-Tex-coated nylon. I was that twelve-year-old kid again obsessing over Air Jordans. After months, I had narrowed my choices down to coats, shirts, shoes, socks, gloves, boots, and pants from Bean or Cabela's, but after my trip to Maine, it would have felt somehow dishonest or unfaithful not to order from Bean. So, one day in mid-October, I picked up the phone on my desk and called the number Mac McKeever had given me for placing orders through the company's Pro Hunting program. Apparently, as a writer with an interest in learning how to hunt, I was given the same privilege as Bean's professional guides. I was walked through the sizing and ordering process and even got a significant discount on my order. The moment I hung up the phone, I began waiting—waiting for the moment when that big box would arrive and I could finally try on the new stuff, the adult equivalent of that old Brewers cap.

The waiting seemed to take forever, so I busied myself in other ways. I sent an e-mail to Steven Rinella telling him about my upcoming trip and this book. He replied almost as soon as I hit send, expressing how happy he was that I had decided to give hunting a try.

"I'm a little nervous," I wrote. "Got any advice?"

"Just have fun," he wrote. We exchanged a dozen or so messages in an hour—I'm still not sure why I didn't just call him—and by the end, he had invited me to join him in California in January for a wild boar hunt on a ranch belonging to a friend of his.

"That seems pretty hard-core," I wrote.

"Man, it's fun as shit," he responded.

I called Mark and confirmed plans and called my dad to make sure he was going to be able to make it. It turned out, he couldn't. Something had come up. I was crestfallen and more than slightly heartbroken. I had planned out this whole trip in my mind. I imagined making up for lost time with my dad, finally joining him in doing something that he had always loved to do. I felt let down. Cast aside. It took me days to realize that proving to Dad that I could be a hunter may have been the initial impulse behind the trip, but it had morphed into something else entirely. I may have wanted to feel accepted as a man by the man I'd always held as the standard before, but after nearly a year of pouring all my free time into this project, I realized that me going hunting for the first time had little to do with him and everything to do with me doing something adventurous, something that scared me, something that I never would have done before.

I won't say that made everything better. It didn't. Of course I wanted him to be there. But Dad backing out at the last minute to deal with the priorities in his life was exactly the kind of thing a confident man would do. So I needed to be confident and not allow all this effort to rest on his calendar availability. I needed to do this for me and only for me. But I didn't want to do it alone.

My friend John jumped at the opportunity. After discussing the Iowa trip with him in the spring, I hadn't done much to firm up plans and had almost forgotten about it. But I called him after I talked to Dad and he made the arrangements to get a couple days off work to join me. He was genuinely excited and I was looking forward to having him along for the long drive and for my first time out in the field.

The Bean box arrived while I was at work, and Rebecca and Jack moved it into our bedroom so that it was there when I walked in around dinnertime. It took everything I had not to run past my waiting wife and children and straight to my new gear, but I managed to hold off on ripping into my package until after the kids were in bed. Turns out, I had already grown up more than what I would have imagined.

After the dishes were done and the kids were asleep, I went straight to the bedroom to take stock of my haul. It was all there, neatly packaged in plastic bags and I laid it out on the bed like a sailor packing his steam trunk for a long deployment. There was: a waxed cotton field coat with orange pads on the shoulders, an orange vest with slash pockets on the breast that fed to a rear game bag, a pair of upland pants with reinforced patches, an orange Gore-Tex ball cap, a gun-cleaning kit, a Boker Upland bird knife, a pair of Bean's signature Maine Hunting Shoes, two pairs of socks, a pair of upland gloves that reminded me a lot of baseball batting gloves, a manly shirt with breast pockets and loops on the shoulders, and a waxed cotton floppy hat for use après-hunt. I stared at all of it for long moments, discarding the sea of plastic bags that had piled on the floor, then stripped off my work clothes and began trying them on in earnest—different combinations of shirt and coat, shirt and vest, coat and vest, both hats. I looked at myself in the bathroom mirror and even snapped a few self-portraits with my iPhone. I must have been at it an hour before Rebecca called in from the living room asking if I was still alive. The truth was that I was more alive in that moment than I had been in weeks. And it wasn't just about getting new stuff; it was about preparing and feeling ready. With each new combination of gear, I practiced the gun mount and movement I had learned in Maine, using a personalized Louisville Slugger my friend Rob had given me as a groomsman gift in place of the Winchester Supreme over-under Dad had given me months before.

After perhaps ninety minutes of pantomime and playing dress-up, I folded everything neatly and tucked it back into the shipping box, emerging from the bedroom with what must have been a shit-eating grin on my face and a sense that I was ready.

The next day, I stopped at the local used bookstore and bought back issues of *Field & Stream* magazine to supplement my reading on the topic of pheasant hunting and butchering and patiently waited for the days to tick off the calendar and my moment to finally arrive.

Two nights before I was to leave, Rebecca, the kids, and I went out to dinner at Bob Evans. The kids, Jack especially, were excited to hear about my plans and I told them what I was going to do in as much detail as I felt comfortable. I still wasn't a gun guy or a hunter and I had tried to be careful not to glorify firearms too much in the presence of my kids for fear of creating an unhealthy or potentially dangerous curiosity. But Rebecca asked Jack and me to stop at the grocery store on our way home from dinner and I couldn't help but feel excited for what was to come.

"Daddy?" Jack said from the backseat. "You're going to Iowa, right?"

"Yes sir, I am," I said.

"And you're going hunting?"

"You better believe it."

"Are you going to bring home a bear?" he asked, and I could sense a bit of wonderment in his tone. I thought maybe Jack was looking forward to having a stuffed bear, like the one in my parents' basement, too.

"No, buddy, I'm not hunting a bear. I'm going after a pheasant."

"A pheasant? Is that like a deer?" he asked and I could tell he had a vision of me stalking large game with a spear.

"No, buddy, a pheasant is a bird."

"Do you eat it?"

"Yeah, buddy, you eat it. It's like a chicken."

Here there was a long pause as he tried to work out the implications of what had just been said.

"Dad," he said—and his tone had gone from "you're my hero" to "you're an idiot"—"you're going hunting for a *chicken*?"

I felt my shoulders sag and the air bleed slowly from my lungs. It sounded so ridiculous when he said it, all this anticipation, all this new stuff and hard work for a bird very similar to one we could pick up at the grocery store.

"Well, it's not just me," I said by way of justification. "Uncle Mark and Tommy will be there."

"Dad," he said, putting his little foot down, "it's going to take three of you to hunt a chicken?"

He was right. I was being ridiculous.

"It's called a pheasant, Jack, and some of them have very sharp claws."

"Whatever you say," he said. "I think we should get some ice cream sandwiches at the store."

Okay, so maybe my big manly adventure was neither big nor manly and it might not even be all that adventurous, but I tried not to let Jack's dimmed hopes of having the kind of father who wrestles bears to submission dash my hopes for my big trip.

The next night, I stopped by John's place to pick up my gun (where I had been storing it in his locked gun safe) and make final arrangements. He met me at the door with some bad news.

"You know that job in Memphis I was talking about at the beach this summer?" he said. "They called me today and they want me to come down for an interview Monday morning."

It was Thursday night. The plan was to hunt Saturday and Sunday and come back Monday. John was trying to let me down easy and he seemed really broken up about backing out. I knew this job was important to him, that the opportunity was one he'd been dreaming about since college. So I couldn't be mad at him. I couldn't hold it against him.

"Maybe I can get them to fly me from Iowa to Memphis for the interview," he said. But it was too late. I couldn't expect him to pass up an opportunity just to join me on my first hunting trip. I collected my gun, shook his hand, and told him not to worry about it, that we'd just go some other time.

No Dad, no John. It seemed that for my first big hunting trip, I would be on my own. Just me and the manliest group of relatives possible and yet I remained excited. I would be leaving early the next morning and I didn't have time to feel any other way.

It was just something I had to do.

# 14

## THE DRIVE TO IOWA
## AND MY MISSING LICENSE

My in-laws were in town to help with the kids while I was gone hunting, so Rebecca and I decided to let them have our bed and, with no guest room for the offering, we blew up the air mattress we use on camping trips and set it up in the living room. When we lay down, my intention was to get some sleep, call it an early night in preparation of an early morning. But instead, we did what we always do. Much to the detriment of a well-rested mind, we flipped on the TV to watch one of my wife's favorite shows, a teenage drama about the sex lives and torment of centuries-old vampires and their human friends. Anticipating a narcotic effect, I set the alarm on my cell phone for 4:01 A.M. and put it in the kitchen of our tiny condo, then nestled down next to my wife.

I've never understood the vampire craze that swept through American pop culture in the early part of the twenty-first century. The idea of a bloodsucking boyfriend and his naive love interest just never carried a whole lot of water. And yet, for my wife, it was catnip. The woman who took more than four months to read my first book managed to read all four books in a popular vampire series in less than two weeks. She waited on line for midnight premieres of new movies from that same series and was constantly on the lookout for entertainment involving forbidden lust and craven wanting. I came to understand that vampire stories were an upstanding suburban mom's secret pleasure, like men who troll the magazine racks at bookstores looking for that lone copy of *Playboy* that someone has removed from the plastic wrapping and tucked furiously—presumably due to the sudden arrival of wife or child—behind a stash of photography and clay modeling magazines.

"These things are all about sex," I told her as we tucked into our fourth episode of *The Vampire Diaries* (she had borrowed an entire volume of DVDs from a friend) during our blow-up bed watch-a-thon. "Why don't they just say it?"

"They are not all about sex. Why would you even say that?" she retorted, an odd sense of offense in her tone.

"This girl wants to be with her boyfriend. She loves him. But he's a vampire and there is, therefore, a chance he will get excited and tear her heart out. It's all about the questions surrounding a girl's decision to lose her virginity to the evil and timeless beast that is the teenage boy."

"Shut up," she said dismissively. "It's not about sex. It's just about vampires."

"Do you think vampires are sexy?"

"Some of them are."

"Then it's about sex. Sex, sex, sex, sex."

She threw a pillow at me and turned the volume up on the TV and I decided not to press the issue anymore. I checked my watch. It was already after midnight and in order to make it to Iowa by midafternoon, I needed to be up in less than four hours, so I rolled over, turned off the light, and left my wife to her vampires.

It felt like my eyes had just closed when the annoying *bleep-bleep* of my cell-phone alarm clock woke me. I've always been amazed by Rebecca's ability to sleep through an alarm, particularly this one. I had set it to the loudest, most-eardrum-crinkling sound I could and nearly leaped off the air mattress to shut it off. I turned to see that my wife had not so much as flinched, looking peaceful with visions of vampires dancing through her head.

I got dressed, having laid my clothes out in the dining room the night before so I wouldn't wake my in-laws up in my room, and, with a kiss on Rebecca's head, slipped out into the predawn darkness.

For anyone not accustomed to getting up this early—and here I have to assume that's most people—there's something genuinely surreal about being on the road before five A.M. Unlike, say, one or two A.M., when you might have to contend with night owls and barflies on their way home for the evening, this time of morning is eerie in its silent emptiness. The sky is especially black. The roads especially open. I grabbed a cup of coffee from the gas station where I normally go on my way to work and found that it was fresh-brewed and delicious. It made me wonder how long the stuff I drink hours later in the day has been sitting there. Best not to dwell on such things. In the thirty or so miles from our home to the Indiana state line, I passed a single other motorist. These are roads that a couple of hours later would be choked with traffic and I had them essentially all to myself. It was wonderful. For someone who loves to drive, what could possibly be better than having an entire interstate all to yourself?

I set the cruise and popped the first CD of John le Carré's *The Mission Song* into the player on my dashboard. The narrator's voice was a silky baritone with a slight central Africa accent. I listened for perhaps a half hour before my eyelids began to feel like antique quilts and I turned to a morning talk show for some relief. I didn't begin regretting that third episode of *The Vampire Diaries* until I neared Indianapolis. I could feel that hollow, empty feeling that comes with sleep deprivation. I tried slapping my face and rolling down all the windows. I put on some hard rock music, but to no avail. I was falling asleep just two hours into my day and with eight or nine more hours of driving ahead of me; I knew I wouldn't make it. So I decided to stop at a McDonald's on the east side of Indianapolis for a fresh cup of coffee, a pee, and some food.

Getting up early for a drive to Iowa is something of a family tradition for me. My dad used to insist that we leave our house in Cleveland in the wee small hours in order to reduce the likelihood of getting stuck in Chicago traffic. Plus, he, like me, loves the feeling of being on the open road. I was going nowhere near Chicago on my route, but traffic was a concern. There was some construction on the west side of Indianapolis that might slow me down, so I wanted to make my stop brief, but when I pulled into a parking spot in the still-dark night and turned my car off, the level of my exhaustion came to bear and I didn't have the energy to get out and go inside.

*Just fifteen minutes,* I told myself. *Fifteen minutes, then I'll get some coffee and be on my way.*

I reclined my seat and, with elbow over eyes, drifted quickly to sleep. I was awakened forty minutes later by a knock on my window.

"You okay in there, buddy?" said a man in a blue dress shirt and dark jeans. The sun had come up, but was still low in the sky and the man's face was pressed close to my window. I must have looked dead, lying there in such an unnatural position. I shook my head and inclined my seat.

"Yeah, yup, fine," I said.

"I wanted to make sure you were okay," he said. "You looked dead."

"Nope, yup, fine," I said and realized that I must sound either drunk or mentally disabled. I wanted to say something clear and intelligent. "Thank you very much for your concern." And with that, he began to walk away, turning to flip a concerned wave in my direction and telling me to have a blessed day. How kind of him, I thought, to show such concern. And then I realized that I was parked in the back of the lot and his car was near the door. There was no possible way he just happened to be walking by and noticed me. There was nowhere to be walking to. With my seat reclined, he would have had to have been peering into my window, casing my possessions in order to see me lying there. By the time I realized that I should probably get the man's license plate number just in case, he was gone and I was once again in the vertical and in need of both a urinal and a pot of coffee.

Apart from a little bit of traffic around the Indianapolis airport, the drive was a breeze. I set the cruise and listened to le Carré's toffee-voiced narrator as the sun rose in my rearview mirror and the Midwest came alive to my right and left.

When Rebecca and I were young and dating, I took her to Iowa for my cousin's wedding. It was a crucible of sorts. Would she be able to remember all my cousins' names? Would it take her as long as it had me—I was twelve or thirteen by the time I figured it out—to remember that Carolyn and Sue are the same person?

Would these fluffy, red-cheeked, good-natured people approve of my cheerleader girlfriend? Would she survive an eleven-hour drive with my parents? We left before dawn—she, my mom, my dad, and I piled into my dad's Buick Park Avenue. Some time around the west side of Chicago, my dad offered Rebecca a challenge. He would buy her a steak dinner if she could keep track of and, upon arrival at my grandmother's house, tell him the exact number of cornfields we passed from the point we crossed the Mississippi River to the time we rolled through Mason City. For the first hour or so, it seemed like she was trying to keep track. Her head swiveled back and forth. She made mental tick marks after every fence line and country road. She must have really loved me early on to want to impress my dad so much.

Eventually, she gave up and when we arrived, true to his word, Dad asked her for the count.

"So?" he said. My family has a way of doing this—loading entire thoughts into single word questions.

"So what?" she shot back, whip smart and unintimidated by my old man.

"How many was it?"

"Do you really know the answer?"

"Of course I do," he said. I fully believed he did too. My dad keeps ledgers for everything: records, notes, accountings. The guy lives for data. I had no doubt he knew the exact number of cornfields we would have passed, and I felt a nervous sweat forming in my palm. I wanted her to be right. I needed her to be right. I loved her that much too.

"Well, I may have missed a few, but I'd say around 547," she said confidently and threw me one of those looks that says *I have no idea what I'm saying and this whole business is ridiculous.*

"Oh, too bad," Dad said. "You were off by just a little bit."

"Oh well," she said. "So how many were there?"

"Two," Dad said. "One on either side of the road."

Groan. Eye roll. It was a joke. One of the better of my dad's career as a merrymaker, but a bad joke nonetheless. It would take me years to appreciate his forethought and patience—he asked her to keep track a good three hours before we crossed the big river and he waited another three once we were in Iowa to follow through. I had to give the old man a little bit of credit; once he committed to something, he certainly followed through.

I think about that joke every time I find myself driving west in the direction of Iowa. And I began thinking about it as I climbed out of the shallow valley of Peoria, Illinois. As a rule, I don't like driving through Illinois. Indiana, sure. Iowa, fantastic. But Illinois is flat, even for the Midwest, and kind of ugly. Plus, the whole state feels somehow neglected once you leave Chicago, like an afterthought. Driving through Illinois, at least the parts of the state I've seen from major interstates, seems stuck between east and west; between urban and rural; between salt-of-the-earth and road salt. My mom hates it. She was born and raised in Chicago and goes out of her way to never step foot in that city. I once had to beg her to accept Rebecca's offer to join her after I had a chance encounter with a man whose daughter was a producer on the *Oprah Winfrey Show* and he had gotten me tickets. Mention the word *Chicago* to Mom and she literally cringes. Perhaps the rest of Illinois suffers in my opinion by extension and association. Except, I love Chicago. Of all the big cities in the United States I have spent any significant amount of time in, it is my favorite.

\* \* \*

Driving across the "Illini Plains," as Kerouac called them, is an exercise in endurance, a man versus boredom fight to the death. Thirty or so miles from the border, my cruise unmolested and le Carré's narrator bringing his story to an end, I was nearly out of fuel and decided to stop for gas and a hamburger. The gas station was just off the highway and seemed to cater to truckers and, judging by the crowd around the soda machine, unwed teenage mothers. It was one of those places so starkly on its own, so out of place among the surrounding landscape, that I couldn't help but ponder the thought process that went into its construction.

> **Developer:** "I've got an idea, let's put a gas station that serves pizza, hamburgers, and Chinese food in the middle of nowhere."
>
> **Builder:** "What do you mean 'the middle of nowhere'? Are we talking near the Danville grain silos?"
>
> **Developer:** "Grain silos? Preposterous! I'm talking way in the middle of nowhere. Nothing else around!"
>
> **Builder:** "Nothing? What about a McDonald's?"
>
> **Developer:** "No way!"
>
> **Builder:** "Burger King?"
>
> **Developer:** "Nope! Nothing! Nothing but fields, baby! And we can have an entire aisle dedicated to air fresheners in the shape of medieval weaponry!"
>
> **Builder:** "An entire aisle?"
>
> **Developer:** "Maybe two!"
>
> **Builder:** "Let's go crazy! We can sell mud flaps and CB radios and pregnancy tests!"

**Developer:** "Can the mud flaps have silhouettes of naked women on them?"

**Builder:** "Are there any other kind?"

**Developer:** "Yes!"

**Builder:** "But wait! Who will come to this place?"

**Developer:** "Truckers and unwed teenage mothers and, maybe, one day, a wayward author!"

**Builder:** "Genius! . . . Well, except the author. He can't come."

**Developer:** "Agreed."

And . . . scene.

I ordered a cheeseburger wrapped in plastic from behind a large, glass-front deli counter and, while the Centers for Disease Control and Prevention might not recommend eating meat products from such a place, found to my amazement that it was, in short, one of the best things I have ever put into my mouth. I'm not joking. Delicious doesn't describe it. It was juicy and fresh and almost enough to change my general opinion about rural Illinois. Almost. And since I hadn't ordered from a clown, king, or redhead with pigtails, I didn't feel like I had cheated my moratorium on fast food. My goodness, can I split hairs.

The stop at Indianapolis had put me slightly behind schedule. I had told Uncle Mark and Tom that I would arrive midafternoon Iowa time—early enough that I could spend some time outside with my cousin before it got dark. So I decided not to stop at my favorite Iowa diversion—the previously mentioned world's largest truck stop—and continued north from Iowa City through Cedar Rapids, Waterloo, Nashua, and on to Mason City.

When I pulled into Mark and Linette's driveway, I was

startled by a large man in cowboy boots and jeans, a T-shirt stretched over broad shoulders and a thick chest. Had I not known I was in the right place, I might have thought I was at the wrong house. The man turned around and to my great surprise, he looked an awful lot like my youngest cousin, who I had seen just four months before.

"What's up, cuz?" he asked.

"Tommy?"

"You made good time," he said. I could not believe my eyes. Mark would tell me later than Tom had grown six inches and gained thirty pounds of raw muscle in less than a calendar year. It was like looking at the Incredible Hulk when you expect to see Bruce Banner. Shocking, and for a moment I felt old. Here was the youngest member of my generation in the family and he had gone from a cute, soft-about-the-edges preteen to a full-grown, corn-fed man in roughly the same amount of time between the All-Star Game and the World Series.

After we unloaded my gear, I told Tom—it felt strange calling him Tommy given his adult frame—that I needed to buy a hunting license, and he recommended we go to a store called Fleet Farm to get me legal before our hunt the next morning. If you have never been to a Fleet Farm, as I hadn't, the best way to describe it is by imagining that a farmer is given magical powers to create a one-stop shop for every single masculine need he might have, save anything to do with sex or church. Though, now that I think about it, there were condoms in the toiletries aisle and I'm pretty sure I saw a few New Testaments on a bookshelf, wedged between the latest editions of *Modern Woodworking* and *Soldier of Fortune*. If Ted Nugent and Bob Villa were stocking a fallout shelter that they planned to share in the event of nuclear attack, it would look very much like Fleet

Farm. The store starts in a front corner, where the clothing section is stocked almost exclusively with tough canvas coveralls made by Carhartt and emanates from there in aisle after aisle of goods designed to set a man's heart atwitter. Hardware, hunting, horticulture (this is Iowa after all), and husbandry seem to be the name of the game. Home decor? Well, they've got some industrial-sized cans of paint. Food? There's an entire row of shelves dedicated to jerky. This was no Walmart or Target. None of that sissy stuff at Fleet Farm. No, this was a store for the red-blooded, God-fearing American male.

I liked it instantly.

In the forty or so minutes Tom and I spent wandering, I saw enough power tools, duck decoys, and pickup truck bed liners to last a lifetime and not a single greeting card in sight. Though, to be fair, we only covered perhaps two-thirds of the store in three-quarters of an hour, so they may have been tucked back behind last year's machetes and chain saws. I had not brought the proper ammunition for my shotgun and needed to pick out some different shells. Iowa, which literally lives and dies by its soil, had implemented stringent regulations regarding the materials hunters may use when hunting on public land in recent years. Lead shot, over time and given enough of it, can damage soil as pellets oxidize and disintegrate, changing the pH levels of the dirt. It wasn't likely that we'd be hunting public land, but Tom thought it would be a good idea to look for a deal on some steel or composite shells to be safe. Not finding one and not wanting to leave any of the three—yes, three—aisles devoted to ammunition of all stripes empty-handed, I bought some new lead shells designed for felling pheasant and offered to buy some for Tom, but he demurred, assuring me that between him and his dad, they had plenty. Then he led me to the customer service desk, where a short, thin woman with leathery skin, feathery hair, and an orange employee vest began walking me through the process of buying a nonresident small-game license.

"What's your zip code?" she barked in a scratchy, I've-been-smoking-since-I-was-nine voice.

I told her.

"And how do you spell your last name?"

"It's Heimbuch," I said. "H. E. I. M, as in Mary. B, as in boy. U. C. H."

She punched some keys on the computer behind the counter. "Have you ever had an Iowa hunting license before?"

"No."

"And what's your zip code?"

Hadn't I just told her that? I told her again and she typed furiously on the keyboard.

"And you've never hunted with a license in Iowa before?"

"No," I said and it was followed by way too much typing. Was she writing a novella while doing this? E-mailing her best high school friend?

"And your last name, how is that spelled?" She had asked me more than a half-dozen questions relating to exactly three pieces of information and with every answer, her fingers flew across the keyboard. And with each subsequent asking, her voice grew increasingly terse. I tried to image the fields on the form she was filling out.

```
Zip Code:
Last Name:
Ever Had an Iowa License?:
Brief Description of General Demeanor in No
    Fewer Than 700 Characters:
```

*Zip Code (in Roman Numerals):*
*Ever Had an Iowa License?:*
*If You Could Be a Kitchen Appliance, What*
    *Would You Be and Why?:*
*Last Name (in Pig Latin):*

The woman asked to see my driver's license and as she was entering the information into the computer (information, incidentally, that included the spelling of my last name and zip code), she casually asked me for my hunter's ID number.

"I'm sorry, my what?" I asked.

"Hunter's ID number," she, well, retorted is the only word for it. "You have taken a hunter's safety class haven't you? They have those in Indiana?"

"Ohio."

"What?"

"I'm from Ohio, not Indiana," I said.

"This says your zip code is in Indiana."

"But I'm from Ohio," I said. "My license is from Ohio. My home is in Ohio."

"Hold on. What's your zip code again?"

After several whole minutes, we finally established that I do live where I have always thought I lived and she again asked me for my hunter's ID number. I pulled the card they had given me when I finished my hunter's safety course from my wallet and handed it to the woman.

"What's this?"

"That's what they give you in Ohio when you pass hunter's safety."

She began looking at the card skeptically. On one side was a photo of a hunter emerging from the woods with the seal of the Ohio Department of Natural Resources. On the other was a statement signifying that I had passed the class, signed by head instructor Arthur—that crazy son of a gun—and myself. But no number.

"This can't be all they gave you," she said. "You have to have a number."

My heart began to pound. Had I really just driven the better part of seven hundred miles and spent nearly a year preparing only to be shut down at the last second by inconsistency in bureaucratic record-keeping? Then I remembered it. A receipt. Arthur had given me a receipt along with my card, and I distinctly remembered packing it along with my books about pheasant hunting and one called *Field Dressing and Butchering Small Game and Upland Birds: An Illustrated Guide* into my work bag, which was in the backseat of my car in the parking lot.

"I think I have it in my car," I said. "Can I just run out and get it quick?"

The woman rolled her eyes and let out an exasperated sigh. "Fine," she said. "We've got to have that number, but you better run because this thing times out in three minutes and I'd hate to have to put all that information back in again."

Tom waited at the register and I took off at a dead sprint out the automatic doors and across the busy parking lot, unlocking my car door with the remote fob and tearing into my work bag with reckless abandon. I couldn't remember exactly what it looked like, but I knew the receipt was yellow and roughly half the size of a sheet of printer paper. It was one of those carbon copies; I knew that because Arthur had taken extra care to print heavily—and slowly—on it. I went through everything. Notebooks. Books. Old receipts for work that I had never turned in and made a mess of my backseat before giving up and walking slowly back inside, my head hung in shame. I was nearly inside, when I remembered that I had created a profile on the ODNR website that stored all the information about my activities so that I could retrieve them later. Maybe it was in there? I was doing a bit of frantic iPhone googling as I stepped back in the store at roughly the pace of an earthworm loaded up on Tylenol PM. It must have appeared as if I had some sort of disability or was engaged in some sort of performance art, but I didn't stop. Forward progress was progress and I was hoping to find the number before stepping back up to the customer service desk now backlogged with a line.

"Craig!" Tom yelled, snapping my attention to where he stood with Old Leatherface, and both were waving at me. Tom's wave was excited, hers had about as much enthusiasm and disdain in it as the nod someone might give to a dentist to proceed with the removal of a bad tooth after the dentist had already removed all the good ones by accident. To her I was an idiot. An out-of-town idiot.

"I'm just going to use your zip code," she told me, and her longing to simply be rid of me was palpable. "I'm not supposed to do this, but if you get stopped, just tell the wildlife officer what happened."

Wait. You mean the number doesn't have to be real? All this time I could have just spouted the first numbers that came to my head? And how was it that now she wasn't asking for my zip code when minutes before I had to repeat it three times while she was looking at my driver's license where it was printed in bold, clear type?

"Thank you so much," I said. "I really appreciate what you're doing."

"Well, yeah," she said. "That will be $128."

"How much?"

"A hundred twenty-eight even."

"Is that a lifetime pass?" I asked.

"Nope, just the few days you'll be here."

"And it's $128?"

"Yup."

"Are the pheasant in Iowa made of gold?" I asked. The price really astounded me.

"Nope, but you're from out of state, so it's more expensive."

I turned to Tom. "How much was yours?"

"Ten bucks for the year," he said.

I handed the woman my American Express and did a silent calculation. With gas, the cheeseburger, coffee, ammunition, and the license, I was already $300 into my hunting trip and the shotgun had never left the case. I couldn't remember the last time I had spent $300 on myself in a day without getting so much as a T-shirt. So far, I had twenty shotgun shells, a piece of paper, a sore ass, and a higher cholesterol count.

"My dad came in while you were working on your phone," Tom said. "He walked right by you and neither of you even noticed."

And it's true, we had not noticed. But then I was preoccupied with my frantic search for a fake number, and Mark had a few other things on his mind. He was in the midst of helping Will (Tom's older brother) get out of a little bit of trouble he was having at school. I won't get into the details here, but let's just say Will—the smart, quiet one—had a run-in with the authorities, the kind of run-in you only have when you're underage and in a collegiate environment, and Mark was less than happy.

That's the big difference between Mark and my dad. My dad

has this quiet resolve. Life is a series of problems to be solved and the only way to solve them is to think through them dispassionately. Consequently, I can think of only one time in my entire life when my dad has yelled at me. Mark, on the other hand, tends to parent more by gut than guile. If Will or Tom screw up, they will know it in the volume of his voice. He'll yell. He'll rant and scream. But unlike Dad, who tends to help solve something and then simply melt away, Mark never seems to get off the phone with his kids angry. Or, he may be angry, but he doesn't seem to let that be the last thing they hear.

I didn't hear him yelling at Will (though Tom would later report that it was Vesuvian and pretty awesome to behold), but I did hear him asking if Will was okay and tell him that he loved him. I can sometimes have a temper. Not a big one, but a temper, and all I can hope is that as my children grow up, my kids know that no matter how mad I may get, I love them with all my heart. I get the sense that Will and Tom know that, that Mark makes sure that they do. And I hope that no matter what Jack, Dylan, or Molly do, I never forget to end every conversation the way I've always seen Mark do it.

Though, as far as reunions go, this wasn't the best I've ever had with Mark. He looked tired, physically worn out and emotionally wrung through. I shook his hand, gave him a hug, and followed as he and Tom went back to look for more deals on ammunition.

We parted ways leaving Fleet Farm. Mark had to run some more errands in town, and Tom and I were heading back out to the house.

"Leave it to me," I said, trying to lighten the mood. "I come all this way and forget to bring my hunter's ID number."

"That was pretty dumb," Tom said, his mouth splitting open into a broad-toothed smile.

"It's just my kind of luck," I said.

"Yeah, rookie mistake."

"We don't need to make a big deal about it though, right?" I said, trying to stave off future embarrassment.

"I'm pretty sure everyone will find out sooner or later," he said. "Besides, you don't know if you'll get anything tomorrow. This could all be good for the book."

"Yeah."

That night, as I was unpacking and laying out everything I needed for my first day hunting, I pulled the book on small-game butchery out to review the incisions I would need to make in order to field dress a pheasant, I found it—the receipt from hunter's safety class. It was tucked between illustrations demonstrating how to remove guts and break off wings. And in large, block letters, it read "IMPORTANT: HUNTER ID NUMBER" followed by five numbers.

So much for my life as a hunter, I thought. I couldn't even track a piece of paper.

# 15

## HEMINGWAY'S SHOT

Uncle Mark banged open the bedroom door and flipped on the overhead light with the suddenness and urgency of a marine drill sergeant waking new recruits on their first Parris Island morning.

"Quarter to seven," he barked. "Time to get up, dude."

He hadn't gotten to "dude" before I had swung my feet off the bed and onto the ground. "I'm up!" I snapped, not rudely but with an avidity I hadn't expected. I wiped the sleep from my eyes and gave a halfhearted stretch to my aching back before standing and heading into the bathroom across the hall for some perfunctory ablutions before breakfast.

I hadn't slept in my cousin Will's room for a decade, and I had barely slept at all on that last trip. My dad, Kosta, my brother-in-law Mike, and I had driven out to meet up with Mark, Will, and Tom and my uncle Paul and his sons, Ben and Mike, before we all drove twenty hours north through Minnesota and western Ontario for a fishing trip. After the trip was over, we stopped in Iowa for the night before making our way back to Cleveland. In one form or another, the Heimbuch family had been making the trip from Mason City to the name-less tract of wilderness near Ignace, Ontario, for more than half a century—ever since my grandpa Robert and his brother-in-law had loaded all the gas cans they could find, some fishing gear, and sandwiches into an old car and driven north until half their supplies were gone.

I made my first Canadian fishing trip when I was ten, the age when young Heimbuch boys were deemed old enough to join the men for a few days of solitude and fishing for northern pike. I sometimes look at the picture taken of me with my first pike on that first trip, which my dad keeps framed on the credenza in his home office, and I wonder whatever happened to that kid. I was so little. So pale. I struggled to hold the moderately sized fish in both hands, my elbows dug deep into my burgeoning love handles to sustain the weight.

I went back a couple of years later with a group of men from the family and got my first real taste of the wilderness and just how naive I was about its power and glory. In those early years, we camped in tents and under camper tops mounted to the back of the family's old Chevy pickups. It was a short walk down a hill to Elephant Lake and my cousin Rob—two years my elder and light years harder and stronger than I, though we called him "Robby" back then—and I were hauling fishing gear down to the boats one morning when we noticed something off in the bushes to the left of the trail.

"Is that a trash bag?" I asked, looking at the lumpy black shape nestled among the undergrowth.

"Probably," said Rob and he went to have a closer look when suddenly the object turned to look at him with big moist eyes and a shiny black snout. "Oh shiiiiiiiiiiit!" he yelled and took off running up the trail. I don't quite remember what I did, apart from leave a streak of excited poo in my Underoos, but family legend has it that the footsteps left in the dirt as my cousin ran away from his face-to-face encounter with a black bear were anywhere between eight and twenty feet apart on the uphill slope back toward camp.

You really must never assume you're safe in the Canadian wilderness.

My fourth and final fishing trip to Canada came the summer after I graduated from college. I was working at a fly-fishing and backpacking store after my postgraduation job at my hometown newspaper had fallen through at the last minute. I had always loved the shop and spent many Friday afternoons in high school browsing around the gear, touching the heavy leather boots and studying the details of the fishing flies in the shadowbox cases toward the back of the store. I was excited to try fly-fishing in Canada and confident that I was the first member of the family ever to make such an attempt apart from my aunt Diane, who had told me about fly-fishing, which she had learned while working as a nurse in Alaska in the 1980s.

"Craig," said my amazing, pleasant, smart, and well-traveled aunt, "fly-fishing is the greatest excuse in the world to stand up to your ass in ice water."

As if I needed one.

I wanted to catch a big forty-inch northern on a fly rod as a way of showing my appreciation for the force she had been in my life.

Everything went fine for the first few days of the trip. We had some luck fishing, though my attempts to land a pike on a fly line were meager and fruitless. I had caught a perch, but the wide-open and windy lakes of western Ontario were too deep and formidable to land a fly and draw the attention of even these greedy and aggressive fish.

A few years prior, the family had abandoned the tradition of sleeping in tents and campers when an old high school classmate of one of my uncles—it's often hard to tell which one—had purchased an old log cabin building school in the Ignace area and set up a guide operation. Having access to such facilities and wanting to help out a guy who could use it, my uncles and dad had been visiting Brother Bruce and staying in his lodges for the annual fishing pilgrimage, which was a real departure for me, since I hadn't been along for a trip in a while. Brother Bruce was nothing like I would have expected from a familial acquaintance. In a family in which the closest thing to a hippie we had were a couple of cousins who had devoted their early adulthoods to the Peace Corps, a long-haired man who smoked pot and often hosted groups of seekers in his sweat lodge in order to make a connection with the Great Spirit Bear was eccentric if not downright absurd. Brother Bruce reminded me of a Vietnam vet who had dropped out of the world and found solace in the Great North Woods, which happened to be exactly what he was. He was an odd bird without trying to be odd. He spoke with the spongy lilt of the upper Midwest combined with the clipped cadence of the masculine woods north of the Trans-Canada Highway. My favorite detail was his dog, a German shorthaired pointer mutt he had found on the side of a Minnesota highway, grossly underweight and with shotgun pellets embedded in the skin of its face, ear, and jowl. He called the dog "Hey You" because that's what he yelled out the truck window when he pulled onto the shoulder of the road and that was all it took for the dog to jump into the cab of the pickup, kick-starting a friendship the likes of which has scarcely been duplicated.

And yet, improbably and incongruously, my self-admitted redneck, right-wing uncle Mark and he got along great. Probably, I remember thinking as I watched the two men talk on the porch of the big cabin on our first night in camp, because they share a mistrust of cities, government, and big business—though for decidedly different reasons—but theirs was an interesting friendship.

Bruce had taken Mark and Dad bear hunting, resulting in the skin rug hanging in my parents' basement. He had taken them fishing, and they had always managed to catch their limit. I think Mark got a discount on Bruce's guide fees for helping out on projects in camp and for bringing supplies up from Mason City whenever he was coming and Bruce had remembered to ask.

We had been in camp a few days, hustling from lake to lake, portaging our small aluminum boats through the woods and catching enough fish to fill the deep fryer Bruce had connected to a propane tank on the side of the house. We decided to forgo a morning trip to a distant lake and spend some time relaxing around the camp. Uncle Mark had brought his three-wheeler on a trailer and Brother Bruce, the psychedelic monk of the north woods, had a six-wheeler and four-wheeler that he used for everything from hauling gear to removing tree stumps around the property. My cousins and I decided to go for a ride.

I got on the six-wheeler and followed my cousins up the narrow two-rut road. In our cars, earlier in the week, the branches from the trees scraped the windshields and doors and there was one place where we had to pull the side mirrors in for clearance. At the top of the hill, we turned onto the abandoned dirt logging road that had once serviced the area and rode for a mile or more before deciding to turn back. It's hard to imagine, but a person can get seriously lost on a road with no intersections or turnoffs in the North Woods and we all wanted to be sure we could find our way back to camp. After missing the narrow entrance to the camp drive a couple of times, we eventually found it and began making our way back down. I went last and was doing my best to keep the six-wheeler in a controlled descent with the left set of tires in one of the ruts and the right on the raised median. I can't remember exact details, but I remember coming to a point where the narrow track veered left and feeling the right front wheels being pulled down into the ruts on the right-hand side.

Try as I have over the years to remember the exact set of events that followed, I have been unable. I remember hearing my cousin Ben call my name and opening my eyes to find myself lying on my back ten yards in front of the six-wheeler. It was as if I had woken in the middle of a terrible dream. My head felt fuzzy and numb and I was, in retrospect, clearly in a state of shock. Apparently, I had tried to right my veering ATV and had nearly done so, but the back right wheel hit a small tree and sent me flying ass over donuts over the handlebar. I apparently lost consciousness, but I don't know for how long, because Ben had been back at camp and decided to ride back to the top of the hill—not to find me, but for fun—when he happened across me. I could have been unconscious for five seconds or five minutes. I had not been wearing a helmet. There's just no way of knowing.

Needless to say, there was some concern over what had happened when Ben and I returned to camp, he on his four-wheeler and me desperately pushing the six-wheeler, broken rear axle and all, with shaky hands. The concern from my aunt Linette— who had broken the "boys only, no girls allowed" tradition on the fishing excursions a few years prior—was for my health. My dad's concern, however, was for my stupidity.

"How could you do this?" It was a statement more than a question. "You were showing off and being reckless and now you've fucked Bruce. He makes his living with that six-wheeler and you've fucked him." He poked me hard in the chest, which brought tears to my already spinning eyes. He yelled at me with reckless abandon for what felt like whole minutes. And he continued to poke me in the chest every time I tried to explain.

"I've never known your dad to lose it like that," Linette said as we made the bed in Will's room ten years later. "He just doesn't do it."

"As far as I know," I told her, "I'm the only one of the four of us who has ever made him mad enough to swear."

"I don't know that I've ever heard him swear since."

"Me neither."

"He was plenty mad."

"That's an understatement," I said. "And I paid for the repairs too. Took cash advances on my credit cards and maxed them out."

"Well," Linette said. "I was afraid for you."

"I remember sitting on the grass and crying with you," I said. "That was the worst trip of my life."

"Me too."

We stopped in Mason City on the way home from that trip and I saw Aunt Diane for what would turn out to be the last time. Resting in a hospital bed on the first floor of Grandma's house—a hundred yards across the lawn away from Mark and Linette's place—she looked skeletal and Zenlike. She told me she wasn't afraid and that the world was a beautiful place, even if she did have cancer, even if your favorite people die too young, before their time. Her insight scared me. She was serene. I lay awake in Will's bed that night, looking out the window across the yard and waiting for the light in Aunt Diane's room to go out. It didn't. She died a few weeks later.

After Mark flipped on the lights to wake me up, I opened the blinds and looked across the predawn dark yard toward the old house, which had been empty for two years. Aunt Diane had died. Grandma died eight years later. And it had been dark ever since, for the first time in more than seventy years.

I put in my contacts and brushed my teeth with the iron-laden well water, then went back into Will's room to lay out all my new gear. Mark made eggs, sausage, and toast for Tom and me. I was self-conscious about my new gear. I felt like a dandy. Dressed head to toe in the clothes I had ordered from L.L.Bean, I felt like a kid getting dressed up for Halloween. Inauthentic. New from the box. Unearned and somehow barely more pretend. Still, I was excited to get out into the field. I had a good feeling about the hunt even though Mark had warned me that pheasant hunting in Iowa wasn't what it once had been. Twenty years ago, it wasn't uncommon for him and my other uncles and their friends to go out to the farm—just outside Thornton, Iowa—and shoot their limit of three birds apiece in the time between breakfast and lunch. Three roosters apiece, like swatting mosquitoes from moist summer air.

But a few things had conspired to reduce the pheasant population of Iowa, namely freezing rain and corn prices over $6 a bushel. Freezing rain is a problem for any bird, but pheasants most especially. Their feathers are thick and full, more like the fur of a Labrador retriever puppy than the slick, linear, and smooth quills of a crow or a sparrow. They are a species tailor-made for adaptation in winter. They burrow under cover and are more likely to run from cover to cover than to fly. And they are natural-born grain scavengers. They can survive a thick blanket of snow by burrowing down in search of corn and grain, then make a little shelter for themselves. But Iowa had experienced three or four years of early winter freezing rain, which froze the birds' feathers and lay a sheen of ice over the ground making it impossible for the pheasants to find food or shelter. A large portion of the once-mighty population simply starved or froze to death, according to my uncle, and those that didn't either fled for places with more consistent snowfall or were tracked down by the resurgent Iowa coyote population. Barn owls, hawks, and other birds of prey also became a problem for pheasant, but the most damaging species to the bird's population has been the Iowa farmer. And it's hard to blame them.

Demand for ethanol, corn plastic, corn syrup, feed corn, and a whole host of other corn-based products (including, one has to assume, corn itself) has made the thick, black Iowa soil more valuable than it has almost ever been. Two decades ago, Mark told me, he sold corn pretty regularly for less than a dollar a bushel, but in the fall of 2011, prices were over $7. It's an attractive proposition to a farmer, to make the most he possibly can with the highest possible yield from his land. This means planting every inch of a farm with corn. Land that may have at one point been too wet or low-lying to plant, and thus left to prairie grass and other habitat perfect for the ringneck pheasant, was drained and planted. The corn itself was harvested to the nub. I remember visiting Iowa after the harvest as a child and young man and seeing miles and miles of dun-colored fields, stubbly with shorn cornstalks and blown over with enough vegetation to allow for a nesting bird; vegetation that would freeze and then be tilled under in the spring to reintegrate nutrients into the soil before the spring planting—sort of like mulching your yard with a lawn mower. I was startled, after we finished breakfast, to drive past acres and acres of pure black soil. What once would have looked like a land made entirely of whole wheat pasta now looked like it was made of a thick layer of used Starbucks coffee grounds.

It's hard to argue against the economics for the farmer. An industry that has been wracked by mass industrialization has devastated the individual farmer. If an opportunity to make a profit and stay alive comes along, he has to take it. He can't be blamed. Not by me. Not by Uncle Mark, who hasn't worked in farming since the demise of the family agricultural chemical business twenty-odd years ago, and not by hunters who have for decades pursued their passion thanks in large part to the kindness of the farmers now faced with this opportunity. But that doesn't mean it's not noteworthy.

We drove for perhaps a half hour from Mason City to Thornton on a two-lane highway. Mark told me the story about the decline in pheasants and how this farm came to be a part of the family. I didn't quite follow all the details, but a friend of his inherited his father's vast tracts (and here it's hard not to imagine the scene in *Monty Python and the Holy Grail* with the father who tries to convince his son of his future wealth despite the son's protestations that he only wants to sing) and there had been a bit of a family dispute. Mark told Uncle Paul, who had said he might be looking for a hobby farm. Uncle Paul called Uncle Roger and before Mark knew it, his brothers had bought the place without him, something I sensed still bothered him though the whole thing had happened more than twenty years ago. It was hard to follow the details because no one in Mark's family drinks coffee so I had not yet had any caffeine.

Add in the heavy, hearty breakfast and my general nerves about the hunt to come and you can be safe in assuming that it was a good thing I wasn't behind the wheel. I've never been able to navigate in Iowa. Though the state is laid out in mile-by-mile grids of roads, I'm constantly lost. Once, while making my way home from a brief visit, I drove a route that was as familiar as my face, noticing farmsteads I thought I knew and recognized. After a couple of hours and running low on fuel, I stopped for gas in a town I thought I had driven through a hundred times throughout my life only to realize—thanks to a glance at the GPS on my phone, that not only had I never been to this place, but I had been traveling almost straight west for more than the hundred miles I thought I had been driving south. It was disconcerting to say the least. Especially since I am actually quite good with directions. It never takes me long to find north and I have, on several occasions, dead-reckoned my way home from unfamiliar places based on nothing but instinct and an understanding of spatial relationships between where I am and where I want to be.

But Iowa is different. Everywhere you look are the same slight, but rolling hills, the same vast fields, the same small, sometimes bleak, towns with the same Casey's General Store and the same grain silo as anywhere else you go. I try to explain this to my friends, and to help them understand, I tell them to imagine being in a maze of subterranean hallways with every surface painted the exact same color tan. You may only make right-angled turns, but after a while you lose track of how many of them were lefts and how many of them were rights. Eventually, you may be back to where you start, but you wouldn't recognize it if you were. In Iowa, you can drive for hours and hours and the only discernible landmarks you may see are the Mississippi and Missouri rivers, but by then you're either in Nebraska or Illinois. If you get to the Mall of America, you've been in Minnesota for at least two hours and if you get to the St. Louis Arch, you're halfway through Missouri.

And yet, it is an appealing landscape and one I could be pleasantly lost in for days. Iowa is far from the flat plain it is often billed as. In fact, the land lilts like an Irish accent, dotted by stands of old gnarly oak and hemlock and broken by hundreds of creeks and rivers with fertile names like Cedar and Winnebago. Crossing over from the dull pancake of western Illinois, I've often noticed how even the air seems different. Cleaner. Thicker. Bigger. Even on an early day like the one I first hunted, the gray skies seem different than they do in Ohio or Wisconsin or Michigan or Virginia or any of the other places I have found myself on gray mornings. Less gloomy. A dreary morning in Cleveland is like having a head cold during a tax audit. But in Iowa the same conditions seem somehow more optimistic. If it rains in Cincinnati, traffic stops and people gripe at work. If it rains in Iowa, it's good because the fields need it. It's hard to say if the culture makes the place in my mind or if the place makes the culture, but either way I look forward to the restorative power of my visits, which keep me grounded and leave me dreading my concrete and faux-brick suburban life.

Mark navigated to the farm by rote. We stopped at the gas station in Thornton, which I estimated made up roughly one-third of the retail economy in this tiny town, and I poured myself a cup of much-needed coffee. I like to put a couple of ice cubes in my coffee. For one thing, I tend to gulp and there really is no pain like a scalded tongue, and two, it tends to cut the acidity of coffee—especially the kind of tar-thick lava-hot java you find at a gas station in the middle of nowhere. I looked for a soda fountain, but didn't see one and asked the man behind the counter if the store had an ice machine.

"No, sorry, don't have one," he told me.

"Really?" I asked. My incredulity was based on the sheer variety of goods the store carried. In addition to the usual bags of chips and twelve-packs of beer, the gas station stocked boiled peanuts, fireworks, rubber gloves, pig chow, live bait, and mesh-backed caps with cornstalks silk-screened on them and, behind the counter, a variety of adult magazines that would make Larry Flint blush. Yet no ice machine.

"You can buy a bag of ice if you're really interested," the clerk added helpfully. I passed and decided I would just have to wait a few minutes for the coffee to cool down before I could take a sip. The man behind the counter nodded at Uncle Mark as he paid for his Diet Pepsi.

"You think you're going to get anything today?" he asked. And in our reinforced pants and blaze orange hats, you didn't have to be a gas station attendant in the middle of nowhere Iowa to catch on that we were hunters.

"I hope so," said Mark. "They're just not around like they used to be."

"No," said the man. "No, they aren't. Well, good luck to ya."

We all said thank you and returned to the truck. It was in this moment that I felt like I was a part of something, some masculine ritual in which the villager bids the hunter a fruitful hunt, sending him off into the field with well wishes and, one assumes, quiet prayers for bounty. I realize it seems a bit dramatic, but that small exchange in the store made me feel like I was going out to be a part of something big, important, daring. It was a small boost of confidence and much-needed caffeine, even if I did burn the tip of my tongue.

When you think of an Iowa farm, you probably conjure a picture of a white clapboard house and a big red barn, an out-sized garage with sliding doors and a silo. The farm belonging to my uncles, Paul and Roger, is nothing like that. There once was a home on the property, but it rotted away years ago. The only sign that it is anything other than a big field is a ramshackle shell of a what used to be a cow barn and a windmill stand-ing above a no-longer-operational well. It's a beautiful piece of property. At 160 acres, it is a half mile by a half mile, and only a few acres had been actively farmed that year—by a neighbor who had leased some land from my uncles to bolster his bumper corn crop.

We pulled off the gravel road onto a flat piece of grass and pulled up next to three other vehicles. Our fellow hunters had al-ready arrived and were standing around, shotguns resting lazily over limp arms, watching two larger German shorthairs—Ava and Jaeger—play and bounce, frolicking in the early cool breeze.

Since this was my first time hunting and because he wanted it to be a special occasion, Uncle Mark had called my cousins Rob and Ben and invited them along. In terms of hierarchy, I fit directly between the two, with Rob two years my senior and Ben three years younger than me. Rob had recently been named Teacher of the Year at the North Iowa Area Community Col-lege, where he taught auto mechanics. Growing up, he was my closest cousin and the brother I had never fully appreciated how badly I needed. When we were young, we used to put on old boxing gloves and rip the tags off our jeans for mouth protec-tion and box in his bedroom. We once joined up with another cousin, Travis, to force-feed our cousin Kevin cookies and red pop, then told him jokes until he quite literally popped, projec-tile vomiting doughy red frosting and fizz all over Grandma's kitchen floor during the family New Year's Eve get-together. It was and is quite possibly the meanest thing I have ever done and also one of my fondest memories. Robby, as we knew him then, became something of a hell-raiser in his teenage years. Uncle Mark told me it was touch-and-go for a while as to whether Robby would make something of himself or spend his adulthood making license plates in jail. It wasn't until he met his wife, Dana, that he settled down. And now the former teenage hellcat is a member of the local school board and was named by the *Mason City Globe-Gazette* as one of the "20 Under 40" making a positive difference in the community, something difficult to imagine at best, worthy of a fact-check in the least, to all of us who knew him when he was driving a Chevy Blazer that required a stepladder to get into and sporting the worst 1980s ducktail haircut you have ever seen.

My cousin Ben and I, though close in age, were not all that close growing up. He was the oldest of the youngest cousins, whereas Robby and I ran in the middle pack while his sisters, Heather and Heidi, and my sisters, Amy and Jill, teamed up with Uncle Roger's three boys—Chris, Dave, and Matt—to form the oldest of the pack. This kind of striation is common in big families. My dad is the fourth of nine children. Mark is his youngest sibling. Mark is only a couple of years older than Chris, the oldest of the cousins. When the oldest cousin is in his late forties and the youngest, Tom, is only seventeen, there is bound to be some division. But if Ben and I didn't spend that much time together growing up, things have changed as adults. It seems every time I am in Mason City, he drives the ninety miles from Waterloo, where he works as an engineer for John Deere, to see me. Tom told me Ben canceled a trip to Kansas City when he heard that I was coming to hunt, a trip Tom believes involved spending time with a young woman. So I was, needless to say, flattered to see him waiting, shotgun in hand, to join me on my first hunt.

I watched the complicated and subtle dynamics of hunting parties play out before me as we stood in a circle making small talk. Someone needed to be the leader, the "Jaegermeister" as Mark put it. When he said it, I assumed we would all be taking a shot of the liqueur before heading out into the field and got excited for a moment, then nervous remembering my hunter's education class and the crusty Arthur's admonition against drinking and hunting. I was both relieved and disappointed when I realized the term referred to the leader of a hunt. Damn, the things I don't know for not having taken that second semester of German in college. Rob spends nearly every weekend bird hunting. The land belonged to Ben's dad, so technically that made him the landowner. But Uncle Mark was the oldest and most experienced and it seemed right to defer to him when deciding our course of action. I wasn't expected to say anything, which is good, because in the thirty seconds or so that it took those three to work out a plan, I felt a jabbing sensation in my neck, reached up, and realized that I had forgotten to take the tags off my new blaze orange hunting vest. I snatched it quickly and said a silent prayer that no one else had noticed before I could yank it off and stuff it into the padding of my gun case, the one Dad had given me nearly seven months before.

"You know what we're doing here, right?" Mark asked, taking me aside as Rob and his friend John tended to Jaeger, and Tom and his friend B.J. tended to Zeke, and Ben and his friend Adam tended to Adam's dog, Ava.

"Sure," I said. My pulse had quickened with the tag incident, and I could feel my palms getting sweaty under my spiffy new shooting gloves. I may have known, then again maybe I didn't. My mind was swirling, and the harder I thought about the hunting techniques section of the hunter's ed class, the less clear it came back to me.

"We're gonna spread out," Mark said, as if it were a reminder and not an education. "We're gonna form a line. Keep fifteen, twenty yards between you and the guys on either side of you. Don't get ahead, don't fall behind. That's how people accidentally get shot. Make sure that if you see a bird and it's a hen you call out 'hen!' We only shoot roosters. If you see a rooster, you can call out 'rooster,' but I won't."

"Why's that?"

"Because I'll be too busy shooting at it. If you hear people shooting, that's a pretty good indication it's a rooster."

Mark patted me on the shoulder, and I half expected him to zip up the last two inches of the soft shell fleece jacket I was wearing under my vest like a mom sending her child off to the school bus for the first time alone. There was concern in his voice. Parental concern. He wanted me to be okay. He wanted me to be safe. But more than anything, he wanted me to have fun. You don't go hunting a second time if you don't have fun on your first trip. As he was walking away, he said, "I talked to your dad the other day."

"Really? What did he say?"

"He told me to watch out for his gun and make sure it comes back in the same pieces he gave it to you in."

"Did he say anything about me?"

"Nope. Seemed more worried about the gun," Mark said, a wry grin coming over his face. His joke—and I'm going to maintain that it was a joke—calmed me for a moment, and I took my place on the left end of the line, between Tommy and his friend B.J. Part of me was glad Dad had thought to check up on me, but more than anything, I was glad Mark told me. I'm sure Dad told him to take care of me and Mark didn't need to be told. He's always watched out for me. And in a lot of ways, I was really proud to be hunting with him.

The brief, touching moment passed and we were ready to start. I'm not sure what I expected. A whistle? A loud cowboy whoop? Some sort of bell or a blast from a small ceremonial cannon? But I was underwhelmed by the start of the hunt. Spread out across perhaps sixty yards, we just sort of started walking. Not even a bugle or French horn. Not so much as a flute and we were off marching.

The dogs were working out ahead of us, bounding, bouncing, and leaping through the tall, windblown dry grasses, which were knee high. Within moments my heart was racing and I could feel the morning chill start to burn off my skin. My breathing got shallow and I felt like I was back on the treadmill at the gym, huffing and puffing, realizing thirty yards into the walk that I had managed to fall five yards behind. This was no leisurely stroll through the bucolic countryside; this was a purposeful double-time march up a small incline through seriously unlevel terrain. I was fully aware of the weight of my loaded gun and carried it with both hands, one on the stock and one on the forearm, out in front of me. I looked up the line and saw Mark carrying his gun easily at his side with one hand. Rob had his slung over his shoulder like a hobo's stick. His friend John carried the same way, as did Adam. Tommy and B.J. carried theirs like they were marching soldiers, one hand under the butt, the barrel resting on their collarbone. I couldn't quite make out Ben's form, but it certainly looked easier than mine. I fidgeted several times, trying to find the right balance and comfort, to no avail. I simply was not used to carrying a gun on a walk. There aren't a lot of opportunities to practice in the suburbs— not without drawing the ire of the local police department or, worse, the homeowners' association.

A few minutes in, I found myself watching my feet, trying to find a good place to put each step. Had I not been carrying a loaded gun, I might have had a walking stick, but as it was, my hands were occupied, so every uneven step or deviation from balance required a tensing of my abdominal and back muscles, a subtle correction so as not to trip and fall flat on my face. Fifteen minutes after we set out I realized I hated this field. All fields really. What is so appealing to behold—the long grasses blowing in the early fall wind, rolling over acres and acres of undisturbed openness—from behind the comfort of a picture window is a real pain in the ass to walk through. The guys down at the right end of the line stopped abruptly, and I followed Tommy as he sped up and began turning. I sped up too, trying to maintain my spacing between him and B.J. We began to swing around, like a giant human door closing and the dogs, which had been frantically moving in S-turns across the width of our line, managed to keep up. Truth be told, on that first stretch of walking, no more than a quarter mile, I had not been paying too much attention to the stated task. A pheasant could have popped up and landed in my hat and I'm not sure I would have known it, so transfixed was I with the ideas of not falling behind, not tripping on my face, not accidentally shooting my young cousin or his friend in the head.

I want to take a moment here to explain how hunting dogs work. If you have never seen a pointer work in a field, then you are missing out on one of the great genetic amazements in the man-made world. Let's take Zeke for example. Zeke is a purebred German shorthaired pointer that Mark bought for Tom at the annual "Hillbilly Sale" outside of Mason City. A hillbilly sale is, by way of explanation, basically a pop-up swap meet. Anyone can bring anything they want to sell and anyone can buy it. There aren't a whole lot of rules. The meets take place in wide-open fields and, from what Mark tells me, there is no reason to go with a shopping list, because in order to get the most out of one of these events, buyers are best served by browsing until they find that perfect thing that tickles their fancy. Care for an illegal iguana? There's a man selling them from the bed of a pickup just over the hill. Have a near-complete collection of spoons from all the world's largest truck stops? Jim-Bob probably has what you need to complete your set. The point is, these things often have little rhyme or reason. They just are what they are.

Seven years earlier, Mark had taken Tommy to the sale to look for equipment for his ammunition reloading hobby. They came across a man with a truckload of chickens. They made some small talk and Mark told him that, while he wasn't interested in poultry, he was in the market for a hunting dog. As luck would have it, the man had a single pup tucked away in a crate beneath the tarp that covered the bed of his truck and his cache of chickens.

For many hunters, training a bird dog involves investing hundreds of dollars and a roughly equal number of hours. They invest in shock collars and while away Saturdays hiding pigeons under bushes and among trees for the dogs to sniff out. They work on commands to teach the dog to pin down a bird— meaning to get it to stay in one place—without killing or attacking it. Zeke required none of these things. So strong was the genetic instinct to hunt that Mark and Tom abandoned training after a couple short sessions. The dog simply knew what to do.

I watched Zeke, who was lither and more energetic than the other dogs, trace long arcs back and forth as we walked, our pace finally beginning to slow, his nose to the ground, his tail nub bobbing. If there is such a thing as pure happiness, as unbridled enthusiastic joy, I realized I was witnessing it. Tom and I, in our positions on the far left of the line, were walking down a long slope along a fence line. Zeke, Jaeger, and Ava seemed to be working independently. Jaeger and Ava might sniff next to each other, but Zeke invariably did his own thing. A stiff breeze blew up for a moment from the left and the most extraordinary thing happened: all three dogs, who had been spread across the breadth of our line, converged upon a single patch of scrub grass fifteen yards in front of Tom. It was like looking down into a shark tank and seeing three tiger sharks swimming around on their own, then putting a drop of blood in the middle of the tank and watching them all converge. At first, my inexperienced mind didn't quite register what was happening. But, after a second or two, when all the dogs began sniffing the same four-foot circle, their tails stopped. They froze into a posture that suggested absolutely focused attention. None of them moved and I heard someone shout from the other end of the line, "Get up on 'em!"

When a bird dog stops dead in its tracks like that, there is undoubtedly a bird in the area. When three of them do, you can very nearly triangulate its precise location. The dogs, through training or instinct, will hold the bird in its place and wait for a hunter to come kick the bird up, which essentially means walking near where the dog is pointing to scare the bird into attempting escape. Without a dog, the pheasant's instinct is actually to run, not fly. But with a dog blocking that option and a hunter approaching, a pheasant will pop up and fly away with the wind or sometimes across it, but never into it.

With the wind moving from left to right, that meant as Tommy approached the spot where the dogs had the bird pinned down, it would more than likely pop up and fly directly in front of me. I nervously clutched my gun.

"You ready?" Tommy yelled.

I nodded. "As ready as I'll ever be."

During my class at L.L.Bean, I got pretty good at these left-to-right shots. My weak eye dominance meant I could keep both eyes open, so I could see the target coming from the left and was able to pick up on it quickly when it moved from my periphery to center view. In fact, of all the different shots we practiced, this was the one I had the easiest time with. As Tommy took another step, my grip tightened and I made sure to keep my face solidly against the stock of the gun. I tried to visualize what was going to happen, put most of my weight on my front foot, and bent slightly forward at the waist. I *was* ready.

A pheasant makes a distinctive sound as it rises from the ground and beats toward safety. It's a sort of staccato exhalation. Imagine spinning a bicycle tire lightly and then holding a piece of notebook paper up to the metal spokes; there's a small, breathy clacking sound as the relatively big bird's wings hammer furiously against the air and its body. I heard the sound for the briefest of moments as the bird, roughly the size (though a fraction of the weight) of a bowling ball popped up as if it were spring-loaded and arched off downwind, directly in front of me. It was such a shock, such a thrill. My pulse quickened and my gun raised instinctively to my cheek. I didn't aim, didn't think about it, just picked up the trajectory of the bird and traced it as it rose and passed in front of me.

"Hen!" yelled Tommy.

"Hen!" yelled everyone but me as the female pheasant traced its exit over the heads and eventually behind our line. I had read about the difference between hens and roosters time and again over the course of my preparation, but trying to distinguish between the two in the field proved much, much tougher. For one thing, a hen is dull in color—brown, taupe, gray. It's smaller, though you would have to know what a rooster looks like to be able to tell, and it has shorter tail feathers. A rooster is a bird of many hues. Black, brown, gray, green, teal, a little bit of red, and a distinctive white ring of feathers around its longer neck. Its tail feathers, too, are much longer and more flamboyant. The idea, according to some of the sources I read, is for the male to distract predators away from nesting females and for the hens to blend in. It worked really well in my case, because I didn't have the slightest clue whether that bird was a male or female. Some things, I guess, come with experience.

"Good job, Jaeger!"

"Great work, Ava!"

" 'At's a good boy, Zeke," said Mark. It was so tender and enthusiastic, the closest thing to coddling I've ever heard coming from his lips. It was never fully explained to me, but I understood that applauding the dogs' efforts, even though the bird was a female, was a means of reinforcing both instinct and training.

I had seen my first pheasant and the experience, while not fruitful in terms of bounty, had been thrilling. It was a rush when the bird popped up and flew past. And I felt satisfied, having heard the "Hen!" call and reacting appropriately by not shooting. My gun was trained squarely on the dun and gray bird. Had it been a male, I would have been able to take two quick and well-placed shots. I had done right and found myself feeling more at ease with the situation. I felt, in short, more like a hunter, like I belonged there.

We walked another quarter mile, before gathering on a dirt road to give the dogs water and discuss our strategy. We would turn north—to the right—along the fence line, spread out, and walk a half mile with the wind at our backs before turning to the east and working our way back toward the cars. Rob had spoken to the men who leased a portion of Paul and Roger's farm for crops. They had another field up the road and a patch of it had been left feral, where they had seen pheasant. We'd try there after lunch. With my first drive out of the way, I felt more at ease. As we started north, I didn't feel quite so awkward holding the gun and was able to feel comfortable with it slung over my shoulder. I'm sure that, had I been watching from a distance, it would have been obvious that I was the new guy and therefore the least comfortable among the group, but for the time being I felt good.

We marched through more tall grass and came to a stand of tall reeds at the base of a small hill. I marched alongside the others, keeping my gun in front of me and my place in the line as the spindly stalks slapped against my nylon-covered vest. After a hundred feet or so, we emerged from the reeds and a strange epiphany came to me.

"I'm about to shoot my first pheasant," I told myself aloud, though inaudibly to the other hunters. I felt my eyes widen and pulse quicken. I had a clear vision of what was to come. The pheasant, with its iridescent and furlike feathers and long spindly tail feathers, would rise in front of me and I would put it down with ease. I began rehearsing in my head as we trudged up the hill. Weight forward. Back heel slightly off the ground. Bend slightly at the waist. Keep cheek firmly against the stock. Move my left hand first and allow my eyes to stay focused on the bird, not the end of the gun. Follow through, don't stop.

We reached the top of the hill and started down across smooth, mercifully short grass. We hadn't taken twenty steps when I heard the breathy flutter of wings against the cold air and looked straight in front of me to see a rooster pheasant rising. He was beautiful—exactly how I had imagined it. He rose straight in front of me and turned his back, revealing a long brown body, black head, the distinct white ring. Green and teal and long tail feathers dragged behind him like a tail on a kite. And, clearly, not a hen. My gun came up instinctively. My weight shifted without thought. My left arm traced the pheasant as it flew directly away from me. I concentrated on the tail feathers and time seemed to slow down. Unlike the first bird, the hen, the dogs had not scared this one up. It had risen of its own accord and directly in front of me. Me! It was amazing, the feeling of absolute focus. I could see individual feathers, make out the shape of the bird's beak, without seeing the end of my gun, without being conscious that it and I were distinct objects, but rather feeling like we were moving in perfect concert. I didn't hesitate to pull the trigger.*

*Ka-blang! Ka-blang!**

The bird dropped straight down, landing not twenty yards in front of me and perhaps one long step to the left, coming to rest in a clump of long grass. The dogs reacted immediately, converging on the spot.

"You got it, Craig!" shouted Rob from my right.

"Nice shooting, big guy!" answered Tom.

"Great shot, Hemingway!" yelled Mark, who had moved to the left end of the line when we made the turn north. Plaudits down the line, then another shout from Mark. "Get on it before the dogs rip it to pieces."

I snapped from my delirious reverie, a postcoital return to the present world. I was a hunter. Before I could eject the spent shells from my still-smoking gun, I ran to where the bird was lying, its lifeless and limp body a trophy of my year spent discovering what it meant to be a man. I picked it up by its neck and was surprised by the weight. It wasn't heavy, just heavier than I had expected—about like picking up a rotisserie chicken at the grocery store. I drank in a long gaze at my first prey, taking mental pictures before stuffing it into the front entrance of my vest's game bag, where it settled at the bottom, on the small of my back. I could feel its heat and was not nearly as creeped out by it as I had imagined I would be. I felt good. Proud. My premonition of moments before had come almost exactly true and I couldn't wait to call Rebecca and my dad to tell them my big good news.

# 16

## THE ASTERISK*

Most of that last chapter was true and as it happened. Right up to the asterisk. From that point forward, it was the way I had imagined things happening, the way they should have happened.

Emerging from the reeds at the base of the hill, I really did have a vision and say to myself *I'm about to shoot my first pheasant.* And I really did rehearse mentally all the things I had learned. And as we crested the hill, which afforded an awe-strikingly beautiful view of the bucolic wonder that is Iowa, the grass did get shorter. In fact, the whole thing went down the exact way I described. The rooster popped up unbidden by dogs directly in front of me, just slightly higher than eye level. I moved as if by rote or instinct, raising my gun and feeling time itself slow down. I felt like I was married to that gun, and for a long moment, my mind went blank of all expectation and insight. I simply was—in the moment, doing what felt so natural.

I selected a small bunch of feathers just above the bird's spindly tail and my eyes focused in such a way that the world itself seemed to disappear. I pulled the trigger without hesitation and this is where the story deviates. Rather than a report of *Ka-blang! Ka-blang!* All I heard was *click, click.*

For a split second, I thought the gun had misfired or that the ammunition was bad, but I didn't have time to think about it before the reports up the line fractured the air. *Boom! Boom! Boom!* Two to my right, then three, and a fourth from my left. The bird tumbled down exactly as I had described.

"Craig, I think you got it," Rob said meekly.

"Nice shot, Craig," Tommy tossed in as if he were throwing the comment away like so much trash. I think they both knew the truth.

"I didn't shoot," I said sheepishly.

"What?" "What?" "Why not?" came several replies.

I looked down at the gun and moved the thumb on my right hand to reveal a switch securely in the "Safe" position. I had forgotten to take the safety off.

"Hemingway wouldn't have missed that shot," Mark chided from the fence line.

"One more reason I'm not like Hemingway," I shot back, but I wasn't in a joking mood and, I sensed, neither was he. I felt like I had let him down, like I had wasted the efforts of all these people who had come out with me that day. I felt like I had dropped the ball, which, essentially I had. Yet I didn't feel sorry for myself. It was more like the kind of embarrassed anger you feel in junior high when someone says something mean about you—something, in my case, invariably true—and you want to both hang your head in shame and run theirs into the nearest hard surface. So much for showing up to my first hunt and surprising the family with a clandestinely earned expertise.

\* \* \*

We continued our hunt for another hour or two, seeing only hens and calling them out as they sprung into the air and flew off un-molested. When we got back to the cars and stood around for a few minutes talking, Mark made a few mocking comments about "Mr. L.L.Bean" missing an easy shot, but it was the sort of gentle ribbing that belies a certain degree of respect and love. Cousin Ben's friend retrieved a knife from his truck and stepped off into some scrubby brush to field dress and butcher his pheasant.

"I don't really remember how to do this," he said to no one in particular as Tom, Ben, and I followed him to where he was going. We stood for a few minutes trading technical wisdom. This was something I had learned how to do. I learned from books and countless viewings of YouTube videos, but my confidence was shot. Everyone knew this was my first hunt and this bird was sup-posed to have been mine. I would have looked like a real jackass had I been pompous enough to claim expertise in field dressing with zero real-world experience. In the end it was Tom who took the knife and made a slice from the bird's anus to its rib cage. He pulled the guts with an ungloved hand, as confident and sure of what he was doing as if by rote. He bent the bird's wings back until the tendons in the shoulder joints snapped and cut them off with a flick of the blade. He cut the pheasant's throat and pulled the head back with a such a deft and strong movement that he removed the head, neck, spine, and skin down to the legs, over which he pulled the feathery skin as if he were pulling off a pair of socks. In less than a minute the entire bird was reduced to two pink breasts, legs, and thighs, which were put into a zipper bag, feet and claws intact for identification by a wildlife officer (male pheasant have heel spurs, while females do not). The rest of the bird was discarded in the bushes for coyotes or foxes to eat.

I went over to the carcass as the others returned to the cars.

I wanted to touch it for some reason, to feel the furry feathers, to see the beak and tails I had thus far only seen in pictures. Then it occurred to me to remove the tail feathers. They made for great fly-tying material should I ever decide to pick that up. But more than that I would have at least something to show my wife and kids for all the trouble of coming out here. I picked the bird up by its feathers, and I could still feel heat coming from the body—moist heat like a baggie of jelly fresh from the microwave and wrapped in one of those boas women get at Mardi Gras–themed parties. I grabbed the tail feathers tightly in my right hand and pulled much harder than I needed to. They came off cleanly and I stuffed them into the slot on the chest of my hunting vest that allows you to put birds into the game bag, which hangs from the back, without reaching around. I hoped no one would see me do it. I felt like a fraudulent brave scalping a victim that wasn't mine. But if they did, I'd use the fly-tying excuse. Hopefully they'd buy that.

We decided to take a break for lunch and drove back into Thornton's block-long central business district and pulled into spots in front of the only business with its doors open and lights on inside, an establishment known only as "The Bar," a name both accurate and appropriate in a one-horse town like this one. Inside it was dark, with the majority of the light coming from a cheap flatscreen hung over the bar and neon promotional signs from the kind of beer companies you only buy from in the suburbs as a gag gift or because you're in college and value quantity over quality. The small windows in the front of the narrow, long room offered nothing by way of illumination or view, and we helped ourselves to a table in the back—like one of those tables you find in a school cafeteria with the cheap metal, padded chairs. Our server offered us sticky, laminated menus, and one glance at the offerings made me love this place instantly. It was hearty food. The kind your grandmother makes for you. The kind she would describe as sticking to your ribs. Chili. Cheeseburgers. Stew. Not a salad in sight. Homemade soup was available some days, and the chili had been made the day before so it was just getting good. Since I'm a sucker for this kind of place and since I can't possibly turn down a breaded pork tenderloin sandwich whenever I'm in Iowa, I ordered that.

We chatted benignly about work and Iowa sports as we waited for our food and about the food as we ate it. My sandwich was as close to perfect as you can possibly get. The tenderloin was pounded flat, breaded, and fried and was roughly three times the size of the bun it was served on. Pickles, a little mustard, a slice of tomato. It doesn't get a whole lot better than this. I'd take this sandwich and an iced tea over just about any meal I've ever had anywhere, except maybe that lobster club back in Maine. That was the best sandwich I've eaten in a lifetime of eating sandwiches. But this tenderloin was awesome too. This with a side of shrimp lo mein would be my death row meal (again, if the lobster club is off the table). It was that good. Feeling full and refreshed, I had a renewed sense of optimism.

Screw what had happened earlier. So what if I made a mistake? It was my first time getting the drop on prey. A rookie mistake. I could learn from it and move on, right? I could still prove my manliness to these guys, still be a hunter, right? It's amazing what a belly full of food does for me. My wife knows to put a sandwich or leftovers in front of me if I'm in a sour mood. It seems that my emotional state is directly tied to how full or hungry I am. If I were to fall on hard times and find myself starving, I would probably end up being the most miserable bastard in the world.

I'm pretty sure a Cheshire Cat smile curled over my lips as we drove back out to the second field we were going to hunt. I was eager. I was ready. I was, I've got to say, pumped up. Rob and his friend had to leave before lunch, which left Ben and his friend, Mark, Tom, Tom's friend, and me to hunt this second piece of land. Mark opted for the warmth of his truck and the Iowa State game on the radio, sending us whippersnappers off to hunt this tiny, triangular spit of long grass in the middle of a three-hundred-acre, black-as-night cornfield. We were piling out of the trucks and readying our guns. Tom was getting Zeke out and Ben and his friend were putting their guns together and giving Ava some water. I stepped in front of Mark's truck, my gun assembled and broken for loading. I was just pulling shells from my pocket when Mark yelled "rooster!" out the window. I looked up to see a rooster thirty or thirty-five yards off rising from the scrub along a fence line and hightailing it toward the piece of property we didn't have permission to hunt. I may have had a shot, had my gun been loaded, but the bird was just too quick on the draw for me.

No problem. Just bad timing. I didn't do anything wrong, right? Besides, a bird popping up this early could only be a sign of good things to come. Surely there would be more in this tiny stretch of land than there were in the 140 acres we had hunted earlier in the day. And to be sure, there were more birds. Six or seven to be exact and all of them as female as Gloria Steinem. I saw all of them, up close.

After walking across a quarter mile of Iowa soil—which is a lot like walking through a foot-thick layer of pulverized Oreos—we came to the arrowhead-shaped piece of land we were going to hunt. The wind had picked up significantly since lunch. The sun was high and bright, the sky clear, but the wind made the day feel heavy. And as if walking into a stiff wind weren't enough, the grass was chest high and thick. Ten feet into the small field, I was breathing like a fat man climbing the Statue of Liberty.

"I think they've got tunnels through this crap," yelled Tom. He was off to the right, walking the fence line. And he was right. Running beneath and through the dense vegetation were Viet-Cong-style tunnels. Every few steps you could see them, openings to a network of tunnels that ran along the ground, weaving in and out of the plants. I had no way, of course, of knowing whether or not these were made or used by pheasant, but it seemed pretty logical to me. The species is threatened by birds of prey—hawks, owls, hell, probably even eagles—which tend to sit high up in trees and take their meals by air. If a pheasant never flies, never exposes itself to the very birds that want to kill and eat it, it has a better chance of living. I secretly hoped they had built the tunnels. I liked the idea of an animal taking its safety into its own hands—not when I was the one trying desperately to kill it, but you get my point. I liked these crafty Chinese sons of bitches more and more by the second.

It took maybe twenty minutes to cover the field, and there was nothing fun about it. The tall grass was so thick, we had to stop a few times to try to find the dogs; so deep and thick in fact that I hardly noticed when a deer stood up less than ten feet in front of me and casually walked off. Ben pointed it out. He was maybe twenty yards away and saw the doe's ears bobbing as it hopped off toward safety and comfort someplace else.

I kept my gun loaded and ready as we walked along the fence line, hoping, no wishing, no praying that I would get one last shot before we were done for the day. I did not.

The day had not gone as I had so long imagined. When I

began planning this trip, I had pictured myself coming home from our hunt with a couple of roosters in my game bag and sitting on a chair outside, sipping gin and cleaning my haul as Tommy told me his favorite jokes. I'd then spend an hour or two in the toasty warm interior, checking my roasting birds, applying additional bacon strips for added fat content and chopping up some vegetables for the roaster. There would, of course, be more gin and by the time I served a beautiful meal to my expectant family, I'd be Thanksgiving drunk—just enough to endure extended periods of family time, but not so much that you can't carve a bird—and swelling with pride.

As it was, however, I found myself sitting in my car, talking to my wife on the phone, and waiting to pick up the pizzas I had ordered in lieu of providing the evening meal with my quick shot instincts and guile.

"So did you get anything?" she asked.

"No," I said, a bit of shame in my tone. "But I came close," I added optimistically.

"What the hell? You drove all the way out there for nothing?"

"There's still tomorrow," I said.

"Well, hurry up and get something, will ya?"

As we devoured taco pizza and a dessert pie, Mark tried to comfort me for my mistake earlier in the day. "Rookie mistake," he said, and "it's better that you walk around with the safety on than to get a bird or accidentally shoot someone. Everyone came home safe, that's the important part." Plus, there was always the next day. Maybe I'd be better then.

We talked until late and until I got a phone call from Rebecca. She was crying. Being in our small condo with the kids, after my in-laws had gone home, and trying to keep them occupied with no backyard, no basement, and a downstairs neighbor who had already twice tried to get us in trouble for noise—apparently she could hear the kids walking from the living room to the bedroom and it disturbed her smoking and watching television with the bass turned to max volume—had gotten to Rebecca. For nearly ten years, we'd lived like single people in small places. We got married young. Had kids young. We had yet to put down any real roots. Not having a house was getting to her worst of all. She could deal without having a ton of extra money and extra things, but she wanted our kids to have a house, a backyard, a basement, a reasonable expectation that they could walk from the living room to the bedroom without risking eviction. And I did too.

When you're a journalist, you understand that you won't make as much money as an engineer or a financial planner. You understand this as a teacher too. But when you're a journalist who marries a teacher for the money and are surrounded by engineers and financial planners, it's like being locked in a candy store and only being able to buy brussels sprouts. It's not that you envy the people who can have candy, it's that you get tired of feeling like you can't. We had made a lot of sacrifices to follow our dreams and to raise our kids, to be able to have Rebecca stay home, and the one that we felt so close to overcoming after a decade of it being a pipe dream was owning a home in the town where we lived.

Rebecca cried for a half hour and we talked for another one after that. I lay in Will's bed and wondered if I were doing the right thing. Wouldn't my time have been better spent delivering pizzas at night or working at a bookstore on weekends to save up our down payment a little more? Probably. But I was here now, lying on a bed in Iowa and thinking about what was to come. I did my best to comfort my wife and put her mind at ease, bidding her a fair night's sleep and going to bed thinking nothing about the next day's hunt.

Sunday morning came with a little less fanfare. I was up before Mark knocked on the door, then dressed and ran into town for a cup of coffee, which Mark and Linette don't keep in the house. That morning had been the fall time change, so my system, already set for Eastern time in this Central time state, was two hours ahead of the clock. I sipped my coffee and read the morning paper, waiting for the others to get up. We had cereal for breakfast and drove down to the farm in Thornton without stopping at the gas station for drinks. Ben and his friend had gone back to Waterloo the day before, leaving me, Mark, Tom, Rob, and his friend and his friend's young son to work the dogs and hike the fields. The wind was a lot stronger that second morning and the conversation thinner while we watched Jaeger and Zeke do their best to pick up scents in the rapidly moving air. It felt different from the day before. The expectation and excitement were gone. I knew long before the end of the day that I probably wouldn't get a bird. I had had my chance the day before and blown it. But I tried to remain vigilant.

We stopped among a stand of pine trees on the leeward side of a small hill and took a break from the wind. Mark, Rob, and his friend started talking Republican politics, while Tom, the young boy, and I watched the dogs.

The conservatism that tends to run in my family is nearer libertarianism than anything that comes out of the GOP headquarters. Especially with the men. Mark and Rob covered a lot of ground—guns, resource management, education, the deficit—but the central theme was that government should stay out of their minds, their hearts, their wallets, and their gun cases. I've never been one to talk a lot about politics. Maybe it was my early training as a newspaper reporter on government beats that made me realize nothing good can ever come from spouting off. Rail against taxes, and the Democrats you cover will clam up. Rail against Wall Street, and the Republicans link you to the "liberal media." Plus, I've never been sure enough in my beliefs to come out of the closet as a moderate Democrat among those I love. My cousin Heather is a flaming liberal, as flaming a liberal as Mark is a staunch conservative. And when they talk, they both hold their ground. I can't imagine doing that. I'm just wired to be conciliatory, to avoid a fight when a fight is coming. So I didn't chime in as Mark, Rob, and his friend talked about deregulation and the welfare state with a tone suggesting they had just bitten into a chocolate cake and gotten a mouth full of lemon juice. Instead, I just took it all in.

There's something beautiful about wide-open spaces, something people don't often get when they live their lives in the suburbs. I was standing on a two-rut road that hadn't been used in years, near a small grove of short, dense trees and looking out across a nearly endless expanse of Iowa. From an elevation of no more than thirty feet, I felt like I could see sixty miles. No interstates. No subdivisions. No office buildings or on-ramps. Just space. The sky felt low with blue-gray clouds that looked stitched to the brown and black earth. I thought about how lucky some people are to have all this, the waving grain, the long blowing wind, the subtle undulations of earth as it meets sky in their backyard. And I thought about what it would be like to move there. When he was alive, Uncle Don always made a point of telling me about opportunities in Iowa. He'd help bankroll me if I came out and bought a small weekly newspaper with a circulation of roughly ten that was having trouble keeping the lights on. Or wouldn't I be interested in taking a job as the lifestyle columnist for the *Mason City Globe Gazette*? And I think part of me always thought I might enjoy that. But I couldn't live out here, not with a wife and kids and job that I love in Cincinnati. *Rebecca would go crazy being out here,* I thought as I watched the seemingly endless clouds roll over my head. Plus, how would I ever really make a living?

I considered the life of a country gentleman for a few minutes until the boys decided they'd had enough politics talk and were ready to get back to the hunt. We followed the same track we had the day before only in reverse. As we walked, I paid close attention to the dogs as they worked back and forth and especially when they stopped moving. Every time our line of walkers paused, my thumb instinctively flipped the switch on the safety and I shifted my weight in anticipation of a bird popping up before me. It never did. While I heard Rob at the other end of the line call out a few hens, I never actually saw one, and when we finished up and headed home, I knew my first hunting expedition was over.

I would not kill anything in Iowa that year.

I felt an odd numbness heading back to Mark and Linette's. I felt like I had studied really hard for a test and showed up to find out it had been taken the day before. But any feeling of sulk, any self-pity, was quickly erased when, after the noontime meal (which is called "dinner" in Iowa and on Sunday is the biggest meal of the weekend), Tom offered to take me out back shooting for the afternoon. Mark and Linette had to go out of town unexpectedly for the afternoon, so my youngest cousin loaded up four or five .22-caliber rifles and handguns into the bed of Mark's pickup and we drove across the enormous lawn to shoot.

You'll think I'm padding the numbers, but Tom and I managed to shoot almost a thousand rounds of .22-caliber long-rifle ammunition in under two hours using a five-shot rifle, a nine-shot semiautomatic pistol, and a nine-shot revolver. Had you been listening from across the street, you might have imagined a war was taking place in the backyard. One of us was shooting as the other was loading and vice versa. I liked shooting Tom's small rifle and even one of the semiautomatic handguns, but it was the nine-shot revolver, the one I had shot with my uncles Mark and Roger, that took my heart. It felt good in my hand and, unlike any of the other guns, I was able to hit targets with it.

Later that evening, when Tom and I were retelling our afternoon to Mark, he got a glimmer in his eye as I mentioned the revolver.

"Well, I think you should buy it then," he said.

"Really?" I said. I had not really considered buying a gun before (except briefly when Mark had mentioned it to me back at the family reunion). I knew I needed one for hunting, but that was a shotgun, not a revolver, and I ended up having one of those given to me.

"I'll cut you a deal," he said, and when he offered me a very reasonable price and offered to throw in a case, I was sold. I gave him all the cash I had as a down payment and promised to send the rest the next time I got paid. I loaded the gun, case, and box of ammunition into my backpack and put it in my trunk. I had just bought my first gun. And I figured having a handgun in the house would be good for the day when Molly started dating. I left early the next morning and had put Mason City long in my rearview before the sun came up.

The trip had not been a total waste after all.

# 17

## HUNTING ALONE

I think I was just glad I wasn't hungover when the alarm went off at six on a Sunday morning in early December. We'd been out the night before, a Christmas party for a group my wife belongs to for Catholic mothers. It's one of those kinds of groups that was probably started to provide support for stay-at-home moms and an entrée into the local community for new women in town, but it's grown into a near-constant commitment of outings, parties, and events. They even went to the trouble to begin scheduling events for all the husbands to get together. And those are awkward.

"Sweetie, I think you should go," one imagines a wife saying. "All my friends' husbands will be there and don't you want to get to know some new people?"

"What do I need to get to know new people for?" replies the husband—me in this case.

"But, honey, you have so much in common."

"Like what?"

"Well, Bonnie's husband will be there and he likes sports. You like sports. It will be loads of fun!"

And so it was that I ended up knowing this group of men, some of whom have become actual friends; others are the kind of acquaintances you can spend a night with at a party never really knowing a thing about—what he does, where he's from, if his name is actually Brian or Jeff. Which is what I did, for the most part, at the Christmas party. I mingled. I moved from bored husband to bored husband and sipped my favorite scotch, checking in every once in a while with my wife, who was drinking vodka and cranberries like Kool-Aid and chatting excitedly with the same group of women she talks to or hangs out with every day as if they had all just come home from decades on separate, but equally deserted islands.

"Hey," said my friend John, who, like me, does not especially enjoy being in a room surrounded by a loud group of mostly strangers and expected to mingle, "I don't think I'm going to be able to go with you in the morning, but I'll get your gun ready and you can pick it up tonight or early tomorrow."

I knew John wouldn't make it even in spite of the fact that he had called me the day before to confirm that he was coming. His parents were in town, and I had a hard time believing that his wife, Anne, would be thrilled about him leaving her alone with them and their three kids to go tramping through the woods with me. I had even told Rebecca in the parking lot on our way into the restaurant where the party was held that I had a feeling he would back out.

"Why would you think that?" she asked me, accused me really.

"Just a hunch."

"Well, that's not very nice."

I felt like going over to where she was standing, highball glass waving with each increasingly drunken gesticulation, to laugh in her face after he backed out, but discretion, when wives and their friends and friends' husbands are concerned, is always the better part of valor. Plus, I know John would have gone in a second if the opportunity had been better timed.

We stopped by Anne and John's house after the party and he handed me my gun and case and told me for perhaps the thirty-second time how sorry he was that he couldn't come along.

"Don't worry about it," I said and went home to catch a little less than four hours of sleep before the alarm woke me with a sudden jolt and the instantaneous relief that my head felt fine. A little tired, but no real worse for the wear. I pulled my reinforced upland field pants, socks, a bush pilot shirt, and a soft shell jacket on and headed out into the predawn darkness.

Hunting alone was something I knew I wanted to try if for no other reason than to reinforce my own impetus. It was all well and good to go to Iowa to hunt with Mark and his boys, and I could see a time when I might join my dad in Michigan to tromp through the woods in search of ruffed grouse. But hunting on my own would mean I had done it; I had become a hunter. Instead of, like the little kid on the playground tagging along with the big guys for a game of pickup basketball, being the consummate guest, the outsider, the pretender. I also knew that I wanted to wait to go on my own until after I had experienced hunting in the safety and comfort of experienced family. Without that, my knowledge was academic. Book learning. No substance. I had spent whole hours watching videos on YouTube and studying diagrams in guides explaining how to field dress a pheasant, but had I not experienced it in Iowa, I would never have thought to bring zipper bags with me for the meat. Some things you just can't learn in a book, and some things you have to do on your own.

When I got back to work after the Thanksgiving break, I

googled "public hunting ground in Ohio" and discovered, to my pleasant surprise, that there was indeed hunting in a state park not far from where we lived. The pheasant were stocked—or released, since "stocking" is really more of a fishing term and tends to take all the masculine self-delusion out of the whole enterprise for me—three times in this park every November, the last instance happening on Thanksgiving Day. Discovering this, I realized I should have tried to muster a hunt before the holiday and worried that the birds might be picked fairly clean by hunters with more knowledge of the area. But I had, at this time, been hunting before without shooting anything, so I was willing to give it a shot.

I've gotten so spoiled having an iPhone. Time was I could read a map and would actually plan my trips before I got in the car instead of punching in an address or landmark at a stoplight and waiting impatiently the six or eight seconds it took for the GPS app to tell me where to go. I had been to this not-to-be-named-here-for-fear-of-making-local-hunters-mad park before, but never to hunt. And it's a big park, built around a Corps of Engineers–created lake. Just because I knew roughly how to find the boat ramp didn't mean I knew where to go to hunt or even where the pheasant might be. But, pshaw. Nothing to worry about. I'll find my way and be just fine, thank you very much. Besides, I could feel that this was my lucky day. This was the day I would go from guy in funny clothes walking around with a shotgun to masculine purveyor of protein. This was to be my vision quest, the day I went boldly and alone into the woods to become a man. It had to be. It was going to be. I was ready.

I followed a two-lane country road north as it skirted its way around the park. From what I could remember from the topographical map I'd looked at on my work computer five days earlier, that section of the park was more grassland than forest and since pheasant like grassy cover and since I didn't want to be mistaken for Bambi's father on the last day of deer season, I thought staying to more open areas was not only good hunting, but good self-preservation. So I meandered around, navigating by instinct and passing at somewhat regular intervals pickup trucks pulled off onto the shoulder of the road. Each one, I figured, belonged to a hunter who either lived closer or was up that much earlier than me, and each represented at least one more gun in the park.

I drove another couple of miles and pulled into a gravel parking lot on the side of the road. There was a truck parked there already and I wondered for a moment or two if I should move on. The last thing I wanted to do on my first solo hunt was charge headlong into a thick bramble of underbrush only to be mistaken for a trophy buck and have my brain removed from my skull by a bleary-eyed hunter who'd been staking his claim to the area since long before dawn. I must have sat for whole minutes, allowing the sky to lighten, before looking back toward the road and noticing a field through a thin stand of trees on the other side. I figured I'd be safe out in the open with my blaze orange hat and vest. Should I be disowned of life and organ, it could only be ruled as homicide as long as my body is found in a field and not in the woods. So, I popped the trunk and began the process of getting ready.

When I first began fly-fishing on my own for steelhead in the rivers and creeks that feed Lake Erie, I came to appreciate the little rituals of preparing for a jaunt into the outdoors. I liked sitting on the lip of my trunk and pulling my waders over the fleece pants and wool socks I wore for warmth. I liked checking the pockets of my wading vest or waterproof jacket to be sure I had the flies I needed for the day. I liked the process of assembling and threading line through the eyelets of my nine-and-a-half-foot, eight-weight steelhead rod and double-checking the trunk to be sure nothing was left behind. It felt like I was getting ready for a contest, a gladiatorial struggle that I'm sure, had I played high school football, would have been similar to the pregame ritual of an athlete. It's like putting on the gear was a way of taking off the world I was trying to escape in order to get myself ready to trek into someplace else.

I had a similar feeling when getting ready for that first hunt with Uncle Mark, Tom, and my cousins. My hands had trembled the first time I assembled the Winchester in the field—or very near it—and once I had made sure all the tags were pulled off my new vest and hat, I enjoyed putting them on. It's ridiculous, I know, to take such a thing seriously, but I did. And I was taking it seriously as I carefully arranged the items in my trunk on my first solo trip.

First, I checked the pockets of my hunting vest to be sure I had the right shells. Then I untied and retied the laces of my Bean boots until they felt comfortable without feeling constrained. I was careful when I opened the gun case and slid the barrels onto the action and fitted the forearm into its proper place with the satisfying *thwap* of Play-Doh being pancaked onto a table. I was all set to go. I just had to use the key on the ring holding my car and office keys to unlock the trigger guard—a medieval-looking contraption that locks around a gun's trigger in order to prevent, say, little kids from being able to fire the weapon—and I would be on my way. Key goes in lock, does not turn. Well, it budges a little, but it's not really going anywhere. I struggled with it for a half hour, feeling like a monkey trying to get into a jar of peanut butter. How could I not open a lock? It's like I was back in middle school trying to get my locker open before Stephanie Hagan walked by and left me speechless. It was one of the cruel ironies of my younger life that the girl whose locker was always next to mine, who always sat in front of me in homeroom and who, I'm quite sure, was made by angels out of clouds and sunshine was the one person to whom I most wanted to speak yet was completely unable to because I was, in short, terrified at the mere thought of doing so. Every time she walked by, my palms began to sweat, my heart began to race, and the numbers on my combination lock became blurred and illegible. Even the simplest of fine-motor skills were out of the question, something that continued until high school when she started dating football players and I settled into life as a burgeoning band geek.

My heart pounded, my palms sweated, as I fumbled with the key, turning it a micron to the right and to the left. It wasn't just about having come all the way to the state park and possibly not being able to hunt; it was about the gun. I really didn't want to break or scratch it, and I certainly had no intention of handing it back to my dad with a stuck lock and a clean barrel.

I grew increasingly desperate as the second half hour came to a close and I still hadn't made any progress. I began sorting through options—call a locksmith. How the hell do you get ahold of a locksmith? And would one come all the way out here? I could call the police, but then I realized they probably aren't too keen on the idea of unlocking a gun for a guy who has no proof that it is his. They'd probably think I was nuts. Besides, this was a powder-coated steel lock, what were they going to do? Pull it apart with that little jimmy they use to open car doors? No. I decided I was on my own.

In a lot of ways, it was shockingly like an experience I had

had in first grade. I was trying to be so cool. So fashionable, or as fashionable as a first grader can be mindful of being. I wanted to impress, to show off. After all, I had left, moved away, and now I was back. Growing up in north-central Wisconsin, you don't often get in early on trends. Not in the mid-'80s anyway. With the Internet, Facebook, and MTV, it's a little easier. Geography isn't the barrier it used to be. Now, you see something on the Web or in a magazine and you hop on Amazon to buy it for yourself. But, back then, things took time to percolate and proliferate. Having gone away and come back, I felt a certain need to share the cultural wonders my journey had afforded me. I was feeling a bit like a nineteenth-century explorer having headed off into the great unknown of the Indian countryside. Upon return, that explorer felt a need to share in the things he had seen and experienced. It was his right, but also his duty.

Parachute pants were my duty. I had to share them.

They were red—as was the custom—with all manner of zippers and snaps stitched at exotic angles into the fabric. They made a very slight swishing sound as I walked and had the bonus curiosity of being convertible pants. With the simple unzipping and snapping of a couple of closures, they would change from pants to shorts and vice versa. How novel. How deliciously cosmopolitan. There could be little question what I might wear on my first day of school. That had been decided the moment they were purchased, the instant I realized we were moving back to Wisconsin.

When the bell rang for recess, I remember my classmates pushing the limits of the no-running rule to get outside while I sidled at a manly gait. No rush. Recess waits for cool like this.

I'm not sure if you've ever encased your body in cheap nylon, but there's a certain lack of breathability that can grow rather uncomfortable. In fact, wrap your legs in cheap nylon and step out onto a sun-warmed blacktop playground and it feels as if you have put your legs into a steam room and are letting them parboil in advance of a good roasting. It took perhaps five minutes for my legs to get uncomfortably warm and sweaty. One boy, a neighbor, noticed my discomfort and began making fun of me. *Well*, I thought, *I'll show him*. I asked the recess monitor for permission to use the restroom and went back into the school with the intention of unzipping my highly engineered pants for greater outdoor comfort. I found a first-floor boys' room and took my place in a stall. I tugged on the zipper and it moved perhaps two inches before stopping. I tugged again, nothing. Again, again, and again. Still, it would not move. I tried to reverse the process, put the legs back on and, still, nothing. Tiny beads of sweat began falling from my forehead as I worked the zipper to no avail. More than ninety minutes of stricken effort passed before I was found in the restroom by a teacher.

I guess this early incident proves my stubbornness; after nearly an hour and a half of wrestling with the gun lock, I was feeling crestfallen and ready to quit. Over the last hour or so, as the sun had risen fully and the world around me had come awake, it had sounded like a war zone. In almost every direction, the sounds of shotgun bursts could be heard. *Boom. Boom-boom. Boom-boom-boom-boom.* Somewhere, not too far off, pheasants' wings were beating their last strokes. Hunters were filling their game bags, maybe even some of the same hunters I had driven past. It's ridiculous to the point of insanity that I would persist as I had, turning the key the same fraction of an inch, back and forth, back and forth. I'd found a small can of WD-40 in my trunk and tried to lubricate the lock into submission, careful not to get any on the wood stock of the gun. I was just about ready to call no joy, to bug out and go home with my head hung between my legs when, in a last-ditch effort, I opened the glove box in my car and saw there my trustiest, oldest pocketknife. It was a rubber-handled, one-hand-open Buck knife with a half-serrated blade that locked and could be released with a thumb switch. I'd bought it when I was working at the backpacking store/fly-fishing shop right out of college. I'd carried it with me every time I'd ever gone into the outdoors except for the trip to Iowa. It was in my pocket when I'd wrecked that six-wheeler and had cut away more tangled fly line than I care to acknowledge. *What the hell?*

I opened the blade and, holding the trigger guard steady so that I didn't bend or loosen it from the gun, jammed the tip into the key slot. At first, I twisted lightly, gently, hoping that by some miracle the lock might pick itself. But as seconds ticked by, I got a little more aggressive. Just under a minute after I had first inserted the blade tip into the keyhole, I took a deep breath and said "screw it, it's only money if I break something," knowing full well that it was about much more than money—my dad's trust, his property, the fact that we didn't have any spare cash to fix a gun I broke out of pure desperation—and twisted the handle as hard as I could.

Jackpot.

The tip of my trusty knife snapped off, but so too did the outer layer of the lock. I pulled broken pieces out and without thinking jammed the knife back into the now gaping lock. I twisted hard again and, again, a layer of the locking mechanism snapped. Three more times and there was nothing left of the lock. I jammed the knife in again and twisted the actual bolt of the lock and both pieces fell away harmlessly from the unmarred, still factory-new trigger. I could have cried. I felt relieved. It was and will be a very proud moment in my life—when I successfully picked a lock meant to keep anyone but the owner of a gun from firing it. I was both MacGyver and, well, kind of a criminal. It felt awesome. My knife may have sacrificed its proud tip, but the little boy struggling in the bathroom to unzip his parachute pants was, at long last, vindicated.

With half my morning gone, I quickly reassembled the gun, which I had taken apart while working on the lock, threw a water bottle into the game bag on my vest, and headed across the road to the field I had seen through the trees. A sign at the road informed me that the field was the property of the park, available for hunting, and used as a location for dog training. It was fairly large, perhaps the size of three soccer fields and ringed on three sides by trees. To the north and south, the stands of trees were fairly narrow, just twenty or thirty yards deep. To the east, the trees demarcated the barrier between field and forest, and along the western edge ran a fence line dividing the public park from a neighboring farm where three hundred acres or more of corn had already been harvested. An open grass field was not, in and of itself, a great location to find pheasant. But the pheasant is a bird that lives near its food—corn—and cover, the trees.

One of the first things the instructors teach about the act of hunting in hunter's safety is to have a plan. Right after the angry and paranoid rants about left-wing conspiracies to remove the trigger fingers from all members of the NRA, like Tom Berenger in that movie *Sniper,* they stress the importance of laying out your moves ahead of time. It's about safety, but also about game management. Wild animals tend to run away from the people stomping through their turf, so you want to be strategic in your approach. You want to push the game in a consistent direction and cover the hunting area efficiently. Given that I was by myself and I didn't have the services of a dog, this was going to be extremely difficult. Pheasant are more likely to run for cover at the first sign of trouble than to conveniently pop up in front of you. They have to feel really threatened in order to do that, and as I weaved my way around this large open space like a sailor two days into shore leave, I quickly came to the realization that I was presenting no such threat. I could have been right on top of a pheasant, standing toe-to-claw with one and I might not have known it. There could have been dozens of them standing just along the edge of the woods, cackling at me, making jokes about the fluffy man in the silly orange hat who looked lost in an area the size of a small strip mall parking lot.

I thought that working along the edge of the field, where the grass was taller and dotted with thorny brambles would give me the best shot at scaring one up. And so I walked three U-shaped circuits along the edge of the woods, hoping a bird would be nice enough to sacrifice itself for the benefit of my plate, ego, and this book. Not a single pheasant raised its claw. Perhaps, I thought, I needed to go deeper into the woods and work my way back toward the field. Maybe that would scare a bird into the open. So I, well, *plunged* is the only word for it, into the dense underbrush that was thick with thorny bushes and low-hanging branches, crouching down low at the waist while taking comically high-kneed steps to clear low obstacles, all the while trying to protect my gun and avoid putting any scratches into it. Eventually I got deep enough into the trees that the ground cover got thin and patchy and I was able to stand up in a small clearing the size of a suburban garage.

That's when I heard it—a cacophony of gunfire that sounded as if it were coming from just behind the nearest tree. Two shots, three, four, eight in rapid succession and over the span of about two seconds. I instinctively, by reflex and without thinking, ducked down onto my knees, cradling my gun and covering my head like a kid in a tornado drill. I don't think I've ever moved so fast in my life or with so much purpose. Sebastian Junger, a favorite author of mine and, in my opinion, the second coming of Hemingway, wrote scientifically and eloquently about this kind of reaction in his book *War*. In the book, he embeds with a forward operating army unit in the Korengal Valley of Afghanistan. He writes about the caveman instinct that takes over when a human brain detects a sudden, loud, and potentially threatening noise. The pupils dilate, the muscles contract and take the body into a crouching position, the hands instinctively cover the head. A seasoned soldier trains his body to react differently, to stand in the face of this base instinct. Hunting in a group, I didn't react when the guns went off up and down the line to fell my pheasant. I expected it. I understood the context. And sitting in my car, hearing the pops off in the distance, it was more of a curiosity than a threat. But alone in the woods, believing as I did that there was no one around, I thought I was under attack.

A couple more shots rang out, and this time I could tell they weren't coming from the south or west, where most of the shots were that I'd heard while struggling with the lock. They were to the north and not by much. It took a second or two to realize that there was another field through the trees to the north and that there must be a group of hunters there who had found some pheasant. My heart rate slowed and I felt my muscles relax. I stood up and immediately thought about that section in Junger's book, adding to his clinical description of the fight-or-flight response another indicator—a single drop of pee in my pants.

I got my bearings and walked through the trees toward where I had heard the shots. You want to be careful sneaking up on hunters when you're alone and unexpected. Blaze orange may do wonders to identify a human over a deer, but it doesn't make you bulletproof. I walked through the trees until I saw six orange figures a couple hundred yards distant. They seemed to be gathering together, I imagined, to look at the birds one or several of them had just shot. I wanted to strut over there, shotgun slung over my arm, and ask, with a manly sniff, "So how we doing today, boys?" But I decided against it. I didn't want to be *that* guy, the computer club president who thinks his job as the water boy makes him equal in physical and social stature to the football team. And, perhaps worse than being seen as a nuisance, I dreaded the off chance that they might invite me to join them. It had taken a bit of courage to join Mark and my cousins for a hunt. The idea of joining up with strangers having never shot anything or having any real, firsthand knowledge of what I was doing mortified me. It would be just my luck that a bird would rise and, apart from doing something idiotic like forgetting to take my safety off, I would do something dangerous like going full-on Dick Cheney and shooting one of the men in the face.

This is not the kind of grounded perspective my dad might have. He'd see a group of experienced hunters offering to take me with them—even though I never got close enough for them to actually do so—as a great way to learn. I saw it as an opportunity to embarrass myself and possibly maim some well-meaning stranger. No, definitely better to get a little more experience on my own. It would be better for everyone involved.

After an hour of fruitless tramping, I came to the realization that I really wanted a dog. A dog would be entertaining. A dog would make this whole process more enjoyable and—dare I consider?—significantly increase the likelihood of actually getting something. But more than just wanting a dog, I wanted Quigley. Quigley was my mom's gift to my dad on his fiftieth birthday, a purebred liver-and-white English springer spaniel and quite possibly the most adorable puppy I have ever laid eyes on. I named him after Tom Selleck's character in one of my dad's favorite movies, *Quigley Down Under,* in which an American cowboy finds himself in Australia dispatching corrupt cattle ranchers dispassionately with the assistance of his trusty Sharps black-powder rifle, eventually riding off into the sunset with a beautiful, if abused, girl played by Laura San Giacomo.

Dad loved that movie. In part it was because Selleck played a red-blooded, sealed-lipped hero, the kind only a person who grew up idolizing John Wayne could really appreciate. And in part because of the gun. The Sharps is one of those big, heavy long-range guns that nearly wiped out the American buffalo. But with its hexagonal barrel and peep sight, it just looked so cool. I've had the opportunity to fire one in my life and while the experience was loud, painful, and completely without accuracy for me, for Dad it was the equivalent of dressing up like Luke Skywalker and playing with a real-life light saber.

Mom and I picked up Quigley from the store where she bought him as a surprise gift. He rode on my lap as we drove home and when we went inside, Mom ordered Dad to close his eyes then brought Quigley around and set him on Dad's lap.

"Nope, uh-uh, no way," Dad said, holding the puppy up as if it had just laid a steaming pile on his lap. "No way do I want a dog, take it back."

It was one of the only times I remember my dad ever being anything less than completely gracious when receiving a gift.

You could present him with a sweater made out of hairballs spit up by a feral cat and he would at least say thank you before throwing it out. But not with Quigley. He did not want a dog and that was final . . . for about twenty minutes anyway.

English springers are hunting dogs, and Dad always said he was going to work on making that dog one. But as the years wore on, Quigley's training consisted more of waiting for a nod from Dad before flipping a cracker off his nose and swallowing it whole. Quigley was Dad's buddy and a great dog. True, as a puppy, he chewed up countless doors and Mom got more new rugs in those early years than perhaps any other point in her life, but eventually Quigs settled down and even came to live with me for a while. In college and for a year or two after, I drove a Jeep Wrangler and it got to the point where Quigley didn't need to be leashed or asked to hop in the backseat when I was going somewhere. He even lived with Rebecca and I after we got married, but our small apartment combined with some health problems that made him throw up on the carpet our newborn would soon be crawling on dictated that he had to go. We did our best to get him healthy, to retrain him, to get him used to his new environment. But, try as he did to improve his behavior, there was little that could be done for his health. I took him to the animal shelter on Good Friday 2005 and had him put down. I had not contemplated seriously getting another dog since, until I found myself wandering aimlessly through the woods trying to figure out just how in the hell I was going to scare a pheasant into becoming a target and, eventually, dinner.

I decided to let the field rest a bit and wait until the group of hunters in the adjacent one cleared out before making another serious attempt, so I wandered deeper into the woods toward where I thought, if my memory of the map I'd seen on the ODNR website a couple days earlier served me well, I would run into a river. Fifty yards or so in, I came across a trail marked with blue blazes and a sign with a figure on horseback. I followed it for a while and the walking was easier. I didn't have to duck under branches or step over thorns—just the occasional bit of mud that, from its color and smell, I suspected to be crushed horse dung—eventually coming to that river. I rested my gun against a tree and peed against another, feeling manly on so many levels it was difficult to comprehend. I had a good long look at the river, tried to conjure up some profound thoughts, and eventually succumbed to an odd blend of determination and anger. It was pure bloodlust. What the hell was I doing having a little stroll along a horse trail? I would never feed my family this way, never accomplish my goal of becoming a hunter.

*C'mon, Heimbuch, get your head in the game,* I thought, though I had to admit that just being in the woods was pretty great. Dad used to talk about getting to a deer blind early, long before the sun comes up, and being there to experience the woods "waking up." The sounds of songbirds, the rustle of leaves, the branches groaning in a light breeze. He was and is on to something there. Those few minutes I spent just standing there, just being, were so peaceful. It's a shame I nearly ruined it with my urgent need for blood.

I worked the field I started on for another half hour, seeing nothing larger than a starling but mounting my gun with every perceived movement on the off chance it would be a pheasant or a grouse, which I had decided to settle for if need be. I could see through the trees that the group of hunters had cleared out of the field to the north and made my way over there, hoping to find a pheasant emerging from cover and picking up some sloppy seconds. I remained on high alert, kicking every clump of long grass, working the field in a zigzag pattern as if I were pushing a lawn mower over it and realizing, with increasing urgency, how badly I wished I had a dog.

I was happy to discover yet another field north of this second one and crossed a narrow but alarmingly deep ditch to get to it. When I pushed through a thin stand of trees and emerged into this third field, I'd swear I heard a choir sing in one of those moments of epic discovery. It was pheasant Valhalla, the holy grail of hunting grounds: tall grass chest high with two rows of corn planted along the woods to the east and heading north; the private cornfield to the west; and breaks in the tall grass to allow for reconnoiter and rest. It was as if everything I had read in the previous year, everything that had been described to me as the ideal habitat for upland game had been made real. My mouth actually began to water with anticipation.

I could hear scurrying through the grass as I moved forward at a snail's pace. Believing them to be grounded birds, I tried to follow them, keeping my gun held firmly in both hands in front of me and my eyes pivoting from side to side. For forty minutes, I was hyperalert. I knew, just simply knew, that at any moment a pheasant was going to pop up and I would finally become a hunter. I worked up a sweat and unzipped the fleece jacket I was wearing beneath my vest. I paused several times to take long pulls from my bottle of water. I gnashed my teeth and muttered unkind things about not having a dog. And, eventually, I ran out of time. I covered only a section of this perfect field and probably not all that well. I needed to get home to see my wife and kids. We had things to do. Errands to run, homework projects, and regular weekend chores. With great hesitation, I ran out of ways to justify staying longer. I knew that eventually

I would come across something, if only I could spend the day. But I couldn't.

I made a vocal vow to return the next weekend and go straight to this third field—no screwing around with horse trails—and I'd already taken care of the trigger lock, so I wouldn't waste any time there either. As I was walking along the fence line back toward my car, my brain registered some movement in the trees separating the first and second fields to my left. I snapped my gun to my shoulder and flipped the safety off, focusing on the point in the low brambles where the rustling came from. I wondered if I should yell "who's there?" or simply wait, and, just as I flipped the safety back on to walk over and investigate, a rabbit took three steps out into the clear. My general hunting license allows me to shoot rabbit. Many upland hunters write about rabbit as an unintended benefit of hunting birds. They can be quite tasty, too, from what I understand. I'd read about them in my book on the field dressing and butchering of upland game. This was the first opportunity I'd had since the safety incident back in Iowa to take legitimate game. And it was right there. I would have had to try to miss in order to miss. I flipped the safety back off and drew a bead on the thing, which was just sitting there, waiting.

I was just about to shoot when I thought about Rebecca and the kids. Had we lived in a place and time that required me to hunt for sustenance, they wouldn't have thought twice about eating a rabbit. But we don't and my wife and Jack, the eldest, are picky eaters. They had agreed only reluctantly to try pheasant and that was because I had assured them it was so much like chicken. A rabbit? Well, that's Easter and Bugs Bunny and hours spent walking through the biggest park in our suburb looking for them and squirrels and ducks. I didn't think I could justify it to them, and I wondered if Jack might think of me as a monster if I were to throw Pete Cottontail on the grill. I had long enough to ponder these and other things, like the possibility of simply lying to him, before I decided not to take the shot.

I was returning, sadly, empty-handed. I got home less than an hour later and Rebecca called to say she and the kids were on their way home from church.

"Did you get one?" she asked.

"Nope, didn't even see one, but I think I've found the perfect spot for next time."

"What the hell? When are you going to get something?" she said, an air of playful frustration in her tone.

"I had a chance to shoot a rabbit. You didn't want me to do that, did you?"

"Well, you better shoot something soon," she said with a hint of disdain. "I mean if we had to rely on you, at the rate you're going, we'd starve to death."

*That's it*, I thought, *the next time I go out, something is going to die.*

# 18

## LUST

Another December weekend and I'm up long before dawn. My brother-in-law and his girlfriend were visiting for a couple of days, fresh from winter finals and delaying as long as they could going home to be with their parents. I could and can identify. I used to love being among a very few students in my college town. Not having to wait for a pool table or a drink, having the run of the cafeteria. But also just delaying that reimmersion into life at home, which can be as shocking, though not nearly refreshing, as jumping from a sauna into a frozen lake. At any rate, I was glad that they were there. Rebecca and I had a party to go to that night and between Christmas and Christmas parties—and the attendant babysitting—this month was already the most expensive of the last year, and it was not, as of then, half over.

So I was up again. The previous weekend had been a good experience, getting out into the woods, feeling my way around the place, and in the days that followed I caught myself drifting off during meetings, imagining what it will feel like to finally and gloriously get my first bird. I had used a couple of lunch breaks that week to watch YouTube videos on how to clean and cook a rabbit, just in case. Rabbit wasn't my ideal in terms of game, but I figured that if I didn't come home with some protein and quickly, my patient wife would begin to assume I was not in fact hunting, but shacking up with someone else. There's only so many times a guy can come home with stories of near misses and forgotten safeties before his wife starts thinking two things: (1) He is an idiot, not a real man. A real man wouldn't flinch in the face of opportunity. He would seize it and come home to be rewarded with admiration and affection. And (2) He is not actually hunting at all, but cheating or, worse and more pathetic, doing something like playing fantasy football with his buddies. Rebecca was not quite to the point of assuming either of these yet, but when I bent down to kiss her cheek before slipping out of our still-dark bedroom, she muttered, "This time come home with something, will you?," before rolling back over and going to sleep.

The weather had changed a bit over the previous week. The previous week it had been chilly, but on this morning it was downright cold. The temperature always drops a bit the farther you get away from the city, but as I headed north out of town, I watched the thermometer readout on my dashboard drop from twenty-six degrees to eighteen before I parked in the same place I had a week earlier. This time there was no problem getting the gun put together, no problem at all. The gravel lot where I left my car was probably a half mile from the field I had discovered at the end of my previous trip, so I stamped my feet and flexed my gloved hands trying to revive feeling in my fingertips as I made a beeline for Bird Valhalla.

My face was thoroughly numb, my fingers burning with the sensation of a million tiny pins being shoved into my skin, like getting angry tattoos from sadomasochists living inside my gloves, when I reached the field. The sun was just cracking the horizon, a slow-moving egg breaking into a pan and I was surprisingly, miraculously, completely alone. Where just a week before there had been parked trucks and flashes of blaze orange in nearby cornfields, there was nothing, no one. I had gotten up early to be sure I could get to Valhalla first, to stake my claim on it, but judging by the complete aloneness, I realized quickly that this had not been necessary. I wouldn't see another soul until nearly ten thirty, and then it would just be a couple of guys in a truck asking if I'd had any luck and, by then, I will have become so accustomed to quiet that the interaction would feel like an intrusion.

Valhalla was everything I had remembered and been quietly fantasizing about all week. Three or four acres of the kind of scrubby grass, winter wheat, and tall brambles that offers a lot of cover for birds, surrounded by a seven- or eight-foot-wide band of millet like a track around a high school football field, offering a steam table buffet for beaked critters. I assume it was planted for the very purpose of giving game birds a place to hang out and eat and make themselves available to be hunted. I made a quick mental note to thank the game warden for this nice little touch if I ever saw him and looked across the field, ringed on two sides by woods, a narrow stand of trees to the south and a dirt road to the west on the other side of which was a harvested cornfield. Lamenting again my complete lack of a canine companion, I contemplated a plan. I could try to zigzag my way up the field working lawn-mower style and hoping to scare something up. Or I could walk up the middle and work my way around. Or I could stand around wasting more time and freezing my ass off trying to decide what to do. I began walking along the millet and fell into a comfortable groove. The sun was up and I could feel my fingers and toes. My face was freezer burned, but I've never really liked my nose anyway, so maybe a little emergency plastic surgery would do me some good.

I walked for a couple of hours around the track of thigh-high grain, ducking occasionally into it or the inner field. I began to understand what Dad was always talking about when he referred to the woods "waking up." From the snapping cold stillness of those moments just before dawn, the field and adjacent woods seemed to change with each passing minute. First the leaves begin to rustle, then the songbirds begin singing their chipper morning tunes. Then the movement starts. The world begins to thaw, and what had been coated in a sheen of matte silver comes to life, the sun a slow drizzle of hot water clearing up the windshield of the world. Jesus, I was beginning to sound like Thoreau. Before I know it I'll be sitting in a stream rubbing mud all over my face and proclaiming the majesty of the potato bug. I'm as romantic as the next guy, as awed by the sight of something beautiful and made by something other than man. I may even catch myself daisy-eyed and dreaming about adventures into the woods, but weepy about a sunrise? Not really, not ever. It must have been the cold or the fact that I hadn't slept well the night before that was warming the chambers of my numb suburban heart. I wondered what it must be like to wake up every day not to the drone of that same oversized alarm clock you've had since college and all the expectations of schedule and responsibility, but to something else. Something more wide open. A life not dictated by all the shit a man has to do to build a career, nurture a marriage, raise some kids who don't end up on America's Most Wanted, and maintain a household. Or perhaps a life where all those things were tied into one. My life at this point felt so fractured, so striated into separate, never-tooverlap streams of need and duty. There was my work life and the hundred or so people involved with it. The meetings, the deadlines, the impatience of wanting to make things go better, run smoother, explore new opportunities and feeling like my hands, my coworkers, and clients simply can't move as fast as my brain, leaving me wrestling with a sense that I could and should be doing better and thus was failing. My fatherhood life and the three kids I was trying awfully hard to spend equal amounts of time with and pay equal attention to. I was getting frustrated a lot. Frustrated about toys not put away. Frustrated at dinners not eaten. Frustrated about having to ask more than once, all the things that go into and along with parenthood. To make it worse, I knew that nothing the kids were doing or not doing was really why I was frustrated. I was frustrated because I hated where we lived and was tired of being the one who had to say, over and over, how lucky we were and hadn't we made it such a long way? And we're almost there. Just be patient. Trying to placate my wife's wants and needs was exhausting and completely artificial, given that I too was frustrated. I really did think we were close—to having a house, to having a yard and a basement, to having the kind of life we grew up with and always wanted for ourselves and our children. Frustrated that we had come such a long way—all the credit card debt and student loan debt and credit counseling and extra work and staying home and late nights writing at Starbucks. I wanted to believe, really believe that it had all been worth something, for something— that things would work out for the best in the end, that the end would come soon, and that the end would really be a new beginning. I knew what I wanted and I couldn't get at it. It's like a bear being put inside of a cage and made to stare at a room service tray piled high with food placed on a table just out of paw's reach. I wasn't sure how long I could claw at the air and keep up hope that one day I would reach the jar of peanut butter.

I felt ridiculous, circling this seven-hundred-yard track over and over, but, to be honest, I didn't know what else to do. If there were birds to be had, I figured, they were in here where they had cover and food. The walking started to feel good, freeing. So it didn't matter how ridiculous I felt, I also felt good. The longer I walked, the more attention I paid to the details around me and the less I thought about the next year's taxes, the meetings I had coming up that week, and whether or not Dylan would ever eat spinach. It was like tuning out by paying attention to something else. I listened to the low cheeping of small songbirds and the creaking of the trees as they swayed in the gentle breeze. I watched the field go from a jumbled mass of brown vegetation to a complicated and diverse ecosystem of varied and distinctive natural architecture—the straight and tall chest-high grass that was almost yellow on the south end; the single tree with bent branches that almost touched the ground in the center; the short grass that looked like it had been mowed, though never watered. I began seeing things in the world around me—opportunities, hiding places, bent or broken branches that led me to believe something had been there. I saw small, narrow stars in the mud, like the Mercedes emblem and came to realize they were footprints left by birds after the last rain. The more I tuned out of my own head, the more attuned I became. In a life where sensory overload is the norm, where every turn is met by a billboard, every thought accompanied by a song pumped in on my iPod, I had forgotten all about what it meant to just be outside. I had forgotten what I had learned as a kid running around in the woods behind my parents' house—that when you are out of doors, you are never without something to watch, something to hear, something to pay attention to; you just have to be willing to notice it.

I had also forgotten about the amazingly free feeling of stopping where you are, unzipping and relieving yourself in the fresh air. It's one of the central blessings of being a man and one of those things I imagine will be as satisfying at eighty-two as it was at twelve. I didn't even move to a tree, just stood where I was, unloaded my gun, unzipped, and let fly. I believe I even whistled while I was doing it. How can anyone be worried or stressed when whistling while whizzing in the wild? It's impossible, I assure you.

After my brief interlude, I realized in a half-dazed sort of way that there were only two things to complain about. The first was an absolute fucking lack of birds and the second was a bunching of my socks under the arches of my feet. It had started a little annoying and worked its way up to a lot annoying and a little bit painful.

They don't exactly put benches on hunting grounds, so I once again unloaded my gun and sat in the grass between the woods and millet on the north end of the field to pull up my socks and retie my shoes. I didn't realize it would feel so good, but after five or six miles of walking in the cold, sitting was something bordering upon orgasmic in terms of sheer physical pleasure. So, I sat. It wasn't like I had much else to do. I still had time before I needed to leave, and I had given up on the idea that I'd get a bird an hour before. Maybe I'd find a rabbit. Maybe. It wasn't that I was ambivalent about it. I wanted to kill something that morning. It was just that I was out there. I was feeling pretty good and, on balance, that was the most I could really ask for with a clean conscience. I sat for twenty minutes or so, taking sips from the water bottle I had been carrying in my game bag and trying to decide the point of diminishing returns between the joy of sitting and the quickly plummeting temperature of my ass. Eventually, the ass won out and I rose, noticeably stiffer, pulled two shells from my pocket and dropped them into the empty chambers of the gun and snapped it closed. I took one step, one tiny step toward the millet, and the quiet morning air was fractured by the sound of five tiny helicopters blasting off from where I was about to step.

That's when it happened. A flush and whoosh of activity as birds sprang out before me from the millet. My heart jumped, my hands moved by instinct, raising the gun to my shoulder and flicking the safety forward. There were five of them. One went to the right along the woods, one took a sharp left, and another buzzed right by my head and straight behind me. The other two took off at an angle somewhere between twelve and one o'clock. I fired—*cli-boom*—and the first shot missed though I had no idea in which direction since I had pulled the trigger before my face was flush against the stock of the gun. I may have just missed or I may have missed by fifteen feet. I have no idea. I was looking out down the barrel when I pulled the trigger a second time. The birds were pretty far away by this point, but I knew they weren't pheasant and thought perhaps they were ruffed grouse. A little smaller and more blandly colored than a cock pheasant, a ruffed grouse is as good a game bird as any and usually very hard to flush. They like to run—even more than pheasant do—so getting them up in the air without a dog is pretty tough. And they're fast. Really fast. The way they took off, it was like they had rockets in their keisters.

I picked out the bottom of the two birds for no reason other than I thought I saw it more clearly. My shot was on target, so pulling the trigger, I expected the thing to drop like a stone into the western edge of Valhalla. I'm pretty sure I hit it, since the grouse dipped a bit in its flight path, but it didn't fall. Shit. I jammed my hand into my vest pocket to pull out some more shells, flipping my gun open like Schwarzenegger in *Terminator 2* and not paying any attention to the spent shells as they ejected and flew smoking past my right temple. I slammed the new shells in and snapped the gun closed as I raised it to my shoulder in one fluid motion. I got my bearings back on the gun and knew the birds were too far away, but my adrenaline was pumping like a swollen river and I couldn't help but squeeze off two more shots.

The smell of nitrocellulose hung heavy around me, that tangy, sweet smoke heavier than the still-crisp morning air. My heart was pounding through my chest, my eyes were wider, and every sound seemed somehow louder, more distinct. Everything I mentioned before about the calm of being in the woods? Yeah, forget all that stuff. That was nice, but I could get those feelings by going for a walk through the neighborhood or listening to a James Taylor album in a dark room. This, this jacked-up rush—a combination of awareness and vigilance, fear and focus—this was what had been missing in my life. I could get used to this. I needed this. Sometime over the last decade of routine and under the constant if relatively slight crush of financial and familial pressure, the world had become a numb and colorless drone, my life like a slight case of tinnitus persistently buzzing in my ear. This new thing—this was a rush. Not an adrenaline surge like the kind you get when you're walking down a dark staircase and miss the bottom step, but an awakening of purpose. Cliché as it may be, I felt suddenly somehow more alive than I had just a moment or two before those birds flooded out of the low bushes. I wanted more.

I popped two more shells into my gun, pausing to notice that finally, after nearly a year of having it in my possession, I had a reason to clean it, looked forward to cleaning it in fact. Obviously, I hadn't definitively killed anything. Not as far as I knew anyway. But I thought maybe I had winged the bottom of the two birds and so I walked off in the general direction they had flown to find out, stalking my prey. To my surprise, the rush held. I walked through the thick brambles and tall grass, down along the dirt road fully aware of my own awareness. I was looking for something—anything—that might indicate there was a wounded bird somewhere near me. After nearly half an hour, I hadn't found anything, though I had managed to put a ring of sweat around the inside of the blaze orange stocking cap on my head and cuts on my upper thighs from walking blithely through the thornbushes, eventually coming to the realization that if I had hit the bird, it was gone and I could not have hurt it that bad or else I would have found it. It was right about this time that those two guys pulled up in their SUV and asked how I was doing.

"Not bad," I panted. "Flushed a few grouse a little while ago and thought I might have hit one."

"Probably tough to do without a dog," said the man in the passenger seat. He was younger than the one driving, and I assumed they were a father and son.

"Yes, sir, it is," I said with a touch more enthusiasm than what would have been acceptably cool.

"Yeah," said the younger man, who, with some further inspection, wasn't that young but probably about my age, "came all the way out here to try and work my dog." He pointed his thumb toward a rear window where the slimy snout of a spaniel was leaving streaks on the glass.

"I'll tell you what," I said. "I'm on my way out. Give me five minutes to get out of here and you can feel free to take this field." It might seem like I was cowering somehow or giving in, but in truth, I wanted to go explore the woods and look for other fields. The longer my fruitless search for the phantom bird went on, the more convinced I was that I could and should shoot a rabbit. I can't explain it other than to say that it was kind of like Vegas. You go to Vegas and on the first day you have grand visions of running a poker table. But you get over to the poker tables and you realize you're not a high roller. *What the hell?*, you think. *Poker isn't really my thing; I'll go clean up at black-jack.* But the female Asian blackjack dealer separates you from most of your money over the course of a couple of days and then you're at the airport. Your flight is leaving in twenty minutes and you are dead-set convinced that you were meant to win something while you are there. So you head to the slot machines looking for something, anything to justify your trip. You have to win. You've abandoned the idea of a big score at the tables. You'll settle for five dollars in sticky nickels. Anything. That's how I was feeling. I came looking for pheasant, but there were none around. I stumbled onto some grouse and took a shot. I won a couple of hands, but ultimately gave up and moved on. Now, I needed a score, something to bring home, to slake this lust that's awoken in me. Rabbit, of which I have seen many in the wild and which are conveniently bereft of wings, would be fine with me.

"Are you sure?" asked the older man, speaking across his son. "We don't want to kick you out."

"Not a problem," I said. "On my way out."

"Thanks so much," he said.

"Yeah, thank you," said the younger man. "And be careful. I know how hard it is to play dog."

I nodded and headed back in the general direction of my car. I was twenty yards away and fully engrossed in the thought of shooting a rabbit before I understood his pun. Following the horse path I had noticed the previous week, I descended into the woods looking for rabbits where I had seen them. The rabbit shot was the toughest to hit and the bane of my time spent on the L.L.Bean range. To simulate the bouncing gait of a rabbit, a clay pigeon was thrown across the ground on its side. It would pick up speed and bounce every time it hit a pebble or an uneven clump of mud. Throughout the day of shooting, I think I may—maybe—have hit one. So I was trying to remember what the instructors had said about moving with the target as I came to the place where rabbits had been the previous Sunday. But the more I thought, I realized that the rabbit I had seen stayed largely still when I walked up to it. In fact, I've walked up on hundreds of the critters while hiking in the city park with Jack and Dylan and, usually, you can get pretty damned close before they scurry off into the underbrush. *I can hit a rabbit,* I thought. *This is going to be easy.*

I spent another hour trudging through the woods, my boots sinking into the muck and mud as the air warmed and the ground melted into a mire of slop. My buzz was wearing off. I was coming down, and, try as I did to convince myself to remain alert, my attention was waning. I was pretty well done for the day. I climbed back out of the woods and crossed the road to where my car was parked. I don't know how I had missed it the week before or even earlier that morning, but I noticed a trail running south from the small parking lot. Or, more precisely, a wide avenue of grass cleared through the trees. It was as wide as a one-lane road and manicured as if it had been mowed fairly recently. Holding on to the notion that I might yet find something to propel lead in the general direction of, I decided to take a little stroll. This part of the park, a promenade really, felt less like hunting than it did an easy meandering. I followed the manicured path for about two-thirds of a mile until it opened on an enormous clearing. Near the end of the trail, there was a sign indicating that this was a dedicated dove hunting area and that the season was officially over. There were four or five acres of grass and about two of the frozen, dried hulls of sunflowers bent against the weight of their own decay. I followed a tree line down a gradual hill and, peering through the branches, was amazed by what I saw.

Stretching in every direction were fields of tall grasses and reeds bigger than me nicely quartered off into manageable one-acre sections. There must have been sixteen of them, all calling out to me: "Craig! Craig! Come walk through me! There are pheasant in me and I want you to shoot them!" If the decidedly smaller field I had spent the morning tromping through was Bird Valhalla, this was the Playboy Mansion, Disneyworld, and the Vatican all rolled into one. It also looked like the kind of place where deer hang out, which made me glad I hadn't strolled this way the week before on the last day of rifle season. The vegetation was dense, but not all that hard to walk through and far enough away from the woods to mean there weren't a lot of predator species—owls and hawks—around to drive the pheasant off. Low-hung grains meant food was plentiful, and the low areas held ankle-deep water that I thought might be attractive to any species choking down a diet composed of raw muesli.

I was already out of time and as badly as I wanted to tromp through there and reignite my lust for the hunt, I had to go. Walking back to the car, I promised myself that it didn't matter how many dishes I had to wash, how many diapers I had to change or *Twilight* movies I had to endure, I was coming back the next day to hunt this ground. My first bird was in there, waiting. I just knew it.

# 19

## KARMA

It turned out that convincing my wife to let me get up early and go hunting a second day in a row was not nearly as hard as I had imagined it would be. I had tried to convince her to be excited about my near miss when I got home the day before, but explaining to someone who is probably not that interested to begin with what a rush feels like is like trying to explain the nuances of Twitter to blind octogenarians—they may understand what you're saying, but they just don't get it. Rebecca has never been impressed by the process. She hates the drive on vacation and doesn't particularly care about the progress I've made over the last decade with regard to cleaning up after myself. She wants results. She wants to be at the beach, not on the way to the beach. She wants no crumbs on the counter after I make a sandwich. She won't be impressed by the fact that there are fewer than there used to be.

Believe it or not, this is one of the things I love most about her. She gets shit done. She makes sure I get shit done. I tend to get lost in the process, to take the long view. We may not be where we want to be yet, but we're on the way. I may not be a bestselling writer yet, but it will happen. We may not be at the beach yet, but look at the mountains, aren't they lovely? The answer, from her, is always no. If she gave a shit about the mountains, we would be going to the mountains for our vacation. She wants the sun, the sand, a drink with a little umbrella, and to be out of the damned car.

This can be tough sometimes, especially when I really am trying but just can't seem to get something done. I hate it, for instance, when I'm working on something and have to step away for a moment to do something with the kids, go to the bathroom, or take a phone call. It always seems like that's the exact moment she decides to check in on me. I'll be midway through the dishes, sink filled with bubbles, counters wet, and dishwasher open. I'll run in to the boys' room to remind them about something or another and she'll be working on the computer in our room. I won't be away for thirty seconds when I hear her call my name.

"Craig!"

"Yes, dear?"

"Um, were you planning on finishing this?"

"Yes, I just had to step away."

"Look, I appreciate that you're trying, but if you're just going to leave a mess, I'll do it myself."

"But I just had to step away for a minute. I am going to finish it, I swear."

"Never mind," she'll say without anger, but loaded with frustration. "I'll do it."

"No," I'll say. "Please just let me finish."

Soon, I'm begging to finish the dishes and trying to convince her that I had a good reason to step away, even if I'm having a hard time, at the moment, remembering what it was. I think it's because Rebecca is such a focused person. People always talk about moms being multitaskers, and they are; she is. When it comes to the kids, she can be in three places at once. It's really pretty amazing. But when it comes to anything other than the kids and their immediate needs, her focus is singular. She can only pay attention to the TV or to me, not both. I annoy her when we're at restaurants and am able—in fact, am incapable of preventing myself from being able—to listen to and follow not only our conversation but the ones going on at the tables around us. I also have a bit of a wandering mind. There are times when I will be in the middle of dishes or doing laundry or any number of other household tasks and find that whole minutes have passed and I'm still wiping the same dish, ironing the same sleeve, vacuuming the same spot. Her mind is linear, mine is tangential. Yet it somehow works for us.

So when I told her that I needed to go back out for a second straight morning, missing breakfast, making beds, and, possibly, church, I was prepared to argue about the need for me to do so in order to write this book, to fulfill my publishing contract. I was ready to talk about all the nights I spend home with the kids while she goes out with friends or how many Sunday mornings I have brought her breakfast in bed just because I love her. It turned out, I didn't need to.

"Just kill something, will you?" she said as I once again kissed her on the cheek in the predawn darkness. "I mean, seriously. How long is this going to go on?"

I didn't have an answer, just gave her another quick peck and headed back up to my hunting ground.

It was even colder on this morning than it had been the day before, but I hardly noticed. I was too determined, too jacked up on expectations and gas station coffee to care. I swung my car into the gravel lot, tied my boots, threw on my vest, and had my gun put together, loaded, and ready to go in less than a minute. I headed straight down the grassy thoroughfare of a trail toward the bird Playboy Mansion with the kind of intensity a Notre Dame football player has when he slaps that sign hanging in the locker room, PLAY LIKE A CHAMPION TODAY. Hunt like a champion. Hunt like a man. Get this done.

When I returned home empty-handed the previous day—again—Jack scoffed and said, "Dad, I thought you were supposed to be bringing home the bacon." Beneath the innocent condescension and latent Oedipal tone was, I think, genuine disappointment. This was no longer about me and my ego, my book or my career. This was about showing my little boy what it meant to be a man. This was about showing my wife that I could get things done and coming home, chest out, boots dirty, and slapping protein on the table with a caveman grunt.

It's not like I was running through the woods or angrily swinging my gun through the air. But I was walking differently. I was carrying the gun in both hands in a ready position instead of slung over a shoulder or rested in the crook of an elbow. And I scanned the horizon like weather radar, trying to pick up the tiniest movement, the slightest hint that I was not alone. By the time I reached the dead sunflower field, I was on high alert. But it was still kind of dark, the sun hinting at its presence over the horizon like foreplay to an actual day. And cold. Really cold. Like didn't-realize-I-couldn't-feel-my-legs cold. I was undeterred. I marched straight toward the frosted amber fields at the bottom of the hill, cut through the narrow row of trees, and plunged, without hesitation, into the chin-high or higher vegetation.

Now, had I been smart about it, had I been thinking at all with my head and not with my outsized sense that I had something to prove, I would have realized that there was probably no way I was going to flush a bird. It was early and cold, and they were bedded down for the night. The ground was frozen. The wind was crisp. There wasn't a dog breathing down their neck. They had little incentive in this thick cover to move at all, short of me physically stepping directly on them. I wasn't going to scare a bird into rising and trying to make its escape by air and I should have realized that, but like I said, I wasn't thinking really. So I charged headlong into quartered field section after quartered field section making my way south, not taking the time to look before I stepped, just continuing on the same determined clip I use when running into the grocery store for milk on my way home from work.

I guess that's why I didn't notice anything when I stepped into the third acre field of the morning. It was in the southwest corner, near the bottom of the field marked exclusively for hunting dove in warmer weather and the low point of the ground I was hunting. I didn't notice the tiny crunch when I first stepped in and must have been distracted by the tall, reedy grass slapping against my face and coat to notice the crunching as I continued deeper and deeper in. In fact, I didn't notice anything about the ground I was walking on until I was in the center of the acre section and found myself in a small clearing about the size of a hotel Jacuzzi, a place where there were no plants at all.

I paused and checked that I hadn't accidentally knocked the safety off on my gun, catching in my peripheral vision a glint off what should have been soil. I looked around the ground and noticed that I was standing not on rich, midwestern soil, but above it. Somehow, I had stumbled onto a patch of ice and before I could say "oh shit," it started to crack under my girth. Spider fractures ran out from under my L.L.Bean boots and I couldn't move. In every direction and leading off into the brush was ice. If I moved, I thought, I might make things worse. I stood stock-still for a long count of ten, considering my options as the ice beneath my feet continued to crack, fracture, and shift. Because it was cloudy, I had no idea if I was standing on an inch of frozen water or the failing frozen skin of a pond. I snapped open my gun and removed the shells, stuffing them into a pocket on my vest and snapping the gun shut again. If this is some kind of pond, I thought I should try to throw the gun away from me if I went in so that it didn't end up at the bottom. That, I worried, would piss Dad off; also, the idea of walking across cracking ice with a loaded weapon just sounded like one of Arthur's caution-ary tales. I didn't want future hunter's safety students to have to listen to the story about the smart-ass who aced the exam but died from acute dumbassedness before he shot anything.

Gun unloaded and ice continuing to crack, I looked around, trying to decide which way to go. I was standing in almost the exact center of the field and it was hard to tell which way to go because the grass and reeds were so tall. I decided to throw cau-tion to the wind and make a break for it, going back the way I had come. I turned around gently and just as I took my first step, the ice under my back foot gave way and it disappeared with a splash, throwing my weight forward. My left foot lunged forward as my right knee hit the ice and broke through and I was stuck precariously in a deep lunge with my gun slung over my left knee, my right submerged in freezing cold water, and my right foot completely under. The only way out was forward.

I pushed hard with my left foot and pulled my right leg up, balancing myself with the gun pressed against my thigh. I turned to see that the water was only about a foot deep, but it was enough to soak my pants. The boots on the other hand, I must admit, kept my feet completely dry and I shuffled my way back across ice, through the vegetation and back on to solid ground, pissed off and with a cold right thigh.

I had a decision to make: continue on in my quest to bring home my son's bacon or do the smart thing, the thing that would reduce the risk of hypothermia, and head for home. I chose, of course, to forge on.

For the next two hours, I pushed through the thick cover, pausing occasionally to listen for movement and hearing none. It was one of those still mornings. Bright sun glinting off the vestigial frost. Crisp air quiet but for the muted *whoosh* of a gentle breeze through the trees a quarter mile away. I could hear myself breathe, each cloud puff of exhalation sounding like a freight train. My leg, cold at first from the moisture, warmed up with exertion and soon I barely noticed my wet pants. I might go home and find the skin blackened with frostbite and falling off in chunks, but for the time being it didn't hurt.

It's strange how your perspective can change when walking through thick vegetation. Come to a high point and look around and you get the sense that you are alone in a relatively vast space, a space much larger than your yard or the supermarket or your cubicle at work. But head back into the stuff and have it block your view and you can feel the world close around you pretty quickly. I tried not to think of the movie *Children of the Corn* and the scenes of those demonic kids appearing mysteriously among the tall stalks. I tried not to think of anything creepy and, really, there was no reason to. But the words *the body was found by a hunter* echoed in my head and left me with a sense that at any moment, with any given step, I would find the grue-some remains of what had once been a drifter or a hooker or a guy who took out a bad loan. That's what I mean when I tell my wife that there are times when I wander off into my own mind and allow my imagination to get the better of me. I simply can't help it. It's why it takes me a little longer to finish the dishes or put away the laundry, why sometimes I can be a little distant on the phone. I don't tune out intentionally; my brain and all its twisted gray goo simply gets the better of me, and sometimes the thing that brings me back is a reaction to my own thoughts.

I was picturing the dismembered corpse—hacked to bits and freezer-burned like a cheap gallon of ice cream—when the hair on the back of my neck stood up straight and a chill ran down my back that seemed to emanate from within. That was it. That was what I needed to bring me back from fantasy to the Bird Grotto and the realization that in two hours of exertion I hadn't seen so much as a cardinal, let alone a pheasant, grouse, or rabbit. Clearly what I had thought would be a perfect hunting ground was little more than a frozen-over swamp, and rather than run the risk of falling again through some ice in order to try and prove my instincts correct, I decided to head back to Valhalla and give it another go in the millet and tall grass. Fuck this place. At least in Valhalla anything or anyone left for dead would be easy to spot and, presumably, avoid.

It was a walk of more than a mile back to Valhalla, perhaps approaching a mile and a half. Back through the thick stuff, up the cleared field marked for dove hunting, and down the mani-cured path through the woods. Getting to my car was halfway, but I didn't stop. I kept walking across the road, passing the field where I went on my first solo hunt, then the one next to it where the eight guys in orange had scared the hell out of me, and across another road to my perfect little spot. I was coming up on the second road when I heard a choked roar approaching from the left and looked up to see an oversize green pickup truck chugging and spluttering toward the little turnaround at Valhalla.

*Shit,* I thought to myself. *I walked all this way and someone is going to jump on in front of me.* I slowed my pace a little and watched as the truck turned around and slowly pulled down the dirt road running along the western edge of Valhalla. I rounded a narrow stand of trees and heard the engine shut off, a door open and slam shut, the yipping wail of a puppy in a lot of discomfort. I was close by now, maybe twenty-five yards away and hidden behind some trees and brush from direct view. I heard a voice, deep, twangy, and nasally muttering frustrated words.

"Shit. Fuck. What the fuck 'er yew doin'? Fuck!"

There was some rattling and clanging. The door opened again and the hood popped. The door slammed with anger. The hood opened. More clanging and more swearing. What was I to do? One part of me said that this is exactly how the scenarios I had been imagining in the big fields began. A well-meaning stranger offers to help a stranded motorist, naively believing in the power of their own goodwill only to end up diced and quartered and left to be discovered by a hunter hacking his way through the underbrush in search of game birds and a little manly vindication. I did not want to be that dead hobo or hooker. But another part of me, the part that encourages my son to follow the Cub Scout promise to help other people, wanted to go over and offer a hand. It's in my nature. I guess, though I can't think of a single memory to back the assertion up, that I was raised that way, to believe that people are innately good. And hadn't Rebecca and I just sat down with Jack earlier in the week to talk about why it's important to help other people in need? On more than one occasion, I've had to rely on the assistance of strangers and friends, and it's always worked out well. But I'm not the kind of person who would cleave a fellow human into bits and strew them about a field. I'm not dangerous. But what if this guy is?

I had the same feeling I did driving to Pittsburgh for the NRA or while lost on the road to hunter's safety. It's a mistrust, a prejudice. I debated silently with myself for a minute or two, then finally decided that if I was going to die, it was better to die trying to do the right thing. Besides, I was armed for God's sake. I had two in the chamber and eighteen more in my pocket. Even if this was some sort of elaborate ruse designed to lure me in for a violent end, my experience shooting at the flushed grouse the day before gave me enough confidence to think I could somehow get the drop on a slack-jawed yokel. And he had a puppy with him. Serial killers don't have puppies. Not live ones anyway. This was an opportunity, I thought, to deal with my prejudice and get over my latent sense of mistrust.

I walked cautiously but directly toward the parked truck and, as I rounded the millet track, and saw it standing there, its driver door open, a puppy huddled under the exhaust manifold and its driver nowhere to be seen, I saw the inside of the door was electric blue while the outside was not simply green, but a hand-painted camouflage of greens and browns and blacks that had faded in the sun into a blurred swirl of putrid.

"Hello?" I called, my gun held firmly in both hands, my right thumb on the safety and my fingers covering the trigger guard. "You okay?"

His feet appeared at the front of the truck. I could see them from the back as he hopped down from the front bumper and stepped around the driver's-side door. He was tall and lanky, dressed head to toe in camo coveralls. His boots were worn and black, the kind that reminds me of those worn by the guys working the quick-change oil, lube, and filter on a Saturday morning. His bottom lip protruded with a massive wad of chewing tobacco, and he grabbed the dog leash from the front seat and yanked his yipping puppy along with him as he stepped toward me with purpose and without hesitation.

"My fuel pump is going on me," he said, abruptly turning and jumping back into the cab of the jacked-up old Ford, and he began cranking the engine. With each successive turn of the key, the engine's effort to come alive was shorter, more spluttering and desperate.

"It sounds like you could use a jump. Do you want one?" I still had both hands on my gun, but the grip had relaxed a bit.

"That would be really great," he said. "Are you sure you don't mind?"

Am I sure I don't mind? This wasn't the kind of thing I expected him to say. I expected him to spit at my shoe and say something along the lines of "fuck yes I need a jump. Take yer preppy ass L.L.Bean shoes and go get yer car." He was so polite. So desperate, I kind of felt a little bad for being as ready to shoot him as I was. Maybe he was changing my mind about the NRA guys, those yokels at the truck stop debating the true meaning of "first cousin," and all the other dirty, aggressive people I've been silently judging for so long. Maybe, with this man's help, I could learn to appreciate NASCAR as something more than loud things turning left. Maybe I'd even begin to understand Toby Keith and American beer. Maybe, but let's not get ahead of ourselves.

"Sure," I said. "I'm parked a couple fields over. Give me a few minutes to get back. Do you have cables?"

"I've got cables. Thank you so much, sir."

The sir, I think, was the reason my grip tightened once again on the gun. No one calls me sir. No one. And not in that every-time-you-call-me-sir-I-look-for-my-father kind of way. They don't call me sir because there is nothing about me that would give a person reason to call me sir. I quickened my pace back around the trees, taking away the direct line of sight to my back that might give him a clear shot if he were reaching for a rifle while I had my back turned, and hustled along the tree line back to my car. Sir. Hmmm. Was he buttering me up? Lulling me into a false sense of security and genuine appreciation? Or was he simply doing his best to be polite? State law dictates that you can't drive around with a loaded shotgun in your backseat, so I popped the shells out and laid the gun broken open across the rear seat, holding two shells in my left hand just in case I got back there and this guy's intentions with regard to ending my life had changed. I opened my bird-hunting knife and put it in the pocket of the driver's-side door for quick access. And I pulled up slowly when I got back to where the truck remained unmoving, a deep sense of suspicion conflicting with my genuine longing to help.

The dirt road was narrow and this guy's truck was parked directly in the middle, so I was forced to pull onto the shoulder and drive through low-hanging branches in order to get around it. I pulled past and watched my rearview for anything suspicious as I went up the road to turn around. I pocketed the open knife when I got out and unlatched the hood. My new friend was waiting with jumper cables already attached to his dead battery when I got my hood open, and he immediately began hooking the other ends to my battery. I got back in my car, shotgun shells palmed, knife ready, and started it, hoping it would provide a quick jump and we'd soon be on our separate ways.

The man, whose name I never asked in an uncharacteristic sign of my unease, tinkered with the wires and tried several times to get his old truck running. After nearly ten long and anticipatory minutes, he unhooked the cables and closed both hoods.

"I'm pretty sure my fuel pump is dead," he said, and I replied something nervous about it being better that he discovered it with people around instead of by himself, trying to subconsciously remind him that I was a person and not a meal. The day before, I had driven Jack and Dylan to play laser tag with Rebecca's brother and his girlfriend and Jack's booster seat was still in the back of my car, my gun on the floor in front. I tried to subtly draw attention to this, to remind this guy that I was a father and thereby had something to live for, something to fight for, something to, and the means with which to, kill for.

"Do you need a ride?" I asked and almost regretted it the second it came out of my mouth, but that's what happens when you start helping someone—you become responsible for them, like spaying the feral cat you gave milk to once on a whim. Once you start, you really should go all the way. You are, in fact, somehow obligated to go all the way.

"I don't live very far and I'd sure appreciate it," he said and quick as a flash went back to close up his truck and scoop up his puppy. I unlocked the door and cleared a couple things off the passenger seat before he got in. "Yeah, I noticed the fuel pump starting to go bad on me yesterday and I guess I just hoped it would last a little longer. I was just hoping to come out and work my new dog a little, get him to chase some squirrels and make him a squirrel dog."

He didn't live far, just ten minutes away, and I drove the unfamiliar roads trying to remember every turn, every name of a street not only to find my way back to Valhalla, but just in case I was in the early stages of a kidnapping and, upon the event of an escape, I needed to lead the police to the scene of the crime. It turned out the guy was pretty nice. He was a longtime hunter and friend of the county's wildlife officers. He liked hunting and eating squirrel—something I tried not to judge him for—as well as deer, pheasant, and the occasional grouse. He liked to fish too and told me, after I made some inane comment about the expense of fly-fishing, that he had tried it the summer before and really liked it. We wound our way down twisting country roads and into a small town where he directed me down a wooded street toward a trailer park. *This has to be it,* I thought. *This has to be his place.* Turned out I was right.

"Good luck; I hope you get something," he said.

"I'd better get something soon," I said, feeling relieved that I was dropping him off safely, but also a little sad that I'd been so quick to assume he was a bad person by the way he dressed and treated his puppy. "Or else my wife will think I'm cheating on her."

He shook my hand and laughed. "That's funny," he said. "Maybe next time I'll tell the old lady I'm out hunting. Thanks for the ride."

And with that he was out of my life forever. I tried not to squeal my tires as I pulled out of the trailer park and realized that, try as I did to pay attention, I had no real idea where I was going. I knew we had gone generally west and a little north, so I looked for opportunities to head south and east.

As I dead-reckoned my way back to Valhalla, I began feeling pretty good about myself for helping out a man in need, for stifling the part of me that had been afraid and doing the right thing. I was in full self-righteous mode when I began to fantasize about returning to the field and dropping a bird. I believe I even muttered a few words about karma under my breath and my hands turned the car automatically and, surprisingly, down the right streets taking me back to the place where we'd left the man's truck as if by rote. I parked in the turnaround on the southeast corner of Valhalla and retrieved my gun from the backseat. I reached absentmindedly in my pocket and felt my still-open pen knife. I nearly lopped my finger off, but managed to retrieve and close it without serious injury.

Dropping a couple of shells into my gun, I began walking north, along the eastern edge of the field through the row of millet. I was walking at a pretty good pace, sloshing and slapping my way through the thigh-high plants and making a lot of noise. My hope was that I would scare a bird into flight, but when I got to the corner and turned west as the planted row followed its tracklike route around the field, I slowed down. I was thinking again about the whole karma thing and dismissing it as self-congratulation. It's pretty pompous to think that God or the Universe or Almighty Thor will repay you for simply doing the right thing. Still, I knew it would make a pretty good story if it happened. Just about then, an errant twig lodged itself in my boot laces and I stopped to remove it. When I bent down to pick it out, I heard a little rustling in the bushes just ahead of me. I stood back up and saw a brown bird a little bigger than a New York City pigeon waddling through the brush three or four feet in front of me. I took a step and it waddled a little more. I stopped and it slowed.

My dad and Mark tell a story about a fall trip to Canada for some late-season fishing and black bear hunting. The story goes that they were walking along an old logging road back to where they had parked a truck when they came across a young boy walking with a shotgun. He had a couple of grouse stuffed into a bag tied to his belt. They chatted him up for a couple of minutes and soon a grouse crossed the road ahead of them. The boy raised his shotgun and blasted the bird before it had a chance to fly.

"Why do you shoot them on the ground?" Dad asked.

"Why not wait for them to flush?" Mark added.

The boy, a local kid who was obviously hunting for dinner and not sport, cocked his head at the two dumbass Americans and said, " 'Cause they're easier to hit on the ground."

This story flashed into my mind with each cautious step in pursuit of the bird walking like a geriatric through the brush ahead of me. After four or five steps, I raised my shotgun and aimed at it. It would have been easy to shoot it on the ground. Really easy. I removed the safety and had my finger on the trigger, about to pull, but decided against it. It would have felt cheap, like I was somehow cheating. I was desperate to get a bird, but I knew I would remember my first for a very long time, maybe even forever, and shooting a bird on the ground four feet in front of me would have been like losing my virginity while black-out drunk. That didn't mean I was going to let this particular bird get away. Not by a long shot. It just meant I would have to figure out how to inspire it to take to the air before I lost it.

I stalked it for another ten feet or so, gun at the ready on my shoulder, safety on. I thought, maybe, that if I paused for a moment then made a quick movement, it might get confused and fly away. I hardly noticed that I was standing in the exact spot where the five grouse had flushed almost exactly twenty-four hours before when I stopped for a short count of two Mississippi then made a two-footed set jump forward about three feet.

It worked like a charm.

Not only did the bird I had been following fly, but so did four others—perhaps the exact same five birds from the day before. And just like the day before, two of them took off in front of me. One went to the right into the woods. One went to the left deeper into Valhalla, and the last went straight back over my head. But my eyes never left the one I'd been following. My physical movements were textbook. First my left hand followed the bird's trajectory, then my right moved the butt of the gun to my shoulder. My weight flowed like water onto my front left foot, and my right heel came off the ground. Exactly as I had been taught at L.L.Bean two months prior, exactly as I had not done the day before. I didn't even notice the end of the gun as my eyes focused clearly on the bird. My cheek hit the stock at the exact moment my right thumb flicked the safety forward and in one fluid, smooth-as-silk and picture-perfect motion, I exhaled and squeezed the trigger without having to remember not to jerk. The bird, all browns and white, tumbled to the ground a millisecond after I heard the shot and twenty yards in front of me.

I had pulled the trigger a second time before I saw the bird go down, so my gun was empty and I flipped the barrel release switch with my right thumb, breaking open the action and digging into my pocket for two more shells as the spent ones ejected and flew past my head. I was walking now. A purposeful walk. A measured walk. An even gait right toward the spot where the bird had fallen. I got to the place I had marked in my mind and looked around, expecting to see the pound-and-a-half bird lying where it fell. I was just starting to believe in the power of karma, just starting to believe in the innate justice of the world when I realized something—the bird wasn't there.

Immediately, I went into a frantic search. The gun was by now loaded and closed, the safety returned to the proper position. My head swiveled back and forth. My steps—moments before even and smooth—became clipped and frantic, like I was trying to guard Isaiah Thomas in a game of one-on-one. Where the hell was the damned bird?

Pausing to look back at the spot where I had seen it fall, I caught something out of the corner of my eye, something that, had I not been so hyperaware and jacked up on adrenaline and prehistoric instinct, I probably would have missed entirely. A tall stalk of a thornbush jerked to my left in a direction inconsistent with the movement of the wind. The little grouse was on the run. Any vestiges of the coolheaded resolve I'd demonstrated in wounding the bird was gone. Suddenly I was in the final scene of a *Benny Hill Show* episode. I could almost hear "Yakety Sax" playing as I bobbed and weaved, walking smack into thornbushes and trying to keep up with the bird's frantic and erratic run for life. It was like that scene in *Rocky*, when the grizzled old trainer makes the young boxer chase a chicken through a Philadelphia alley to improve his agility. Only I was no fighter, this was no chicken, and as evidenced by the slaps to the face I was taking from the prickly flora, this was no alley.

Through the lens of hyperrealism, the chase felt like it took hours, though I'm sure—judging by the meager distance actually covered—that it was over in thirty seconds. The bird changed direction one time too many and found itself coming straight back toward me. I had the gun to my shoulder, stalking it like a SWAT officer storming a meth lab, and was ready to fire when once again I thought of the young boy in my dad's

Canadian story. I stamped my boot down six feet in front of its beak and it made a weak attempt to fly—more of a hop than anything. It was, perhaps, eight inches off the ground and less than two yards in front of me when I pulled the trigger for a final time. It went down immediately and twisted and writhed for a couple quick seconds before settling down, wings over its head and claws splayed behind it as if tragically failing an attempt at a cartwheel, for the final time.

In the immediate aftermath of my first kill, I was awash in conflicted feelings. I stood stock-still, only moving to flip open my gun and allow the single spent shell to arc behind me, removing the unfired one and stuffing it into my pocket. If I'm honest, I was a little scared. The way the thing flopped and writhed in its final moment of life freaked me out. I didn't want to get too close, let alone touch it, for fear that it might spring to life and make one final, desperate lunge at me. I know. I've seen too many horror movies where the killer is believed to be dead, only to pop back out of the water and drag a freshly deflowered teenager with him to the deep. But it was a strange thing to see, especially that close and in the three dimensions and Technicolor majesty of a crisp winter morning right in front of me. I wondered if I felt guilty, if I had any remorse about taking another creature's life with such wanton eagerness, but was able to answer my own question: No. I didn't feel bad that the birdie had died and I had been the one who made it do so. I did feel a strange pang of anticlimax, though, like I should have felt more victorious than I did. I did not feel like I had conquered nature. I did not feel like Francis Macomber dropping the wildebeest. I felt more like I had conquered man, actually. Like I had stepped up and done something hard.

It was a similar feeling to the one I had after I took Rebecca's parents out to lunch and asked for their daughter's hand in marriage. It was something I had been dreading. I knew I loved her and I wanted to spend the rest of my life with her, but it's never easy for a guy to confront a girl's parents and ask for their blessing to take their baby girl away. Just like then, I had spent a long time preparing, getting ready for any situation or question. I had rehearsed what I was going to do and practiced how I was going to behave. And when the moment came, it turned out to be not as hard as what I had built up in my head. That lunch was easy. A few questions about my career prospects, a few wise words about the relationship between love and commitment. I picked up the check and it was done. It was the same with this. A few rough experiences and a few thoughts of failure, but then the moment came and I did exactly what I wanted to do, what I needed to do. I got the bird to fly, shot it, and stalked it until it was dead. It wasn't like climbing Everest or any other feat requiring a tremendous amount of physical skill and mental experience. And when it was done, I felt a weight had lifted, like I had confronted something tough and made it out alive.

I still didn't want to pick the damned thing up though. That was the hardest part. When I was sure that its tiny heart had made its last beat, when I was sure that it didn't have any fight left in it, I walked over slowly and squatted down, catcher style, with it between my boots. There was a small amount of blood, about as bad as when you cut yourself shaving and dab it off with some toilet paper, on its wing. I poked at it at first, flipping it over with the tip of my gloved finger and revealing the damage that had been done. My intention was to shoot it in the head, knowing full well that the meat, such as it was, was in the breast and thighs. I had missed by an inch or two, blowing the upper half of the breast, neck, and throat completely off. The small head was attached by the spine and a little skin wrapped around it. Nothing more. With a little more confidence, I picked up a claw between my thumb and forefinger and flipped it over. It was stunningly light and my gun, which was a twelve-gauge and much too big for such a small bird at such close range, had made it all the more so.

Grouse are pretty birds, I thought. Not pretty like a parakeet or majestic like an eagle, but pretty like the endless Iowa cornfields I had come to enjoy driving through over the previous year. I examined it closely, looking at the place where I had shot it and noticing how much it looked like raw chicken. This might seem like a pretty obvious thought to have, and it was obvious, but up close and in the moment, it seemed somehow interesting, like finding out that your mom had been pretty in high school. One of those things that makes you utter an audible "huh," then move about your day. I turned it over, laying it in my left hand, my gun resting on my thighs, and spreading its wings. The creeped-out fear that moments before had kept me standing in one place was gone, replaced by no small measure of curiosity.

After a couple of minutes of examination, I stuffed the grouse into the chest entrance of my game bag and felt it slide down to rest just above my hip. I could feel its warmth through the vest, through my soft shell jacket, my shirt, and base layer. It was a strange feeling, to have the sensation of warmth passing out of one body and onto your own. I'm not one who puts a lot of stock in the notion, considered orthodoxy by many Native American tribes, that animals have spirits and by killing them you are releasing those spirits into the world. But feeling how that bird's body heat radiated through my clothes and onto my skin, I understood how they came to believe it. I reloaded my gun, forgetting to go back and pick up my three spent shells, and walked for another twenty minutes in a halfhearted attempt to track down the other four grouse. My head just wasn't in it. Had I not been alone, had I had someone to share the moment and more than a couple of high fives with, I might have gone on. But, alas, I was done. I gave a quick thought to going off in search of a rabbit, but dismissed it as quickly as it had come. I was calling it a day.

I unloaded my gun and walked back to my car, glad I had decided to leave it so close after dropping the stranded motorist off at home. I put my gun in the backseat and popped the trunk, where I had a large plastic bowl, paper towel, an aluminum bottle full of saltwater, latex gloves, and freezer bags waiting. I pulled off my vest and laid it on the ground, then switched my golflike hunting gloves for a pair of the disposable latex ones and pulled out the Boker bird knife I had ordered from L.L.Bean.

Now, all the videos I had watched and diagrams I had studied relating to the proper technique for field dressing and butchering upland game birds involve making a slit in the skin just above the poop shoot and creating an opening to reach in and pull out the guts. They also demonstrated how to make an incision just above the breast and cutting the skin around the neck so that you can pull the head back and remove everything but the breast. These were intact birds. Mine was like John Cleese's character in the *Harry Potter* movies, nearly headless. Given that my bird was missing half its breast and that the head was liable to fall off with the slightest tug, I knew this was going to be difficult. I pulled it out of my vest and looked it over, trying to devise a strategy. I knew I had to get rid of the guts because the heat from them takes a while to dissipate and is the single biggest contributing factor to spoiling meat. I jammed the tip of the knife between the hips, feeling oddly perverted for doing so and made an incision, which I widened with my Italian sausage fingers until I could reach in and physically eviscerate the bird. I cut away the aforementioned poop shoot and considered my next move. Pulling the head back, I tried to remove the spine, but there wasn't a whole lot there, so I ended up slipping the tip of my knife between the breast and the skin covering it, making a notch, then used my hands to pull it apart as delicately as possible. I then put one knee on the bird's outstretched wing and sort of tugged and pulled until what remained of the breast pulled free.

I felt like a serial killer and half expected Frances McDormand's cop from *Fargo* to come up and ask if it was my partner in the wood chipper. The legs were still intact, so I pondered for a minute or two what to do. I knew the skin would slip off like a sock if I were to remove the lower, scalier portion below the knees. A lifelong love of lobster did nothing to prepare me for the sensation of grasping the thigh in one hand and knife in lower leg in the other and bending back the knees until they snapped then running the connective tissue over my knife to remove the lower section of the leg. I did this twice, then tugged and pulled on the skin and feathers until the thighs came clean.

Right about the time I was promising to never again eat at KFC, I noticed the smell, a raw, acrid stench of gamy meat, blood, and internal organs. Not powerful, exactly, but pungent. I repeated Han Solo's line from *The Empire Strikes Back* as he cut open the beast to make a warm bed for Luke Skywalker— "And I thought they smelled bad on the outside"—as I separated the salvageable meat from the nasty bits of bone, feather, skin, blood, and beak and threw the latter into the woods next to me. I rinsed the meat in the saltwater to help pull any remaining blood out and the water clouded immediately. I did my best to cut away any remaining chunks of skin, pull off any residual feathers or other indications of nastiness, then patted the meat dry with paper towel and put it into a gallon freezer bag to take home.

There was shockingly little in there.

Had I been able to salvage the whole breast, we could have gotten a meager meal out of a single bird. But combine my misplaced shots and amateur-at-best skills in the field of butchery and what I was left with was slightly more meat than what is on three or four buffalo wings. Paltry. But at least it was protein. I had gone out into the field and was coming home with meat. I would cook it and feed it to my family. Did it matter that it wasn't exactly enough to tide us over from breakfast to lunch, let alone through an entire winter? Not to me, my friends, not to me. The only thing that mattered was that I had found, shot, killed, and cleaned an animal for my family to consume. Mission accomplished.

I was a hunter.

# 20

## VINDICATION

Hunting became a weekend ritual for me. Every Saturday and Sunday through December, I got up before dawn, pulled on my L.L.Bean clothes and gear—which were starting to feel less shiny and new with every use—and headed north toward the public grounds that were becoming familiar. Most days, I didn't see anything. Other days I didn't look all that hard and simply enjoyed being out in the woods or walking purposefully through a field of overgrown scrub brush. Six or seven times I went out and six or seven times I came home empty-handed. Every once in a while, I would come across another hunter who would tell me how the DNR had released more than a thousand pheasant into the area where we were and had I only been there the day before I most certainly would have gotten something. I'd thank them, shoot the shit for a moment or two, then move on.

At first these little interactions made me uncomfortable. I didn't like the idea of an armed stranger approaching me, but in time I realized I was armed too and that most hunters are actually friendly, approachable people.

I hadn't so much as seen a pheasant since Iowa and after

looking through my pictures a week or two later, I realized the bird I had shot was not a ruffed grouse as I thought it was, but a bobwhite quail. The two species look almost nothing alike, which is testament to my inexperience and, had I recognized the quail, I might have realized that the season for hunting them had ended three days before I pulled the trigger.

Christmas was approaching, just days away, and Rebecca took Jack, Dylan, and Molly up to Cleveland to spend time with family. I would join them in a couple of days. I had work to do, had, actually, to be at work since I'd burned through my vacation days on trips to Iowa, North Carolina, Maine, Iowa, and, sadly, Pittsburgh. We do this every year. She takes the kids and goes to see her family for most of the break from school, and I join them when I can. By this time, I had felt my yearlong adventure was coming to a close, but there was still something that eluded me. I'd been hunting with family, I'd been hunting on my own. I'd taken the classes, read the books, and confronted the NRA, but I still didn't have my pheasant; that unchecked item on my to-do list was pulling at me, poking me like an annoying reminder of unfinished business. My family had left on Wednesday. Christmas was Sunday. I had to work Thursday and Friday and had planned to drive up to join Rebecca and the kids Friday night. It didn't leave much time.

I checked my schedule and realized that if I were to squeeze one more trip in before the end of the year, it would have to be Thursday before work.

I got up long before dawn, dressed, and poured a cup of coffee in my travel mug before setting out north toward Valhalla. I hadn't so much as heard any of the pheasants others told me had been released there, but I didn't have a lot of time to hunt before work and going someplace new was out of the question. I needed to go someplace familiar to get the most out of my limited time. I arrived just as the sun was turning the sky from black to purple and parked my car in a circular gravel drive, next to where the remains of a deer had been left by a hunter back in November. They were still there, though most of the meat had been picked over, leaving an eerie set of bones and teeth. I assembled my gun quickly and waited for the sun to come up a bit more before setting off. I wanted there to be enough light, should I come across something, to distinguish between an out-of-season quail and anything else that might fly by. Truth be told, I knew the effort was futile. I had the same feeling I did that second day back in Iowa and had resigned myself to not getting a bird this season.

"That's okay," I told myself through chattering teeth in the early morning cold. "There's always next year."

Ten minutes later, the sun had risen enough to begin walking. I set out along the now-familiar path of millet, walking away from my car, generally north toward the woods where I had gotten my unidentified quail. I got maybe twenty-five yards away from the car, walking slowly and pausing every few feet to listen for rustling among the sounds of mourning doves and other birds waking up, when I decided I needed another pair of gloves. I couldn't feel my fingers, the tips were well beyond numb, and I remembered a pair of light wool gloves, the kind you buy from a freestanding kiosk in gas station convenient stores, in my trunk. So I turned back and had nearly reached my car when something stopped me in my tracks.

Thinking back, I have no idea what it was that made me stop. I don't remember hearing anything or seeing anything. I don't remember anything grabbing my attention, but for some reason, my senses were heightened. I was suddenly aware of the sound of my own breath, the beating of my heart. My head turned as if guided by someone standing behind me with hands on both my ears, toward the trees on the other side of the gravel drive. I had never paid much attention to the woods at Valhalla, believing, as I had read, that pheasant tend to avoid the woods for fear of predatory species that live in the taller branches. But something drew my eye in that direction regardless of what I had read.

It took me a minute to make it out, to distinguish it from the dark shadows of the woods, but there, walking among the trunks of oak and elm, was a rooster. I did a double take, but there it was. It was walking slowly through the clear forest floor, seemingly unaware of my presence. Fifteen yards. Maybe sixteen, but close. It was big, much bigger than I would have thought. I didn't have a lot of time to see the one in Iowa. It got up and flew so fast and by the time I examined the body after the hunt, I wasn't paying much attention to scale. But there it was. Right there. Right in front of me. After a year and thousands of miles, hundreds of hours spent reading and studying, learning, walking, waiting, stalking fruitlessly through the tall grass, it was there. Right there. I was only out of the car for twelve or thirteen minutes. I had given myself an hour and a half. I had planned on walking four miles, and it turned out I only had to walk a few feet. This was my chance for a pheasant. This was my chance for redemption. This was my chance to put a period on the end of my project.

I didn't want to startle it by moving too quickly. I took two steps away from my car and raised my gun to my shoulder. I drew aim and waited. Do I shoot it now? On the ground? Do I wait for it to fly? Can I make it fly? After a few long seconds' contemplation, I decided such considerations were the luxury of the experienced, the privileged sportsman for whom there would always be another hunt. Was it selfish? Sure. Morally ambiguous? Maybe. But I made my decision and was willing to live with it. I took my time, carefully sliding the safety switch forward and following the bird as it moved slowly from my right to my left. I took a deep breath and let it out slowly. I felt the pressure of the trigger against my finger, and just as the pheasant was about to step behind a thin two-year sapling, I pulled the trigger. Immediately, the pheasant hunched over. It's not like in the movies when the hunter fires and all that is left is a puff of feathers. That would defeat the purpose of hunting. And I wasn't so close that the bird went flying. Instead, it slumped to one side like it had tripped and began flopping and flailing.

The adrenaline kicked in. I took a few steps forward, breaking open my gun and letting the spent shell eject past my face. I didn't take my eyes off the pheasant. It looked like it was going to get up and make a run for it, so I slammed my gun shut, raised it, and pulled the trigger.

*Click.*

It took a moment for me to realize I had not reloaded the top barrel and had thus pulled the trigger on an empty chamber. I tucked my cheek against the stock, keeping both eyes open and pointing the gun at the bird. I put the weight on my front foot, bent slightly at the waist, and lifted my right heel slightly off the ground. This time when I pulled the trigger, all motion was stopped. The bird slumped, jerked slightly, then stopped. I snapped my gun open and put two new shells in the barrels before snapping it closed again, never breaking stride, but walking purposefully toward my quarry. When I reached the place where the pheasant lay, I stood a couple feet away, gun at my shoulder, waiting for it to move. I stood with my gun shouldered, even though I knew the pheasant wouldn't hurt me, but I didn't want it to get away. I couldn't live with myself if I merely wounded an animal and let it get away.

I waited for perhaps a minute before unloading my gun and resting it against a tree. I knelt down and looked at it. It was beautiful. The feathers were black and brown, white and teal, a complicated mosaic that formed a complete picture that was enough to make a man marvel at the mystery of the world. After another moment, I felt something welling up inside my chest and without warning or forethought, I released what Whitman described as a "barbaric yawp." I shouted at the top of my lungs nothing in particular. Just a release that lasted maybe five seconds and what followed was a mixture of elation and pride. I had gone into the world bigger than myself and emerged more alive than when I had entered. I was carrying my pheasant—it was no longer "the" pheasant or "a" pheasant, but "my" pheasant—out of the woods toward my car when the green pickup truck with the Department of Natural Resources seal on the door pulled up. My first thought was that it was a wildlife officer, so I laid my gun across the elbow of the arm holding my pheasant and dug into the pocket of my hunting vest to retrieve my driver's and hunting licenses. When the truck pulled up, I proffered my papers and held my pheasant up high.

"I finally got one," I said. "First one of the season. First one ever. But I got one. You need my license?"

"No, that won't be necessary," said the man in his late fifties with the thick walrus mustache of salt and sand.

"Are you the Warren County officer?" I asked.

"Nope," he said. "Just turning around."

"Oh," I said and put my identification back into my pocket.

"Nice bird, though," he said.

"Thanks, it's mine," I blurted and instantly felt like a jack-ass. Was he really there to confiscate the pheasant on behalf of the state? Sometimes I don't know where this shit comes from.

"Yup, sure is," he said and pulled away.

It took me longer to field dress my pheasant than it had taken to hunt it and when I was done, I was left with perhaps two pounds of breast and leg meat. I left the lower legs and claws attached on the off chance that I might have to prove to a game warden that it was a rooster and put the whole of it into a gallon freezer bag and closed it in my trunk. I called Rebecca as I pulled away, but it was still early and she didn't answer her phone. I tried calling Dad but got his voice mail too. I sent my wife a text reading simply "I got one," and an hour or two later, after I had stopped at home and put the meat in the freezer, showered, changed, and had gone to work, I got a text message back from her reading "Finally. It's about time."

My God, I love that woman.

I waited until after Christmas to cook my pheasant. I was home alone; my family was still in Cleveland, and I had planned to meet them in a couple of days to celebrate New Year's. After months of reading recipes and books about pheasant cookery, months of reading about game and eating healthy, I had decided on a simple roast with roasted vegetables. I dog-eared the page in my book with the recipe and made a list of ingredients to get the next day on my way home from work. I moved the frozen meat, claws still attached, to the refrigerator to thaw and settled into bed to watch a little Anthony Bourdain. He was in Vietnam. It was a rerun, but one of my favorites. In the episode,

Bourdain waxed poetic on the perfection of the simple Vietnamese delicacy pho. Essentially a noodle soup with vegetables and meat, pho was something I had always wanted to try and that night I went to bed dreaming of the salty, savory soup. All the next day, it was all I could think about. It seemed so easy. Stock. Vegetables. Rice noodles. Protein. Hot sauce.

All of a sudden a roasted pheasant didn't sound all that good to me. I began looking up recipes for pho when I should have been working, and while I didn't find one specifically calling for pheasant, I did find a few that looked easy enough and stopped at the grocery store to pick up the noodles, some chicken stock, bok choy (which I had never tried, but looked a little like spinach and cabbage and seemed appropriately Asian) and went home to mix it all up in the slow cooker. My pheasant had nearly thawed, though I helped it along a bit by running the freezer bag under some warm water for a few minutes. I rinsed the meat to get rid of feathers and got out the cutting board and our biggest knife. It was harder than what I had thought it would be to remove the claws. They didn't come off quite as neatly or quickly as I had imagined and touching them, admittedly, sent a shiver up my spine. The rest of the bird looked so familiar, so much like the rotisserie chickens I had practiced on. But the claws were something out of a horror movie. I hacked at them until they were removed and put them back into the freezer bag, burying it in the bottom of the trash can and forcing myself to not vomit.

I put all the ingredients into the Crock-Pot, added salt and some hot sauce, and set it on high. I set the oven timer for two and a half hours, figuring that would give it enough time to cook through and for everything to get soft and delicious. As it cooked, an earthy, savory smell began to fill our small condo. It wasn't an unpleasant smell. I actually kind of liked it. It was different to be sure, but with each passing moment my anticipation grew stronger. All year long, ever since I interviewed Steven Rinella, I had worked on changing my eating habits. I ate more lunches brought from home. I spent less time at drive-throughs. I'd lost some weight and ran my first 5K. I had even resolved to eat no fast food in 2012 and was looking forward to the challenge. But this, this meal warming in my slow cooker, was the pinnacle. This was something I had sourced, something I had hunted and killed, something I had provided. And I was excited to know what it would taste like. I found out when the oven timer went off and I opened the Crock-Pot, ladled out a bowlful, and picked up a piece of the meat, some rice noodles, and bok choy with a pair of chopsticks I'd stolen from a Chinese restaurant.

It tasted like shit.

The unfamiliar bok choy had infused a manure flavor into everything else, and the salty broth and hot sauce formed a burning film on my tongue and teeth. The meat was firmer than a chicken and oddly dry. I bit into a tough piece of leg meat and nearly broke my tooth on a piece of shot from my gun. I pulled the meat out of my mouth and smashed it between my fingers until I found the small lead BB. I took a second bite and tried my best to swallow it, but couldn't. I should point out that I have never once sent a meal back at a restaurant, and the last time I failed to finish my plate during a home-cooked meal was sometime during the Bush/Quayle administration. But I simply couldn't do it. Not only was it bad, but I was suddenly aware of the claws in the bottom of the trash can and couldn't shake the thought of them. I spit what was in my mouth into the bowl and pushed the whole of it through the disposal in the sink. I unplugged the slow cooker and let it cool for a while before dumping the contents into a couple freezer bags and walking the whole thing down to the trash. My first great experiment in hunting my food and eating what I hunt was over.

In the end, I ordered a pizza.

# EPILOGUE

It's been two months since I shot my pheasant and, despite a couple attempts late in the season, it was my only one for the year. Dad's shotgun is still in its case, cleaned and oiled, and sitting in my trunk along with a couple boxes of ammunition and my orange L.L.Bean hunting vest. When the weather warms up, I'll probably take the gun and shells over to John's house and lock them away in his gun case, where the pistol I bought from Uncle Mark has sat since I got home from Iowa.

Rinella has left the Travel Channel and is the host, as of this writing, of a show on the Sportsman Channel called *MeatEater*. It's a good show, similar to *The Wild Within*, but a little more poignant for the channel's audience. I reached out to him and his production team after my Iowa hunt and was able to get Uncle Mark a set of DVDs, which I'm sure he'll watch on rainy Saturday mornings for years to come.

I never did get an opportunity to go hunting with my dad. We made loose plans to get together either near where I live or at his and Mom's new place in northern Michigan, but time just ran out. I hope next year we'll get together for a pheasant hunt. We'll just have to see. Uncle Mark tried to cajole me into joining him in Wyoming for an antelope hunt in the fall, but I passed. Dad will join him and Will and Tom and a few other uncles and cousins, and I'm sure they'll have the time of their lives.

I hate to get all *Doogie Howser, M.D.* here, but I once heard someone say that a man doesn't truly become a man until his dad dies and, if it weren't for this last year, I may have agreed with it. But setting out to learn to hunt made me realize that manhood is not a destination, but a process. Being a man is not singular. There is no one way. I didn't need to learn to hunt in order to feel like a man. I simply needed to do something else, something outside of my comfort zone, something disruptive. I did, and now I feel lucky that I'll be able to share experiences with my dad I may never have, had I not set out on this journey. I'll get to know him in a different way. I'll understand him better and I feel truly blessed for that.

I've been asked several times by friends if I plan on teaching my sons to hunt, and the answer is that I simply don't know. I will probably still do it a few times every year. I'll drag myself out of bed early on a Saturday or Sunday morning, put on my L.L.Bean gear, and grab a cup of coffee before heading up to Valhalla or some other place in search of pheasant. I'll probably go back to Iowa for a weekend bonding with my uncles and cousins. If there comes a point at which my sons want to join me, I'll gladly take them along. But I'm not going to force it on them. This project, this whole last year was not about hunting. It was about immersion. It was about understanding the relationship between men and the things they are passionate about. Hunting happened to be what it was for the men in my family. If my sons feel called to it, I will gladly embrace that and do everything I can to encourage them finding something they love. Just as I would if it were baseball, art, or music. It doesn't really